Healer

Healer
The Remarkable Life
Of A Hometown Country Doctor

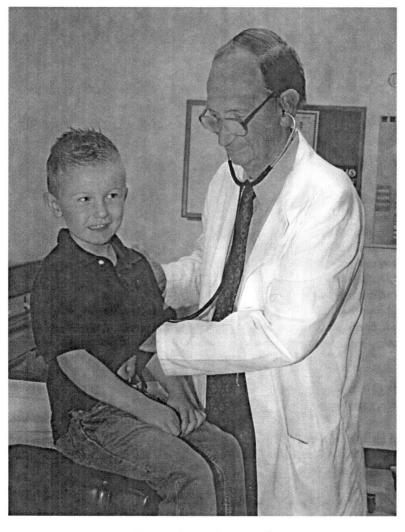

Rudy Reed

MILL CITY PRESS, MINNEAPOLIS

Mill City Press, Inc.
212 3rd Avenue North, Suite 290
Minneapolis, MN 55401
612.455.2294
www.millcitypublishing.com

ISBN-13: 978-1-938223-94-5
LCCN: 2012921088

Edited by Robert J. Reed
Cover Design by Kristeen Ott
Typeset by Mary Nelson

Printed in the United States of America

Dedication

To Bertha A. Reed
1896–1973
for tending so well to the growing
of a hometown country doctor

And to Janet Myers Reed
1932–2008
loving, devoted wife and full time assistant
of a hometown country doctor

A Note To Readers

All of the stories included in this book are real stories. With one exception, all of the people whose names appear in the book are the names of real people. All of the patients of Dr. Jim Reed whom I talked with were more than happy to contribute to this book about their family doctor. Finally, the two people pictured on the book's cover are real. The young, sparkly-eyed lad is Mason Griffith, who lives in Farmington with his parents, Patrick and Mallory Griffith. The elderly gentleman is Dr. Jim Reed.

Over the span of more than half a century, Dr. Jim Reed has been involved many times over with the full spectrum of human life, from the glorious to the gruesome, the inspiring to the inhumane. Jim and I were in agreement that his experiences with the dark side of life—with a couple of notable exceptions—would be excluded from the book. We both agreed that to include them would serve no purpose and thought most readers would find them distasteful. Suffice to say that when confronted with those most difficult situations, Jim fulfilled his ethical duties as both a physician and a human being in doing the best he could to be of service.

Throughout this book, when I refer to doctors in general, I have elected to use the phrase, "he" and "his" rather than the more proper "he or she" and "his or her." I have done this simply for ease of reading. When Jim Reed entered medical school in 1950, his class of 100 included only five women. It pleases me to report that women now comprise about 50% of the student population. I happen to believe that will result in an improved medical profession.

CONTENTS

Introduction

It was Sunday, the last day of February in 2010. Winter had been long and tough, with above average snowfall and below average temperatures. But last night the weather finally broke. Today, it was 41 and sunny, a great day to kick back and contemplate the coming of spring. I picked up the phone to talk with my older brother, Jim.

Just seven weeks from his 83rd birthday, Jim long ago earned the right to do nothing except relax and enjoy his twilight years. But that wouldn't be Jim, which is why, when I phoned, he was working. Jim's a family doctor and he was making a house call, a habit he'd started some 55 years earlier, as an intern. After I hung up the phone, it occurred to me that he might have been the only doctor in America making a house call on this Sunday morning.

Dr. James M. Reed began practicing family medicine in our rural, central Illinois hometown of Farmington (pop. 2,500) in 1956. Now he's 84 and in his 55th year of caring for patients in ways seldom-if-ever-seen, anywhere at anytime. This book is the story of his life. At its heart, it's about how he grew into the doctor he became, and how, over the course of half a century, he gained the deep admiration, respect and total trust of many thousands of patients.

Unless you've been a long time patient of Jim's, you'll find the stories in this book difficult to believe. After all, how many doctors have ever done even one of the following:
- performed life-saving surgery in a farm field with only a pocket knife, or
- unknowingly become involved with a bank-robbing gang, or
- in the middle of the night during a power outage, saved the life of a miner trapped beneath an avalanche of dirt in a tiny cabin of a huge steam shovel, or
- examined a patient while incapacitated, flat on his back, at home.

I know that much of what I've written in this book will be hard for readers to believe because I found it hard to believe myself and I'm Jim's own brother!If that sounds a little far-fetched, let me explain. Jim is eleven years older than I. When he enlisted in the Navy in WWII, he was eighteen and I was only seven, so I'd never spent much time with him. By the time he returned home from his schooling, in 1956, I was eighteen and leaving for college. After that, we'd see each other only briefly a couple of times a year. As a result, I never got to know Jim very well.

Over the years, I hadn't heard much about Jim's doctoring career. I had never been one of his patients, nor had I ever talked with any of his patients. But I can recall the day all that changed. About 1995, I was in a restaurant in Peoria when I ran into Vic Venturi, an old childhood friend. After exchanging pleasantries, Vic just blurted out, "You know Old Doc saved my life." Turns out, he'd had a life-threatening heart condition that Jim helped him with. When I heard Vic compliment Jim, I was deeply moved; to hear a comment like that from a dear childhood friend about the brother I had idolized was a very emotional, heartwarming experience—it really stuck with me. But it was still several more years before the idea for this book was truly planted in me. I can remember the day.

It was one of those beautiful, crisp autumn Sundays, in 2001. My wife and I were at Jim's for a visit when he suggested a drive through the countryside where our ancestors had roamed, a few miles west of Farmington. It quickly became apparent that somehow Jim not only knew every turn in every road, but also who had lived in every farm home for the past several generations, as well as many details about their lives. Then it hit me that he had been traveling these roads for fifty years. He pointed out barren land where he said small towns, now extinct, like Ellisville Station and Troy, had once stood. At Jim's request, we stopped for picture taking. He seemed to be saying that if families didn't take the time to do what we were doing, the personal histories might die out. He was clearly enjoying giving us this tour. We passed several tiny cemeteries, some barely visible, tucked among hillsides and shade trees. Jim seemed drawn to the cemeteries and I wondered if it was because he had been involved in so many of the stories buried there.

As we continued to navigate the country back roads, Jim suddenly brought his car to a stop, seemingly in the middle of nowhere. I looked around and to the south noticed a tiny white cottage nestled back among some large trees. Without a word, Jim leaned over, grabbed his ever-present little black bag, opened the door and moved slowly toward the house. I turned around and asked Jim's wife, Jan, what was going on. "There's an elderly lady living there alone and he just wanted to stop by to see how she was doing." I was stunned, so I asked Jan if this sort of thing was unusual. "Oh my no," she said. After a few minutes, Jim came walking slowly back toward the car. Jan asked how the elderly lady was and Jim just said she was fine. He placed his black bag back in its place and we continued on our way to London Mills, where Jim was born.

While Jim drove, I was going over in my mind what I'd just witnessed. Here was a doctor taking time on a Sunday to make a house call for a non-emergency matter—for a patient who hadn't even asked him to come to her home. And I would bet my Stan Musial autographed baseball that the lady was never charged for the call!I wouldn't have believed it if I hadn't seen it for myself. That experience became the inspiration for a poem I wrote about Jim for Farmington's 2004 citywide celebration honoring his 50th year as a doctor. More importantly, it was the day the seeds for this book were strewn.Still, they lay dormant because both Jim and I had some doubts about proceeding.

Jim would need a couple of nudges before he could feel comfortable with the idea of a book about his life. Most kids like Jim who grew up in small towns during the 1930's, 40s, and 50s were humble. That's just the way life was. That doesn't mean you didn't try to excel or take pride in doing so. It just meant you didn't gloat about it or do anything that would call attention to yourself. That was true for both kids and adults. Sure, there were always a couple of kids or adults who weren't humble, but they stood out—and weren't very well liked. Kids from small towns who continued to live there as adults usually remained humble; Jim Reed was one of those. That's why he needed a nudge about this book.

For about thirty years Jim had been a volunteer member of the University of Illinois School of Medicine at Peoria, where one of his roles was to present lectures to students about his experiences as a family physician. He told me that invariably, after talking to the students, some of them would approach him to let him know they'd never heard such interesting tales about medicine. That was one nudge; the other nudge came from outside medicine. Jim's wife had a high school classmate, Carolyn Thompson, who went on to earn a doctorate degree in education and teach at the University of Kentucky. Dr. Thompson met Jim for the first time over dinner a few years ago, and after an evening listening to some of Jim's medical tales, she suggested to him that they'd make rich fodder for a book.

Those nudges freed Jim to express a concern to me—he never honestly felt the medical profession fully understood what the life of a modern country doctor was really like. In fact, over the years, he said that when he would mention something unusual that he had done, his colleagues would often express their disbelief. So in that regard, he began to feel that a book might 'set the record straight,' as it were.

Jim wasn't the only one who needed a couple of nudges. In the area of writing I had good reason to be humble. I had never written a book before, at least not a book of prose. I had written a lot of poetry, but this was entirely a different matter. So I experimented. I wrote a couple of possible chapters for the book and showed them to a few friends. They encouraged me so I decided I could take the leap. (But I still didn't feel real comfortable about writing glowing things about my own brother.)

On the other side of the ledger, I thought I had a couple of plusses going for me. One, this venture would be a pure labor of love for me because I had idolized Jim all my life.(I had seven older brothers and had idolized all of them, for different reasons.) The other plus, as it turned out, was what I said earlier about not really knowing Jim all that well over the years.I had a thirst to make up for that lost time. My curiosity and commitment would be greater. What I didn't know before I started, however, was that while it would be a labor of love for me, it would indeed be a lot of labor.

With both Jim's and my own reservations out of the way, I set off on this journey, in January of 2008. I thought the road ahead looked pretty clear and the goal straight-forward: I'd write a book about my brother's remarkable life. That supposed clarity didn't last very long. Before I'd gone down the road very far, I felt like I'd been using the wrong map. I ran into major detours. My path became congested with new perceptions, emotions and possibilities. I found myself floating about in uncharted territory; I was inside myself for a while, and it was both a little scary and good at the same time, kind of like a twilight zone. I felt like I was missing something important about the book. Then the haze began to lift. I think I know when it happened.

I was driving around Farmington one day when all of a sudden I heard a loud honk from right behind me. Startled, I looked around and noticed that my car had been barely moving. The impatient guy in back of me wanted me out of his way. So I pulled over and stopped. Then it dawned on me what I had been doing. I'd been going at a snail's pace because I was looking all around at everything except the road. I had been looking for places that had been here in the 1940's and 50s when I had grown up. Places like Petrini's Confectionary, the Princess Theater, Jim Fresia's Clothing Store (with our clubhouse in the back) and Dee Massingale's Cream Station, where my brother Harp and I had spent half our lives.I looked for those and more. But they were all gone, and I felt like my own past was gone, like it had never existed. All of that went through my mind in a couple of minutes. Then, just as quickly, it all changed.

On my way to the home of Mrs. Lavonne Welker for a book interview, suddenly I drove right by a remnant of my past: Alexander's Lumber Yard.

(It was the place a lifetime ago, where, when they closed down for the day, my buddies and I waged many a hard-fought rubber gun war among stacks of lumber, sand and building materials.) A minute later, I arrived at Mrs. Welker's. As soon as we exchanged introductions, she said she had known Jim since first grade, and she started talking about both our mother and father. I could barely control my instant reaction, warm and emotional. I managed to keep it inside me until the interview ended and I was on my way back home. During that 100-mile drive I thought about Mrs. Welker, our parents, and all the places in the past.

Now it was beginning to dawn on me. I realized I'd been missing the big picture of the book. My focus had been too narrowly on Jim. The big picture wasn't Jim. The big picture was Jim AND his patients. In fact, they were almost inseparable. Since I now was seeing Jim and his patients as somewhat inseparable, it would be a mistake to write the book as if it weren't the case. Including Jim's patients would therefore imply including everyone in Farmington, which meant me and our family. It seemed to me the only way to make the book feel real and genuine.

My road to the book was now clear. It would need to include Jim's patients nearly as much as it included Jim himself. So I contacted over 70 of his patients and colleagues. I scheduled in-depth interviews with nine patients who had known Jim for an average of an astounding 58 years. What I heard amazed me (as I hope it will amaze you). Their tales of Jim's exploits were heartwarming and inspiring. Added to Jim's own first-person accounts, they presented a life story of a courageous, selfless, highly skilled, humanistic doctor the likes of which the profession of medicine has seldom seen—and may never see again.

After these interviews I finally understood the only piece of advice Jim offered when we started on this journey. When we sat down together for the first time, he told me to talk to his patients. I didn't know what he meant at the time. Now I did. I think the secret of what had been going on in Farmington was that Jim had never separated himself from his rural hometown, from its people and from his youth. He had never tried to be someone else. He'd always been at peace with himself, with his hometown and with its people.

There are thousands of people in the Farmington area who don't need this book to know Jim Reed. They know better than anyone, including me, what he's done for them for more than half a century. They know he's an unusual human being, a hometown country doctor totally dedicated to their care. Hopefully those readers who've never known Dr. Jim Reed will feel like they do by the end of this book.

Part I

Growing A Hometown
Country Doctor

"Life is lived forward but understood backwards"
–Soren Kierkegaard
Danish philosopher and theologian
1813-1885

Chapter 1: Spoon River Roots

Jim Reed was nearly born on the Spoon River. Seventy feet of scrub grass and a one-lane dirt road was all that separated the river from the Reed family home where he was born. "I used to stand on our back porch and fling rocks into her," our older brother, Red, recalled. As rivers go, she was small, flowing southwest from her headwater near Kewanee, Il. about forty miles to the Reed homestead at London Mills, then another forty miles southeast to Havana where she spilled into the Illinois River.

The Spoon River would've remained as anonymous as other Illinois streams like the Mackinaw or Kickapoo, had it not been for a lawyer-poet from nearby Lewistown. In 1915, Edgar Lee Masters published "Spoon River Anthology." His poems about the fictional lives of town folks buried in the local cemetery gained national acclaim and brought sudden notoriety to Spoon River country. (At the same time, known only to scholars of zoology, the Spoon River was rich in clam life; twenty-three years after Jim's birth on her banks, that treasure trove of aquatic life was key in his admittance to one of the world's leading medical schools.)

On April 15, 1927, the greatest sports figure in U.S. history, the larger-than-life Babe Ruth, hit his first home run of the season. Before his year ended, the Bambino had established the most famous event in the history of sports: 60 homers in one season. Meanwhile, folks in New Orleans experienced the largest 24-hour rainfall in U.S. history: 14.94 inches. While all that was going on, Mrs. Bertha Reed was totally consumed with a more personal matter.

On April 15, 1927, James Medill Reed was born in his family's white two-story clapboard house in London Mills, Illinois. Then a tiny hamlet of 400, London Mills is situated on the north side of route 116, about 35 miles due west of Peoria. The attending physician was Dr. C. R. Essex of Galesburg. Jim's birth rated the standard one-sentence announcement in the local newspaper, The London Times. Jim was greeted at birth by his proud parents, Cyril and Bertha Reed, and five brothers and sisters. Virginia was ten; Quentin (Cotton), nine; Willard (Red), seven; Hubert, five; and Barbara Jeanne, four. The firstborn Reed, Elizabeth, had died from cholera in 1919 at age five. Two years after Jim's birth, our family grew again, but this time from tragedy. Our mother's half-sister, Sylvia Pippett, died from cancer, leaving four young children, unable to be cared for by their father. Various relatives took the children in, with six-year old Madeline gladly welcomed into our family. She stayed with us for three years, at which time she was reunited with her three sibs, her father and his new wife.

The London Mills home of Jim Reed's family from 1913-1933

The Reed family migrated to Illinois from Pennsylvania in 1878. William Reed and his family settled in Gilson, a small town fifteen miles north of London Mills. William, our great-grandfather, became sheriff of Gilson. Generations later, one of William's escapades as sheriff remains a favorite piece of family lore. One quiet Sunday in Gilson, nearly everyone was in church. Two career crooks thought that would be the perfect opportunity to enter a home and make off with money and valuables. Tragically, the robbers chose a home of an elderly couple too ill to attend services.

Taken by surprise, the thieves panicked and committed a terrible double murder. Then they mounted their horses and headed south. What they didn't know was the town they picked for their crime had a very determined sheriff. As soon as he learned of the killings, William Reed packed a few provisions, said his quick goodbyes, and saddled his horse.

The chase took William all the way to St. Louis, a distance of nearly 200 miles. After several days of riding, Sheriff Reed finally returned to

Gilson with his captives to avail them of their fair trial before hanging. My hunch is that the appreciation and admiration the Gilson citizenry felt for William Reed was probably on par with how the folks of Farmington feel toward his great, great, great-grandson a century and a half later.

William Reed, the "law"in tiny Gilson, Illinois

Beginning with William's election as sheriff, the Reed family remained closely involved in politics for several generations. (Their leanings fell strongly toward the Republican side of the aisle). Our grandfather, also James Reed, had the honor of once serving as a delegate to the Republican National Convention. So devoted to the party's cause was our father Cyril that he chose Medill as the middle name of his newborn, James, after the publisher of that Republican newspaper bastion, the Chicago Tribune.

Jim Reed was named after his aforementioned paternal grandfather, a successful grocer with stores in Middlegrove, Uniontown and London Mills, Illinois. Cyril Emmons Reed, our father, was born in London Mills on July 8, 1892. After graduating from London Mills High School in 1910, Cyril went to work in his father's store in nearby Middlegrove. Eight years later, the spring of 1918 saw the coming of the greatest health crisis in recorded history, the worldwide Great Flu pandemic. (Before its mysterious disappearance in 1919, it claimed 675,000 lives in the U.S. and at least 20,000,000 worldwide.) For some reason, Cyril Reed, only 26 at the time, took it upon himself to prescribe mega doses of aspirin for his wife, two children, and sundry relatives. Nearly 100 years later, Jim feels strongly that had a lot to do with the fact that none of the Reeds contracted the killer disease. He explained that to this date, aspirin, even though it's one of the greatest drugs ever invented, largely remains a mystery drug, in that science doesn't completely understand how or why it works.

In 1928, Cyril Reed was rewarded for his family's longtime support of the Republican Party when he was appointed Postmaster of the London Mills post office. Unfortunately, political appointees are also subject to political dismissals; his job would be a casualty of the Great Depression and Franklin Roosevelt's victory over Hoover in 1932.

One of the three small groceries owned by Jim's grandfather, James Reed

Jim Reed's mother was born Bertha Alpaugh on September 2, 1896, in a farm house south of London Mills, near the little burgs of Troy and Ellisville Station, both of which are now ghost towns. Her mother, Kate Martin, was one of twelve children—six boys and six girls—born into the financially secure Jacob Martin family, owner of twenty-four area farms. (Each child eventually inherited two farms.) When she became a young lady, Kate fell into family disfavor with her liberal choice of male companions. And there were pregnancies. She moved to nearby Abingdon and, as a single mother, Kate reared her three children, Bertha and her half-sibs, Sylvia Pickett and Waldo Cain.

Jim's maternal grandmother Kate Martin, left, with her twin Cora in 1915

Kate's daughter Bertha, a good student with an inquisitive mind, completed high school in Abingdon. The curricula of high schools at that time resembled present day colleges more than current high schools. For example, Bertha studied four years of Latin. (By the '50s most schools offered no more than two years of that classic language and by the '70s they'd abandoned it altogether.) The study of Latin, the bedrock of our English language, undoubtedly played a key role in Bertha's superior command of vocabulary and grammar. Not only did she display an uncanny ability at completing newspaper crossword puzzles, but when the board game Scrabble became the rage, she destroyed all challengers—including the likes of Jim's close friend, Russ Risdon, holder of two degrees from the University of Illinois, who repeatedly left the games quite frustrated.

    The formal education of our parents may have ended at high school, but most likely both were blessed with more than average basic intelligence. For example, when our father began managing a gambling casino (legal at the time) he quickly mastered the ability to keep track in his head which cards had been played during a blackjack game. Of course, that skill is so desirable that Las Vegas casinos eventually began banning such players as 'card counters.' Dad's favorite daily pastime was sitting in his comfy chair, poring over the Chicago Tribune, loudly making editorial pronouncements for everyone in the house to hear. (Unfortunately for our mother, Dad's booming voice was surpassed only by the ungodly volume of his nightly snoring rampages!)

Jim's parents at age 18 : Bertha Alpaugh(in 1912) and Cyril Reed(in 1910)

In the early 1900s, the most popular social events in rural towns were Saturday night dances. It was at one such social occasion that Jim's mother and father first met. After a few months of Sunday afternoon rides in a horse-drawn carriage—a photo of one such ride remains a family treasure—Cyril and Bertha Reed were married in 1913. But before our father won the heart of our mother, there were other challengers for her affections.

On one date, Dad took Mom to a large festive political rally and a young, handsome man with political ambitions from nearby Pekin showed up. His name was Everett McKinley Dirksen. In 'working the crowd,' as politicians say, our mother caught Everett's eye and he proceeded to strike up a conversation with her. Not being the shy type, he flirted with her and asked her for a date. Mom's version of the whole affair was that while she might have been a little tempted, Dad won out in the battle for her affections because, "he had a nicer horse and buggy."

Dirksen, one of the most popular republicans in the history of Illinois, went on to become a Senatorial fixture in Washington, earning the nickname of"The Silver Tongued Orator." For years, Mom kept a photo of Senator Dirksen on the wall of the back porch of our home. My guess is that Dad only allowed it to remain hanging because he was such a staunch republican.

Already a large family when Jim was born in 1927, the Reed clan grew even more with the addition of Phil in 1929, Marcia Lou in 1930, Greta Gay in 1931, and Clayton (Sonny) in 1933. In 1934, Warner (Harp) became the first child born in Farmington, followed by your humble narrator in 1938 and, finally Alicia Rose, in 1939.

I believe there were three important factors that helped our mother successfully cope with the gargantuan task of rearing fourteen children. One was that ever since she was a child, she regretted never having had a full-blooded sibling. Secondly and perhaps most importantly, she had lost her beloved first-born, Elizabeth, at the tender age of five. And lastly, she always had a deep unabashed love for children. It was a joy and love that never waivered at any time of her life. It's no exaggeration to say she placed a greater value on her love of children than she did on religion or her country or any other aspect of life. She seemed to have that rare innate sense of how to relate to young children. I became fully aware of this only when, as a young teen, I assisted with her day care center which she founded in the early '50s. Evidence of the respect young mothers felt for her was the long waiting list of parents hoping for an opening in her center. Her love for children was so deep that she would become upset when anyone used the term, "kid." "A kid is a baby goat and a young human is a child," she would admonish us. "And you don't raise a child, you raise an animal and you rear a child!"

While Mom's love of children was unquestioned, her and Dad's method of child- rearing differed markedly from that of later generations. The rule of thumb in their day was the "hands off" style of parenting. When the children weren't at home they weren't supervised by parents, who felt no need to know what a child was doing at all times.

The hands-off parenting which Jim Reed and most all other children experienced fit in very nicely in small town America from the '20s through the '50s. Children could wander all over town without any fears from their parents about where they were or what they were doing. There was in fact very little they could do to get into serious trouble even if they wanted to. Everyone knew everyone, and knew everyone's business. There was very rarely crime. Doors weren't locked. Life was slow, secure and satisfying.

Those heartwarming, trademark characteristics of small town America were suddenly dealt a crippling blow on October 29, 1929, the day known in history simply as "Black Friday." The catastrophic effects of the Great Depression wrecked havoc on the rich and the poor, in towns large and small. If any group of people escaped the ravages of the Great Depression, it was young children, because they're a different breed.

They are not simply small adults. Their minds work differently from adults and that was their saving grace during that most stressful time in our country's history. Their developing psyches are not concerned with responsibilities and thoughts of what the future holds. Renowned author (and schoolteacher) Frank McCourt said that "children are almost deadly in their detachment from the world." That is their blessing and accounts for their great resiliency and ability to survive. So it was for the growing clan of Reed children.

Even though Jim Reed was just six and a half when his family moved from London Mills, he left with many fond memories. Close by the home where our family lived stands a very tiny barn. As I viewed it with Jim all these years later, he was dumbfounded at how small it was, saying, "it had seemed so large when we were kids, playing hide and seek and cowboys and Indians in and around it." Then he showed me the nearby piece of land where he saw his first Hollywood motion picture, a Buck Rogers cowboy silent.

Our older sister Barb recalled the most popular activity in London Mills was America's Pastime; next to the Reed's London Mills home was an empty lot large enough to accommodate neighborhood ballgames—but there was one drawback. According to Barb, "there was an old maid named Jane Norville living on the south side of the field, and if the ball rolled into her yard and she happened to be outdoors at the time, she would rush to scoop up and confiscate the ball, thus ending an otherwise joyful outing. Our parents wouldn't let the boys go after the ball and I was too scared to do anything!" Kids of that era kept people like Jane Norville in mind when Halloween rolled around.

Semi-pro baseball teams were very popular in small midwestern towns in the thirties, forties and fifties. Many players were skilled enough for professional ball but player salaries were so meager they instead worked regular jobs, playing ball just for the fun of it, often two or three games a week. These were free, well attended social events. Our Dad managed one such team, and Jim vividly remembered one game: "I was sitting on the bench next to Dad, close to the action, when a screaming liner off the bat came at me so fast I didn't have time to duck and it smacked me square on the head." Luckily, he didn't suffer any serious injury, but it did teach him to pay closer attention to the ballgame!

The young Reed children took great pleasure playing in the shallower part of the nearby Spoon River; but it was a constant source of worry for our mother, forever fretful that she might lose one of them. Her fear only increased when, just a week after Jim's birth, torrential rains wreaked chaos on folks living by the Mississippi River. In what was the greatest natural disaster to that point in U.S. history, about 700,000 people suffered terrible privation. Being about 60 miles east of the Big Muddy, London Mills escaped the disaster—but the flood still exacerbated Mom's fears. She tried to keep all her kids away from Spoon River but it was a difficult task. Jim spent a lot of time down there searching for firewood, and Barb remembered that "whenever one of the kids went missing for awhile, Mom would always send one of us down to the river to scream out the wanderer's name."

For decades in small Midwest towns, the annual social highlight for children of all ages was the Fall Festival. Those carnivals had all the essential ingredients for unbridled allure and excitement, starting with the beautiful calliope music, heard for blocks around. Added to that was the sky-high explosion of bright lights in the middle of the dark night. For children, it had all the glitz and glamour of the Las Vegas strip. Then there was the irresistible appeal of the many rides and games, all the way from the fright of stopping at the very top of the giant ferris wheel arc to the impossible challenge of knocking down all the dirty milk bottles with a baseball.

London Mills was too tiny to support a carnival of its own, so the closest one was in Farmington. In the late summer of 1932, when Jim was only five, he and his three brothers were determined to take in the excitement. Undaunted, they set off on foot—even though their goal was a distant fifteen miles away! Cotton was all of thirteen, Red was twelve and Hubert ten. There they were, the Four Musketeers! According to Jim, "making it there on foot was no problem because we all were filled with adrenalin from the anticipation of the awaiting excitement." After hours of fun (in spite of having very little money to spend) they started home. But with that adrenalin all used up, fatigue set in for young Jim, and so his three brothers had to take turns carrying him piggyback for several miles! For the Reed boys, one big advantage in their upcoming move to Farmington would be a walk of several blocks instead of 30 miles round trip to the carnival.

Jim Reed was only six and one-half years old when his family left London Mills. So you'd probably think nothing there would hold much meaning for him. But Jim has always had an attraction to and appreciation for the past, and he's been returning to London Mills from time-to-time for 75 years. There's really only one reason why: these are sentimental trips that make him feel emotionally good about the distant past, as well as the years in between. And the great thing is that thanks to the miracle of memory, all the good times can be recalled in the blink of an eye. (In an odd coincidence, Dr. E. K. Dimmitt, a beloved Farmington-born doctor who combined with Jim to provide their hometown with over 100 years of continuous medical care, had his first office in London Mills, in the early 1900's.)

Once in a while, Jim's feelings about his birthplace became so strong that he'd think about buying his old home. He told me that once he even inquired of the owners whether they might be interested in selling. (They weren't.) When I asked him what he would have done with the home, his answer was revealing: he said he didn't know. I think the reason he didn't know was that he had simply acted out of strong, fond memories and deep emotions instead of logic.

Chapter 2: Life and Lessons in the Great Depression

Three of Jim's older sibs, in 1923.
From left to right: Virginia, 6,
Hubert, 1 and Quentin, 4

On the left is Jim at 12, in 1939,
with his brother Phil, 10

Willard, 4, in 1924

Barbara Jeanne, 6, in 1929

From left to right, in 1939:
Warner, 5, Clayton, 6, Greta Gay, 8 and Marcia Lou, 9

The youngest Reeds, in 1943,
Rudy, 5 and Alicia Rose, 4

There was nothing approaching 'normality' during Jim Reed's childhood. From the time he was 2 in 1929, until he was 19 in 1946, our country was engulfed in the two greatest national crises since the Civil War. The Reed family's involvement in WWII will be covered in a later chapter. For now, let's see how they managed during the Great Depression.

October 29, 1929, was destined to change the course of American history. 'Black Friday,' as the beginning of the Great Depression came to be known, was the first day of the greatest non-war crisis in U.S. history. No one was spared: rich or poor, black or white, urban resident or small town dweller, including all the folks in London Mills.

The Age of Rugged Individualism had exploded. President Hoover's response that "prosperity was just around the corner" couldn't have been further from reality. Just five short months after Black Friday, unemployment had risen by 500%, and by March, 1933, it had risen by an incredible 900%. Running in the 1932 election, Franklin D. Roosevelt promised Americans a "New Deal." Hoover was swept out of office and FDR's chief policy advisor, social worker Harry Hopkins, proclaimed "the primary job of government is to help people."

From 1929 until 1933, the Reed family got by pretty well because Cyril Reed had remained on as postmaster of London Mills. However, when the Republicans were voted out of the White House in 1932, political patronage job holders such as postmasters were also relieved of their positions. Seeing no future in London Mills, Cyril Reed relocated to Farmington with the hope of finding some type of work in the grocery business through connections his father had had in the Peoria area.

In the late summer of 1933, the Reeds borrowed an old truck, loaded up their belongings and headed off to Farmington. Jim Reed has a clear memory of that day.

"I left town with a handful of Bull Durham tokens I had stashed away under the front sidewalk of our home. When I accumulated them in sufficient quantity, I could exchange them for pennies." It's noteworthy that Jim does not recall being particularly upset about the move. "It was an age," he continued, "when kids were seen and not heard and everyone in the family simply viewed it as something that had to be done and so there was no point in becoming distraught." The trip itself brought some joy because the children were permitted the thrill of riding on the back of the truck, high upon the household furnishings. Jim told me his other most vivid memory of the move was that "all I had to eat the whole day was a banana. In fact, my strongest memory of the next few years of the depression was one simply of hunger."

The Reed's moved into a rental home on the northeast corner of Court Street. Cyril Reed, like so many others, was unable to find steady employment and had no alternative but to apply for welfare. He would remain unemployed until the largest public works program in U.S. history, the federal Works Progress Administration (WPA) was implemented, in 1938. Our father's assignment was in helping construct the Farmington Lake. The project was built completely by hand. Even men with other jobs took any available part-time work. One of those jobs for Dad involved walking five miles to Trivoli to pick corn all day, then walking the five miles back home. His pay for that day's work was $1.00.

Like most men of his generation, our father was a rather reserved man not given to expressing inner feelings and anxieties. In retrospect, it's impossible to measure the damage done, but two important factors helped ameliorate the crippling psychological effects of the Depression. One was that the millions of men put out of work for years knew they weren't responsible for the conditions which had resulted in their debilitating status. Secondly, since nearly everyone in small towns found themselves in the same dire straits, there was much less social stigma and embarrassment attached to their status. But however they did it, Cyril and Bertha Reed kept themselves and their family from slipping into the despair that swallowed many others.

In 1933, when the Reeds settled in Farmington, if the older Reed children didn't already know the meaning of work, they were about to find out. Virginia was 16, Cotton 14, Red 13, Hubert 11, Barb 10 and Jim was 6. "I had two jobs," Jim said, "one was walking the railroad tracks looking for fallen lumps of coal from the passing train cars and the other was scouring the two downtown back alleys for cardboard boxes to be used for burning for house heat." Of course, there was never any money to spend on anything except the absolute essentials. "One Christmas," Jim said, "all that we had under our small Christmas tree was an orange for each of us."

In 1935, Virginia became the first of the thirteen Reed children to graduate from Farmington High School, and she immediately got a job in Peoria as a nanny. Cotton got part-time work at Ingold's gas station across from Chapman School, graduated in 1937, and continued working there until he entered WWII. Red worked part-time at Jackson's Drug Store and Butch Bernardi's grocery store, graduated in 1938, then worked a year at the Clayton Dry Goods store before entering the University of Illinois in 1939. Hubert dropped out of school a year to work at Bernardi's and the bakery before returning to complete his senior year with his sister, Barb, in 1941. Barb worked in the bakery, and like others in the family, also delivered newspapers. She entered Western Illinois University in 1941 and earned her own way with a scholastic scholarship and a job in the Dean's office. The Reed children held so many jobs all over town that sixty years after the Depression, one of Red Reed's coffee klatch buddies told him that when he was a kid he knew there was no use looking for a job because the Reeds already had them all.

The human bedrock of the Reed clan, Bertha Reed, had known what hard work was all about even before the Depression (caring for 7 kids). Now, in addition to running a large household, she began doing washings and ironings for the Presbyterian minister. She also made delicious sugar cake doughnuts which the children would then sell door-to-door on their paper routes.

By listing the many part-time jobs held down by all the Reeds, it becomes apparent that only by everyone pulling together did the family manage to scrape by. Jim recalled that "no one ever had a pair of shoes without holes in the bottom, covered by cardboard." And he added, "no one ever wore new clothes, only hand-me-downs. Twice a year it was a happy occasion when large boxes of clothes would arrive from Mom's aunts who lived in Amarillo, Texas and Pasadena, Cal."

People are very curious animals. Every toddler's favorite word is "why?" We want to know what makes people tick, especially the unusual ones. Whether it's another school shooting or a heroic pilot landing in the Hudson River, we want to know what made them do it. And what makes the question more interesting is that we know there are no pat answers, no sure things. There are no parental or educational molds for producing an assembly line of people with all the desirable characteristics. So what made Jim Reed?

It isn't hard to identify the ways that Jim is different from most people. For example, there's not much doubt he was blessed with quite a bit more pure native intelligence than most of us. But that's nearly all genetics and beyond anyone's control. What about the all-important personality traits like his unusually strong work ethic? And his total devotion to his profession. What about his genuine humility? And the depth of his feeling of responsibility. What about his sense of sharing? And his total dedication to his patients. Where did it all come from?

First a bit of overview is probably in order. We all want what is best for our children. But parenting is anything besides easy, and there is much disagreement about how to best parent. In the first half of the last century, the "how to parent" mania had not yet swept the country. Then, pushed primarily by child psychologists in the early 1960's, the fad became one of protecting young children from any situation which might place them under stress. This new theory of child rearing held that the every child's psyche was delicate as origami and easily disturbed. As a result, the child's universe came to be placed at the center of every family. Educators also swallowed the new theories whole hog. So of course, many trusting and inexperienced parents jumped on board the bandwagon.

The only problem was that nearly everything about the new parenting movement was wrong. Well intentioned, but nonetheless wrong. The misguided efforts, theories and school changes produced a couple of generations of poorly educated, self-centered adults. Fortunately, there remained a few flashlights in the dark, such as the nationally syndicated psychologist, John Rosemond, who had the unmitigated gall to suggest that what we needed was simply a return to the 'good old days' of child rearing, when common sense and not a child's ego ruled the roost.

Perhaps we need to pay heed to the medical research suggesting it is best for a child's developing immune system to be exposed to a less-than sterile environment when young so they will be better able to ward off problems later. Doesn't it make sense that the same strategy might also work for a child's developing personality? Now, let's see how all of this might have affected young Jim Reed.

One of the most harmful results of the overindulging parents of the last 5 or 6 decades has been the spoiled child, the self-centered, selfish child made to feel superior to everyone else. Clearly, Jim Reed, like nearly all kids of that previous era, was not even close to being spoiled. As the seventh of fourteen children, there was no time or money for any spoiling. If a spoiled kid grew up to become a doctor, he would likely be one of those who emits an air of superiority. He would not like to have his opinion questioned—by anyone. And he would likely not have a good bedside manner.

Sharing is a concept that Jim Reed grew up with. In a large family during tough times, sharing was mandatory—all the time. Everything was shared: food, clothing, time, jobs and space. Jim didn't sleep alone until he went to Navy boot camp when he was eighteen. Sharing became embedded in all the Reeds and would last a lifetime. Just three years out of college, Red bought the family a home in 1950. Hubert took one of his nieces into his Chicago home for many weeks when she needed extensive medical care. Cotton provided his sister Greta Gay a job and a home for several months in Sikeston, Mo. And those are just a few examples.

The extensive work histories of the Reed children described earlier can only lead to one conclusion. The highly prized American work ethic was nurtured in every Reed during their formative years. Nearly all parents today—as well as many psychologists—would be shocked and dismayed at the idea of twelve, thirteen and fourteen-year-olds holding down part-time jobs. But I would suggest there is a much different way—a more positive way—to look at those experiences.

Each time Jim Reed successfully completed an assigned task, a building block was put into place for his self-confidence and self-esteem. Most importantly, this was taking place at a subconscious level, the side effect of doing a job, as opposed to the more modern theory of trying to 'teach' this type of personality development by repeating cute mantras, like 'I'm special' in school or plastering bumper stickers on cars saying, 'my child is smart.' That approach produces a false sense of (annoying, cocky) self-confidence. This calm sense of accomplishment that grew slowly inside Jim, day by day, would result in an adult whose response to being described reverentially by his patients was to simply say that "I was just doing the job I was trained to do."

Today's parents would view part-time work for their young child as an imposition on their desire for all sorts of activities. That was not the case back in the forties and fifties. Children then could work and still have time for friends and activities. There were no TV's and computers to mesmerize kids for hours and cause addictions. And kids were not taking soccer, golf, tennis or swimming lessons. There weren't any fields, courses, courts or pools. Back then, kids were on their own .

In small-town America in the 1930's, 40s and 50s, almost everyone knew everyone else. Maybe not intimately but at least as a passing acquaintance. If the Depression did nothing else good, it tended to bring people closer together because of a shared sense of suffering. There is no question that in our emotional lives, the closer we feel to people—be they relatives, close friends or casual acquaintances—the more compassion we're likely to feel for them. And it has a kind of steamrolling effect. Once it reaches a certain level that compassion tends to be extended to complete strangers. For example, as hard up as our family was, Barb Reed recalled that, "The train ran close to our home on Court Street and Mom could not turn away any hobo who'd show up at our doorstep." This genuine type of compassion and sharing with those less fortunate was a model of behavior, and surely influenced the way Jim Reed practiced medicine, offering the same high quality of service to a stranger as he did to patients of fifty years.

We've seen how Jim Reed, as well as most folks of his generation, developed a strong work ethic. Another important quality that went hand-in-hand with that work ethic was mental toughness, a toughness of both the mind and the heart. It's a way of approaching life, of looking at day-to-day problems, dissecting them, attacking them and not giving in to them. I'll never forget the time I experienced that first hand with our mother.

It was 1950 and we had just moved out of our downtown apartment into our home at 154 North West Street. Mom was excited about having a yard again, but knowing financial resources were meager, she had to come up with a shrewd landscaping plan. She was familiar with the nearby Higgins farm. She knew there were many small shrubs there and that Pa Higgins would never miss them. But how to get them? We didn't have a car, but we had an old child's wagon. (Keep in mind that Mom was 54 at the time.) She threw a shovel in the wagon and with me in tow, set off walking to the farm, digging up several shrubs and hauling them back home! Then we transplanted them—and they thrived. That type of dogged determination was passed on to her children. And later we'll hear story after story from Jim's patients about his dedication to their well-being, and his attitude of never giving up.

In this chapter, we tried to show some of the ways Jim's personality and character may have been molded by the environment in which he was reared. That environment included his family life, his community and a major event shaping those times. The glorious thing about children is that given half a chance, they will succeed at growing up good. Jim Reed was given that chance, just to be a kid. In the next two chapters, we'll see what Jim the kid was like.

Chapter 3: Dick and Jane Days

Few events in the life of a child are more memorable than the first day of school. Or at least that's what American folklore would have us believe. Once we grow up and become parents, we learn that most of that was just fantasy. When you stop and think about it, the determined resistance many children exhibit upon being forced to begin their school careers makes more sense than the fantasy scene of kids merrily skipping down the sidewalk with their smiley faces. Jim Reed was one of the resisters and he would not bow to compulsory education without mounting a gallant fight.

The resistance shown by many children stems mainly from their being pulled away from the friendly confines of home. In my profession of social work, we called it separation trauma. In Jim's case, he experienced a double dose of trauma since our family had moved to Farmington just a couple of days prior to the start of the 1933 school year.

When that fatal first day arrived, our poor frazzled mother not only had six children to get off to school, she had to do it while also tending to the never-ending needs of four preschoolers. So the older kids frequently fended for themselves. But as the time grew nearer for the school bell, Mom knew she had better check on Jim. Alas, when she went searching for him, he was nowhere to be found! Seems that while all the commotion was going on, Jim saw his chance to go hide underneath the dark, secluded front porch. Not knowing this, of course, Mom summoned ten-year-old Barbara Jeanne to go hunting for him. "I finally found him," Barb recalled, "fished him out and watched him like a hawk all the way to school."

Once Barb had him safely at the front door of Chapman School, Jim was greeted by Mrs. Marietta Pettyjohn, the wonderful first grade teacher (there was no kindergarten in Farmington.) Even her name was appealing, rolling off your lips like a Gershwin lyric. She was stout but not obese. She looked like she could have put in an hour gardening before she came to school. With short-cropped, curly, whitish hair, she had that special twinkle in her eye which said she really liked children. Our mother had the same twinkle around young children. I think they found children to be intriguing people. I cannot guess at Mrs. Pettyjohn's age because when we were kids, all adults looked old.

She easily had the most pleasant personality of the entire Chapman School staff, which included Miss Palin, Mrs. Higgs, Miss Wasson, Mrs. Hedden, Mrs. Gentle and the principal, Mrs. Burns. Nearly all of these teachers spent many, many years at Chapman School and taught eight or nine of the Reed children. Moreover, each of them remained in Farmington during their retirement years, and Jim would eventually care for them all in his medical practice. I had to ask him specifically about Miss Palin because I'd never seen her smile. I was taken aback when Jim described her as "a very sweet person. In fact, all of the teachers were good patients and I particularly recall Mrs. Burns because she was one of the few patients who always took notes when she would see me."

Jim remembered being surprised "when I discovered how accomplished our music teacher, Mrs Moore, was as a pianist. She was every bit as good as Liberace." As the doctor for all the teachers, Jim's fondest memory was "the day I was summoned to one of their homes for some minor illness, and when I arrived I found all of them gathered there engaged in a game of bridge." So they did socialize outside the school!

Seventy-five years after his first day of school, Jim had no difficulty recalling the experience. "The boy sitting right next to me was crying," Jim said. "He was upset because he had been held back to repeat the first grade." One could speculate that psychologically, Jim's memory of that event sticks out because, even at that young age, he was demonstrating an ability to empathize with someone who was suffering.

Jim's other memory of that first day provided one of the most surprising revelations of his life story. He vividly recalled, "looking toward the front of the room, up toward the ceiling, and seeing a long line of symbols or drawings stretching all the way from one side of the room to the other. I had no idea what it was." Jim had no inkling they were letters of the alphabet! In other words, Jim's life had been void of any attempts to prepare for school in any way, shape or form: no bedtime stories, no Sesame Street, no pre-school, no intellectual stimulation, period.

The thing is, in that generation, unlike today, there was no feeling at all that a child needed to be "prepared" to go to school. The prevailing attitude of parents was, "It's the school's job to teach, not mine." Parents back then valued education but differed from modern parents on how to achieve it. Even if Jim's mother had wanted to do something to "prepare" Jim, she wouldn't have had time to do it, what with ten children and a Great Depression to cope with. Ironically, seventeen years after Jim entered school, his mother would establish the first pre-school center in Farmington, with yours truly as an assistant and close-up observer of her magical charm with young children.

It seems Jim could be a poster boy for that old saying, "It's not where you start out that counts, it's where you end up." When I asked him how long it took for him to begin recognizing the letters and learning the alphabet, he had a ready response: "One day." He thought he was reading within a few weeks time. From that point on, school lessons came quickly and easily for him, and even though it seems a little unbelievable, he told me, "it would be my freshman year in high school before I ever received a grade of anything other than "A." At the same time, Jim made a very relevant point that during his elementary school years, grades "didn't mean much and kids just didn't pay much attention to how smart anyone was." I knew what he meant. I recall that teachers had a system of pasting little sparkling stars next to each student's name on a poster. The blue ones—the ones I usually got—were for the highest scores. But I always wanted the red or green ones because I thought they were prettier.

Going back to that first day, Jim had yet another strange experience. Keeping in mind that he had absolutely no idea of what school was, when Mrs. Pettyjohn announced it was time for morning recess, Jim—not knowing what recess was—saw all the kids leaving for the door and he thought school was over, so naturally he proceeded to head on home! And don't think that just because lessons came easy to Jim right from the start meant he was in love with the idea of school.

At a young age, Jim had a little fear of storms, and combined with a less-than-enthusiastic interest in school, he chose stormy days to occasionally stay home from school. He didn't recall ever getting into trouble for this and claimed "the schools didn't make a big deal out of regular attendance." With each passing year, Jim said he did become more aware that school was easier for him than others, and by the time he started junior high he was a little self-conscious about it, thinking that the other kids might like him less because of it. "It got to the point," Jim said, "that by the time I entered high school, I stopped volunteering to answer questions in class. Some of my teachers made the problem worse. They would call on others but when no one would know the answer, they would look at me and say, 'okay, Reed, what's the answer'?"

When Jim was in the eighth grade he became a patrol boy, and at the end of the school year—because of his service—he was chosen to attend a week-long summer camp in Wisconsin. He didn't pull any punches when I asked him how he liked it. "I hated it! It was the first time I'd ever been away from home overnight. I wrote Mom a postcard the second day I was there begging her to come get me. I told her I was going to die!" Well, Mom didn't rescue him and Jim didn't die. A short six years later he had matured to the point where he enlisted in the Navy without even telling Mom!

All eight Reed boys experienced the same type of slow physical maturation process, which is to say we were all much smaller than most of our classmates. Ted Farmer, a close friend of Jim's, now living in Topeka, Kansas, recalled that, "Jim was the smallest kid but also the fastest kid on our teams." In fact, in junior high, his lack of size was a positive on the basketball court because they had three different teams: the featherweights, lightweights and heavyweights. Jim was the only kid small enough but yet skilled enough to play on all three teams.

Jim's childhood friend and junior high basketball teammate, Ted Farmer

Chuck Thomas—a father
figure to Jim—and his dog,
Popeye

Bill Thomas with his dog,
Monar, and Jim's brother, Phil

Like most other kids, Jim's fondest memories of his growing up years centered on his friendships and non-school activities. Disinclined to be there or not, on his first day of school Jim made his first friend in Farmington, a classmate named Billy Max Thomas. Billy Max's parents, Chuck and Dorcus, owned and operated Thomas' Tavern, located in the building directly south of the Princess Theater. Even though the Thomas' lived above their tavern, they had a surprisingly large backyard second to none in terms of a place where kids could have fun.

Their backyard was untraditional, filled with waist-high weeds—tailor-made for games of hiding. Sitting in the middle of the yard was a full-sized streetcar filled with a wide range of collectibles like chairs, tables and lamps. In addition, there was a small shed, providing the most sought-after hiding spot: a rooftop. The Thomas yard backed up into the yard of the blacksmith shop, which always had two or three old rusted-out machines on display. A block-long back alley ran along the south side of the yard, and a decrepit, six-foot wooden fence separated the yard from the alley. This paradise of weeds, nooks and crannies became the playground for the post-Jim generation of Reeds when the family moved from Vernon Street in 1940 to an apartment above Betty Anne's Bakery, right across the alley from Thomas'.

In retrospect, Jim felt that Billy Max, an only child, was always a little embarrassed that his parents had a tavern. Jim on the other hand never shared Billy Max's conflicted feelings, and recalled the tavern "being so clean, free of bad influences and language that my elementary teachers would sometimes have lunch there." Of all the stories in this book which were borderline unbelievable—and there were many—that one actually ranked near the top for me. I was utterly unable to picture either Miss Laura Palin or Miss Ellen Wasson ever setting foot in any establishment serving alcoholic beverages. Another reason I had trouble swallowing Jim's story was because our brother Harp told me his standard Saturday night entertainment was sitting on the flat roof of our apartment building with a bird's eye view of the entrance to the aforementioned Thomas' tavern. "Just like clockwork," Harp said, "a drunken brawl would break out there every Saturday night." When I confronted Jim with Harp's less savory image of the tavern, Jim started laughing and granted that Harp's story was accurate; but "the same guys who had fought on Saturday night would be back drinking and joking around together the very next day."

Besides Billy Max Thomas, Jim's circle of friends included Ted Farmer, Lloyd Albert Smith, (son of the local jeweler) Tom Anderson, (son of the funeral director) Harold Colvin, who later graduated from the Naval academy and flew fighter jets, Bill Jackson, Francis Vandervoort, (son of the druggist) Donnie Smears, who later worked with Jim at the bakery, Don "Peelie" Swartword, and John "Bud" Toft, one of Jim's two closest remaining living friends. In addition, there were two tomboys who were as athletic as most of the boys: the Tiezzi sisters, Frances and Nancy, a good friend of our sister Barb.

Jim was like most other kids all over small town America in the thirties and forties in his enjoyment of what he called "good, clean harmless fun." Cops were never involved. The term "delinquent" was never heard. And parents usually had no idea what their kids were doing. (My strong suspicion is that had she known what was going on, our mother would not only have not objected, but would have experienced a little vicarious pleasure. She liked seeing a characteristic in kids she often referred to as "gumption." In an adult, it's what Ed Asner meant when, on the very first episode of one of TV's historic sitcoms, he told Mary Tyler Moore she had "spunk.")

The only drawback to the escapades of Jim and his friends was that someone had to be the butt of their pranks. Often, that victim was Francis Vandervoort. While other kids didn't really hate Francis, he was far from the most popular boy in town; he was considered by most kids to be the town nerd. And he tended to have a little air of superiority about him. Now it just so happened that there was an outhouse behind the drugstore owned by Francis' father. On one particular night, Jim and his buddy, Mervin Kelly, hatched a scheme guaranteed to teach Francis a lesson in humility.

They quietly and carefully lifted the outhouse off its foundation and moved it back just far enough that the infamous "hole" was now situated right inside the door. Then, after hiding behind the outhouse, they let out with a loud scream for help. Hearing the SOS call, Francis immediately bolted out of his dad's store and headed for its source: the outhouse. (At this point, it would be in poor taste to describe in messy detail what happened next. Suffice to say the deviously clever practical joke went off exactly as planned.)

Francis found himself in a terrible spot. It was too deep for him to escape from without help. Jim said that Mervin "favored a course of action called 'getting the hell out of there,' but I convinced him we'd better lend Francis a helping rope." Hard as it is to believe, Jim added that "Francis took the joke in the mood in which it had been intended." If that was the case, then I think we can all agree that Francis was a better kid than anyone had given him credit for being.

Our own sister, Marcia Lou—younger than Jim by four years—was the butt of another of Jim's ingenious pranks. Behind the Reed's home on Vernon Street was a back alley accessing the back entrances to the businesses on Fort Street. One of those businesses stored a few large concrete containers for funeral caskets. The shed holding the containers had no door, since no one was about to walk off with such a heavy load.

Now, it so happened that storage shed was on the direct path Marcia Lou would take to get home in the dark from the Princess Theater, where she was a frequent moviegoer. Jim and his buddy, Chick Jacobus, waited until a horror movie was playing. Then, as the ending time for the movie approached, they climbed inside one of the concrete containers, propped open the lid a few inches, and prepared for Marcia Lou to pass by. Alone. Just as she did, they let out blood-curdling screams. The rumor is that Marcia Lou established a new world's record for getting home, and that she never again set foot in the back alley, at least after dark.

Halloween tricks were so commonplace they were not only expected but always went unpunished. It was often seen by kids as a time to get even with some adult you weren't too fond of. Jim recalled the time a couple of kids walked out to a farm under the cover of darkness and, um, borrowed a cow. Then they led the confused Guernsey into town and tied her up on the front porch of Mr. Huff, the school principal. What the kids hadn't known was that earlier in the day, the cow had apparently eaten something that disagreed with her. So she deposited quite a mess. Not Mr. Huff's favorite memory, no doubt. Or the cow, for that matter.

Jim was good friends with the aforementioned Bob "Chick" Jacobus, who lived across the street from the Reeds. Chick was three years older than Jim but in those days, in a small town, age differences didn't mean much because all the kids knew each other. The friendship between Jim and Chick developed from their mutual love of the outdoors. Now, BB gun shooting was a popular sport, and Chick was a crack shot. He took the time to teach Jim how to shoot and handle a gun. Jim mentioned the thrill when Chick finally saved enough money for an old second hand .22 rifle. It was deemed a definite step toward manhood.

Bob "Chick" Jacobus, several years Jim's senior, was a big brother figure, instilling a lifelong love of the outdoors in Jim

The Fourth of July was more fun for kids in the thirties and forties because there weren't many restrictions on fireworks. Big, powerful firecrackers called M-1's were commonplace and could easily take a finger off a careless kid. As it happened, Chick had a kid-hating old maid living right next door to him. Jim said "the only thing she liked was her precious, fancy marlin birdhouse perched high atop a pole in her backyard." On this particular Fourth, Jim and Chick decided to get even with her for acts like keeping their baseballs that were hit into her yard. So Jim got a couple of small green apples and carefully carved a hole in each just large enough to tightly hold a M-1 firecracker. Then, deadeye Chick loaded one of the atomic apples into his trusty slingshot and took aim. At that point, Jim lit the M-1. "Chick's first volley was a tad off," said Jim, "but then, after making a slight adjustment in his aim, he hit the bullseye, blowing the hell right out of the birdhouse." Chick and Jim continued to hunt together (but not for birdhouses) right up to the time that Chick went into WWII. "On his first test on the firing range," Jim added, "Chick got a perfect score and was assigned to an elite sniper unit."

One of the most popular kids games throughout the thirties, forties and fifties was kick the can. Any number could play, all ages could play, and all you needed was a tin can and some space. Now, the Reed's front yard was a gathering place for kids, including games of kick the can. And in that front yard, there was a small gas pipe sticking about four inches up out of the ground. One day, Jim was the "it" guy. He purposely captured everyone except—you guessed it, Francis Vandervoort.

At that point, Jim placed the can over the gas pipe. (For those readers unfamiliar with the rules, kids who hadn't yet been caught could free everyone if they beat the "it" kid to the can and kicked it before the "it" kid got there and jumped over it.) Once Jim spied Francis in his hiding spot the race to the can was on. Of course, Jim slowed down to let Francis get there first. When that happened, the unfortunate Francis kicked the immovable object, and went tumbling. Asked if Francis didn't break his toe, Jim's laughing response was, "not that I recall!"

Another popular game was "rubber guns." Basically, it was a version of cops and robbers for older kids. Like all games back then, it was cheap. All it required was some discarded pieces of wood and old car rubber inner tubes, free for the taking at Switzer's or Schuler's gas stations. Your gun, hand made, was just a block of wood with another small trigger-release piece of wood nailed to the back. The bullet was a thin round piece of inner tube, cut and stretched tightly across the gun. It was then fired by releasing the trigger. The bullets were capable of high speeds, distance and pain infliction. But no one in Farmington ever had their eye put out. Or, err, not that I recall.

In small towns all over America, one of the most popular of all extracurricular activities was participation in the school band. Since many of Jim's junior high friends were band members, he naturally joined up, even though he had never demonstrated any interest in music. During the once weekly music classes, Jim pulled his trumpet out of its case and gave it his best shot. But his heart was never really in it. That's why during the week between music classes, his trumpet never left its case. So, when he entered high school, his music career ended.

Jim stands below and to the right of principal Miss Mary B. Wright, holding his trumpet

We should not leave Jim Reed's Dick and Jane days without again emphasizing that all the kids around his age, all over America, were growing up during the worst domestic crisis in United States history: the Great Depression. The fact that Jim, and millions of boys and girls across America could, under those grave conditions, lead pretty normal childhoods speaks worlds about the amazing resiliency and optimistic nature of children. And it is also a great credit to parents whose families could have so easily collapsed during those tough times.

Chapter 4: F. C. H. S.

**Farmington Community High School opened in 1926. All thirteen
Reed children graduated here, from 1935-1957.
The school was vacated for a new grade K-12 mega campus in 2004**

When Jim Reed and his freshman classmates entered Farmington
Community High School in the fall of 1941, they had no idea that in
three short months their country would be engulfed in war. Instead, their
main concern was how to survive the time-honored tradition known as
"Freshman Initiation."

Initiation was a one-day school event in which each freshman
was assigned—by lotto draw—to one senior whose job it would be
to publicly embarrass and humiliate him or her to the highest degree
possible. For that one day, roughly a month into the school year, every
freshman was required to totally obey every command of their senior,
no matter how disgusting or dangerous, within reason. All the while,
the sophomores, juniors and—worst of all—the entire faculty (!) stood
around doing nothing except enjoying the spectacle.

It's difficult to overstate the lurking fear that the impending day
pierced into the hearts of the freshmen. Weaker high school plebes

considered such drastic alternatives as dropping out of school or infecting oneself with some contagious disease. On the other hand, seniors who'd waited three long years to do unto others what had been done unto them, took softly sadistic pleasure in what was about to happen. First of all, the freshmen were made to wear the ugliest, nastiest costumes imaginable, designed by their senior leader. On top of that, you usually had to carry around something stupid all day long. Something, say, like an aromatic necklace of garlic cloves. Also, you had to stand at the feet of your senior all day long. (Of course, it just seemed like a week.) You had to honor their every command, no matter how pointless. Something, say, like running two laps around the track while carrying an armful of books, or singing some stupid song, out loud, in front of people.

Two of Jim's closest, lifelong friends, John "Bud" Toft on the left, and Virgil Hedden at high school freshman initiation in Sept., 1942

Bud, on the left, and Virgil pose for their 1946 high school graduation photos

Jim Reed was one of the few very lucky freshmen. The senior who'd drawn his name was a gentle soul named Rudy "Bud" Rolando. Bud had a part-time job at a shoe store and fortunately for Jim on the day of initiation Bud needed to make several deliveries to customers. Basically, that's all he made Jim do. He didn't have to dress up in some ridiculous outfit. Personally, I think Bud was just lacking in imagination. Unfortunately for Jim's little sister, Marcia Lou, Jim wasn't lacking in imagination.

When Jim became a senior, and it was his turn to do the initiating, he fixed the draw so that he just happened to get his sister's name. Jim knew that Marcia was a little skittish and easily frightened, which made his task all the more inviting. First, Marcia was blindfolded. Then Jim and a buddy brought out a small bowl of water with two oysters in it. Marcia was told she was going to have to pick two eyeballs and eat them. Then they slowly put her hand into the water to touch the oyster. Then, Jim's friend let out a blood-curdling yell which only got worse as Marcia put the oyster in her mouth. At that point, fearful that Marcia might be having a heart attack, they pulled the blindfold off her! Apparently she responded well to resuscitation and was able to survive the day.

During his high school years, Jim continued to build on personal relationships formed during his earlier school years, with kids like

Bill Thomas, Bud Toft, Tom Anderson, Dick Westerby, Don "Peelie" Swartward and Ted Cramer. At the same time, he began forming friendships with farm kids he hadn't met before high school because they hadn't attended elementary or junior high in Farmington; one such farmboy was Art Pille. Art was a year behind Jim and quickly became best friends with fellow classmate, Dick Westerby. Art and Dick were actually closer to each other than they were to Jim—but they all became close when Jim and Art roomed together in college. Art was a brilliant student and succeeded Jim as high school valedictorian. He grew up on a farm near Hanna City and as a farm boy, he had a choice of high schools. (Art's older brother, Bob, had instead elected to go to Peoria Manual High School; Bob went on to become a well-known Chicago newspaper sports writer.)

Two more of Jim's close childhood friends, Don, "Peelie" Swartwood, on the left, and Wayne Doubet

Wayne Doubet came into F.C.H.S. from a farm near Middlegrove. It wasn't until then that Jim learned he and Wayne were second cousins. The Doubets were a large clan and had married into the equally large family of Martins. (Jim's maternal grandmother was one of six Martin sisters.) While wartime rationing limited teenage access to gasoline, Jim and his buddies did manage some infrequent outings. Jim recalled when "a bunch of us loaded into someone's truck and headed for the skating rink in Canton. There weren't enough seats for everyone so Wayne plopped down on top of a paint can. And when we arrived, he stood up and had a ring of paint around his rear." Bud Toft felt free to admit after 65 years that "one reason we were able to make a rare trip out of town was that me and Vigil Hedden would occasionally siphon off gas from Garth Wilcoxen's car while he was working inside the bakery with Jim."

Virgil also lived on a farm near Middlegrove, and was forced to miss an entire year of school due to rheumatic fever (thus, he was a year behind Jim.) Along with Jim and Bud Toft, Virgil shared among other adventures, the trio's hobby of pigeon collecting. Now, the only place to capture them was in a farmer's barn, so the guys would wait until Saturday night when all the farm families spent the evening in Farmington. Key to the capture is that when you shine a flashlight directly into the eyes of pigeons, they're momentarily stunned, giving you just enough time to grab one by the legs and drop the dumbfounded bird into a waiting gunnysack. The pigeons were found in the haylofts of the barns; since they perched on a small ledge near the top of the barn, reaching them was not a simple matter. One small misstep and serious bodily damage could have resulted. Once captured, the birds were cooped up in backyard cages, simply to be admired. Little did Jim know at the time that he would later develop a lifetime hobby of collecting homing pigeons, famous for their role in both World Wars.

Jim, Bud, and Virgil also did a lot of winter trapping, mostly for muskrats but also coon and fox. They spent the majority of their time in strip mine areas north and west of Farmington. Trapping there was a tough, cold job, so they built a big sled with sides and a top for hauling traps, and for sitting in to shield themselves from hateful northwest winds. They would sell their catch to the Perardi Fur Company. Muskrats brought about $2.00 apiece.

Also during winter months, ice hockey games were hotly contested on a pond west of the old Higgins farm near the railroad overpass. The only cost was a pair of blades which just clipped onto your street shoes. You made your own hockey stick and anything could serve as a puck. Jim still sports a small scar near his chin where a tin can puck clipped him over sixty years ago.

While the outdoors was his first love, Jim also enjoyed an indoor activity whose popularity was largely due to the war: assembling complex model planes. In those days model building was not done with plastic parts. Instead, each part—and there could be hundreds of them—

was made of lightweight balsa wood. Each piece had to be cut by hand from a large master drawing and individually glued into place. Some of these behemoths had a four-foot wingspan. The propellers were hand wound with a big rubber band, but still the planes could stay airborne up to two or three minutes. In spite of the elaborate nature of the planes they were relatively inexpensive, at about $3.00.

Like every one of the eight Reed boys, Jim was small and skinny as a teen, weighing a staggering 105 pounds as a freshman. But he was fast and he was fearless. So, in spite of his size, he wanted to try out for the football team. Early on in the fall practices, one of the drills was to have the running backs field long, high punts and try to elude two large onrushing linemen. Jim made the wrong move and was simultaneously smashed by both of them. As he lay motionless on the ground, Walter Grebe, the football coach, rushed to his side.

Legendary Farmington coach Walter Grebe and Mrs. Grebe

Coach Grebe could tell right away Jim had sustained a serious shoulder injury and was in need of emergency help. He carefully picked Jim up and placed him in his car. Before he took off for the hospital, he sent a kid to tell Dr. Dimmitt to meet them at the hospital. And he sent another kid to break the bad news to Jim's parents. Upon examination at the hospital, Dr. Dimmitt decided to hold off on surgery for two weeks to see how the shoulder might heal. For most teachers, that would have been the end of their involvement. But Walt Grebe was not most teachers.

Coach Grebe knew that Jim was about to experience the longest, loneliest two weeks of his young life. He also knew the Reed family was poor and did not have a car. So, for the next 14 days, what Coach Grebe did, every single day, was to give one of Jim's friends the keys to his car, and have him take one of the cheerleaders and drive down to visit Jim. (A little beauty never hurts.) And he also arranged to have Jim's mother driven down to visit him several times. These acts of kindness and consideration demonstrated the kind of man Walt Grebe was and Jim Reed would never forget it.

When Walt Grebe came to Farmington in 1937, he didn't know anyone. The student manager on his first football team was our brother Red. It was customary for the noontime service club to invite new teachers to their meetings, and they were asked to bring along a student. Before he was even in high school, Jim was chosen for that honor by Coach Grebe. To this day, he doesn't know why he was chosen. His hunch is that Red had something to do with it. Coach remained a quiet, private man throughout his life, and Jim considered it intrusive to ask him about it.

Little did Jim know in 1941 that only fifteen years later, he'd become the doctor for Coach Grebe's family and begin paying him back for all he'd done. He doctored him for 39 years before Coach passed away in 1995 at age eighty-seven. There are a couple of indications of how close their relationship became. Coach was one of the few people Jim invited to accompany him to horse races, once to the Quad Cities and once to Chicago. In retirement, Coach's passion was to work on the upkeep of Farmington Lake, and Jim helped him by purchasing the necessary chemicals. Then, late in life, Coach was elected into the Greater Peoria Sports Hall of Fame. Jim was surprised and honored when Coach told him he wouldn't attend the induction ceremonies unless Jim accompanied him. Walt Grebe had attained legendary athletic status in the state of Illinois. He was elected to the Western Illinois University Sports Hall of Fame, as well as to the Illinois High School Association Sports Hall of Fame. For six consecutive seasons, from 1945-1950, his football teams compiled (at that time) the second best six-season record in the history of the state, losing only twice. But those of us lucky enough to have known Coach well will remember him best as a compassionate, fair, kind role model for children of all ages. And no one remembered that better than Jim Reed.

The second man that Jim got to know very well as a result of his football injury was Dr. E. K. Dimmitt of Farmington. After two weeks of what Jim described as very painful watchful waiting with the hope that his arm might heal naturally, surgery was performed by Canton surgeon Dr. Coleman. Following that came four weeks of intensive physical rehabilitation. Unlike today's comprehensive physical therapy departments in modern hospitals, with treatments performed by professionally trained specialists, Jim's therapy was performed by Dr. Dimmitt himself in his own office. Jim said the therapy sessions lasted about an hour and consisted primarily of Dr. Dimmitt (a strong, tall man) leaning Jim against a wall while he placed a lot of pressure on Jim's back and shoulder. Since each session took an hour, Dr. Dimmitt had Jim come up to his office every night at 9:00 P.M., just as his office was closing. Looking back, given the state of the rehab profession at that time, Jim has no complaints about the care he received; and as was the case with Walt Grebe, Dr. Dimmitt ultimately became a patient of Jim's.

The premature end of Jim's football career marked the beginning of his four year work career with Betty Anne's Bakery, a local institution known far and wide for the superior quality of their delicacies, especially their raised glaze doughnuts. People came from miles around to indulge themselves. Mrs. Helen Gasparovich Gray is a Betty Anne historian, having worked there from 1944 until it closed in 1972. "One group of folks," she told me, "regularly came all the way from Kewanee, 40 miles away, just for the doughnuts."

Jim worked as a doughnut glazer for several hours every day after school. He was so short he had to stand on a box to do his job. The piping hot doughnuts were dumped into large vats of glaze where Jim—and his classmate Donnie Smears—had to flip each one over so both sides were glazed. Some other workers were Sam Yancik, Garth Wilcoxen, Mae Wilson and the head baker, Harry Blackmer. With no air conditioning and hot ovens working overtime, the temperature was nearly unbearable. But even in those tough working conditions, it was not all work and no play for Jim and his partner in mischief, Donnie.

You see, some of the doughnuts would accidentally fall to the floor, and it seemed wasteful to Jim to just throw them away. So he came up with an ingenious prank plan. It so happened that the back of the bakery was directly across from the front door of Thomas' Tavern. The key to the prank was the location of the bakery's huge exhaust fan in direct line with, and just a few feet away from, Thomas' front door. "When we'd have a lull in our work," Jim said, "we'd take the discarded doughnuts, sit in front of the fan, wait for a slightly tipsy patron to exit the tavern and then throw the doughnuts into the exhaust fan. The fan then chewed up the doughnuts and spewed them out all over the unsuspecting patrons who never knew what hit them." But there was one day when the timing of their escapade couldn't have been worse.

The bakery staff regularly walked down the back alley to get back and forth from the retail store to the production shop. On the particular day in question, Jim and Donnie were in their "firing" positions with their eyes glued to Thomas' front door at the exact same time that Clyde Barley, co-owner of the Bakery, happened to be coming down the alley. As luck would have it, he stepped in front of the fan at the same time a patron was leaving Thomas' and sure enough—WHAMOO—he was splattered! Jim's recollection was that Clyde took the incident with a good laugh and did not deal out any disciplinary action to the guilty parties.

The owners of the bakery knew full well they were breaking the child labor laws when they hired 14-year-old Jim Reed. And therein lies one of the great folklore stories of the bakery's history, according to Mrs.Gray, to whom the story was told by co-owner, Leo Lint. "The Department of Labor staff," she says,"was notorious for dropping in unexpectedly to check up on us. One day a nice lady who worked at the diner called the bakery and told Mr. Lint an inspector had just left their place and might be on his way to the bakery. Leo's first thought was to hide Jim Reed. Nearby there was a huge, nearly empty flour barrel. Someone had the brainstorm to stash Jim inside the barrel. So they did and then covered the top with a big tray of jellyrolls. The inspector soon showed up but his search of the bakery for violations proved fruitless."

There were many personal connections between the bakery and the Reed family. The bakery was co-owned by Clyde Barley and Leo Lint, and took its name—The Betty Anne Bakery—from the name of Clyde Barley's youngest daughter, who was a classmate and close childhood friend of our sister, Alicia Rose. The Barley's oldest daughter, Ruth Anne, was a classmate and close friend of our sister, Marcia Lou. The Barley's son, Dick, was a childhood friend of our brother, Sonny. The head baker was Harry Blackmer. His daughter, Ruth, was a good friend of our sister, Greta Gay. His two sons, Norm and Dale "Jasper" were friends of Sonny and brother Harp. Harp recalled going to the Blackmer home on Christmas day because "they always got a lot of neat games." Other Reeds also worked in the bakery. Barb worked in the retail shop. Hubert drove a bakery delivery truck. And when Jim left for the service in 1945, his brother Phil took his job.

Jim recalled that he made about $21.00 a week at the bakery, big money for a 14-year-old kid in those days. His take from his wages was just 35 cents a week, and he blew that amount on a daily Milky Way candy bar. (A nickel per Milky Way, obviously.) The rest of his wages went to our mother. We'd be remiss in leaving the Betty Anne saga without mentioning that to this day, some Reed family members hold a grudge against Jim for not preserving the mystical formula for the best-ever-made-scrumptious Betty Anne Bakery glazed doughnuts. We should also note that Jim provided medical care to Mrs. Harry Blackmer from 1956 until her death in 2009 at age 100.

It's not uncommon for high school juniors and seniors to spend many hours wondering what their immediate post-high school life will be. But that wasn't a concern for Jim and his high school senior buddies. They knew exactly what lay ahead and it wasn't pleasant.

Jim Reed's high school graduation photo, 1945

Part II

The Education Of A Physician

"The true student possesses in some measure a divine spark which defies definition, but there are three unmistakable signs by which you can recognize the genuine article. First is an absorbing desire to know the truth. Second is an unswerving steadfastness in pursuit of the truth. And lastly an open, honest heart, free from suspicion, guile and jealousy."

--- Dr. William Osler, M.D.
"The Father of Modern Medicine"
McGill University School of Medicine
Class of 1872

Chapter 5: The War

December 7, 1941, started out like every other wintry Sunday for fourteen-year-old high school freshman Jim Reed. He'd just completed home deliveries of the thick, heavy Sunday edition of the Peoria Journal Star. It was a tough job for a young kid and help never came from a parent or a car. A kid would either use a wagon or make two out-and-back trips on foot or by bike, taking only half the route at one time. Regular customers numbered about one hundred. Shortly after returning home from his route, the phone rang. It was a supervisor at the Peoria office of the paper telling Jim to be ready to make another delivery. The paper was printing a rare special edition with news of the Japanese bombing of Pearl Harbor.

From a "date which will live in infamy" until the surrender of Japan nearly four years later, Jim's life, and those of most Americans, would be dominated by World War II. Upon first hearing the news of Pearl Harbor, Jim recalled his immediate reaction was one of, "Please let it be over by the time I graduate from high school." That would not come to pass. Civilian life in small towns went forward but it was different. Jim recalled that school went on pretty much as usual but "there was a different feeling about it."

In Studs Terkel's remarkable oral history book, "The Good War," that feeling was poignantly captured by a fourteen-year-old girl when she recalled "What I feel most about the war, it disrupted my family. That really chokes me up, makes me feel very sad that I lost that. On December 6, 1941, I was playing with paper dolls: Deanna Durbin, Sonja Henie. I had a Shirley Temple doll that I cherished. After Pearl Harbor, I never played with dolls again."

Jim Reed didn't recall that a lot of time was spent talking about the war at school or at home. It may have been an attempt to escape from reality. But there could be no escape. News of the war dominated the radio, the papers and, to a lesser extent, the movie theaters, the only place where real war scenes could ever be seen. Jim remembered learning of the first casualty of a person he knew, Walter Blessing, a young neighbor kid from just down the street. But there was another reason Jim couldn't avoid the harsh realities. He had three older brothers in the Armed Services.

Top row: left to right, Quentin "Cotton" and Hubert
Bottom row: left to right, Willard "Red" with our mother, and Jim

Our oldest brother, Cotton, enlisted in the Air Force in the summer of 1941, when he was twenty-two. Since his graduation from high school, Cotton had been working at Thede Ingold's gas station across the street from Chapman School. Cotton lucked out, spending his entire tour of service stateside at bases in Illinois, Missouri and Texas.And even though he'd never been inside of an airplane prior to the war, by the time his tour was over he was teaching instrument flying.

Hubert Reed enlisted in the Navy in the summer of 1942, when he was twenty years old. (He had been working at the Betty Anne Bakery after high school.) Hubert saw heavy combat activity while serving aboard a fuel tanker in the South Pacific as a machinist's mate. In 1945 when his ship was in the vicinity of Iwo Jima, it came under heavy Japanese Kamikazee attacks for an interminable thirteen consecutive days and nights; Hubert was fortunate to escape that barrage without incurring any wounds.

Our brother Red was drafted into the Army from the University of Illinois in the fall of 1942, at the age of twenty-one. He was a member of the Allied Forces Normandy invasion. His 30th Infantry Division landed on the beaches on day 17 of the invasion. While serving as a forward artillery observer, Red received a leg wound at the battle of Hodge Row at St. Lou on July 9, 1944. He was discharged with the Bronze Star, the Purple Heart and a limp which would be with him for the rest of his life. Red spent a year in rehab in the Hines VA Hospital near Chicago before returning to the University of Illinois, where he received his accounting degree in 1947.

In December, 1941, Jim Reed was only two and a half years removed from having spent his first night away from home and writing to his mother that he was "dying" in summer camp. Now he was only 3 ½ years away from spending his first night in the Navy and "never again feeling homesick."In December, 1941, Jim Reed had no idea that for his entire professional life of 56+ years, he'd be closely involved in the treatment of many physical and emotional injuries suffered by American veterans of war, scars which are too often forgotten by many of us.

A staggering, unimaginable total of 16,000,000 American men and women served in the war. With few exceptions, nearly every able-bodied man from the ages of 18 to 40 was destined to serve. For high school kids like Jim Reed, it became apparent nearly every classmate would be called to duty. There were at least three powerful psychological forces at play in teens and young adults feeding into their willingness to join the cause. First and foremost was the normal desire of every male teenager to prove and demonstrate his approaching manhood. Without war, this is evidenced in activities like drinking, smoking, a fascination with cars, dating and, of course, contact sports. But there was no more visceral way to channel those inevitable urges than with guns and conflicts. Secondly, teens want to emulate the behaviors of those they admire and respect, like parents, uncles, brothers and friends. In times of war, that translates into, "if they're all signing up, then it must be the thing to do." And then there is the patriotic pull on the heartstrings of fighting for Old Glory, country, the survival of democracy and our way of life. As a result, the nearest Armed Services recruiting station was a popular destination for Jim and all his classmates, while they were still in high school.

For those of Jim Reed's patients who've felt for years that he was infallible, not truly human like the rest of us, here is where the bubble of fantasy and wishful thinking is burst. Jim Reed was about to lie. It may have been white in color—and justified by the times—but it was still a lie. And to make matters worse, it was an official lie to the U.S. government! It happened at the Armed Services Recruiting Station in Springfield in the Spring of Jim's senior year. Now, hundreds of thousands of guys were lying about their ages in order to be accepted into the service. But some, like Jim, lied about their medical conditions.

Jim's fib was different from most. Since he was applying for the Navy, one of the questions asked was if you had ever walked in your sleep, because they didn't want someone walking off the side of a ship in the middle of the night. Jim answered "no" when in fact he had sleep walked! He recalled his first incident at age fifteen when we were living in our downtown apartment. "In the middle of the night, wearing nothing but a pair of shorts, I strolled down the stairs right onto the sidewalk and over to the front door of Betty Anne's Bakery, where I worked. When I woke up I was trying to open the door." (My own theory is he was after more of the scrumptious glazed doughnuts made at the bakery.) Jim did have an episode in the service, but fortunately it happened at Great Lakes and no one became aware of it. (His last episode ever took place while he was in Med school.) With his fib secure, Jim passed his physical exam and was accepted for assignment to the Great Lakes Naval Training base and ordered to report the day after graduation.

If I were on a college debate team and had to take sides of who suffered most in the war, I'd opt for the side arguing on behalf of mothers. The boys in uniform were kept busy most of the time, a key to warding off the debilitating effects of constant anxiety. In addition, they were always part of a group of buddies. But the mothers had to fend for themselves, 24 hours a day, consumed with not knowing what was happening to their sons. And for our mother, those feelings were multiplied by three—and when Jim left, by four. Most soldiers weren't allowed to reveal either where they were going or what they were doing. Every letter home was censored. Under such conditions, it was not unusual for mothers to think the worst was happening. Jim's recollection was that our mother wrote Red, Cotton and Hubert nearly every day, even though it might take several weeks for a letter to reach them. On the other hand, her sons did not write home very often. Jim felt "we just didn't have that much to say."

Of course, before soldiering Jim had been a teenager not unlike so many others. One difference, though, was that for earning valedictorian honors as the top student in his high school class, Jim won a scholarship to the University of Illinois. But before he'd graduated, the school principal, Russell Troxel, confronted Jim with the harsh realities of war. He put it to Jim that "since there was a chance you might not return from the hostilities, would you agree to surrender the scholarship to the highest ranking senior girl." Jim conceded.

Jim's enlistment agreement stipulated he would report for duty the day following his graduation. That's what he did; sixty-three years later he can still vividly recall those first two days with Uncle Sam. With his bag packed, he remembered "being disappointed my parents didn't even walk with me down our apartment stairs to the bus station." Like most young people, he was unable to understand the agony his parents were experiencing at sending yet another of their sons off to war. They could not bear the burden of seeing him leave. (Coincidentally, just one month after writing those words, I was watching a PBS Masterpiece Theater play about Rudyard Kipling sending his only son off to WWI. And as the younger Kipling was leaving to report to duty, his mother could not bear the agony of leaving her home to see him off.)

With his well-worn satchel in hand, Jim boarded the Blue Line bus in front of Petrini's Confectionary and headed for Peoria. There he boarded the Inter Urban electric railway to the recruiting station in Springfield. He was accompanied by his friends and fellow enlistees, Bill Thomas, Bill Brentz and Ted Farmer. On the way to Springfield, there was some excitement in the form of a small fire on the railway—but happily no one was hurt.

After spending the night in Springfield the recruits boarded a train for the ride to Great Lakes Naval Base, just north of Chicago. They reported to the top floor of a six-story building, where they were ordered to strip down and wait in line. It was Jim's first experience at being treated like cattle. The long line of young recruits moved slowly down each flight of stairs, receiving part of a thorough physical exam on each floor. Following that, they waited in line to receive their new wardrobe, which was not tailor-made. (As they passed by each station, they were simply quickly eyeballed and tossed shirts, pants and shoes.) By this time it was nearing midnight and as they began the long march to their barracks, Jim recalled the "veteran" recruits hanging out their barracks windows hollering "you'll be sorry!"

The primary goal of boot camp was to instill a strong sense of discipline, and the road to that goal was through a regimen of physical training. Great Lakes was the largest Naval training base in the country with thousands of recruits, broken down into companies of 100 men each. At the initial fitness test, Jim achieved the highest score in his company. He said there was no question that high school coach Walter Grebe had done a great job getting his students in top physical condition. As a matter of fact, Mr. Grebe had seen an Army film on physical training and duplicated it at the high school.

Boot camp did not include much classroom instruction. There was a course in learning to identify enemy warships and Jim learned it so quickly they made him an instructor. In addition to training in small arms fire and artillery, there was also instruction in firefighting since it would be an essential skill when aboard a ship in battle.But Jim personally felt the most difficult experience in boot camp was watching film footage of combat action. It was thought this was the only way to prepare recruits for the horrible realities they would likely be facing. Jim would never forget watching a Japanese soldier holding up a bayonet, twirling it around, with an infant on the end of it.

While Jim was at boot camp, our brother Red was recuperating from combat wounds at the nearby Hines VA Hospital. Younger brother, Harp, 11 at the time, recalled going there once with our mom to visit and not being allowed in to see Red because of his age. During boot camp there wasn't any time for socializing, since their day began at 4:00 A.M. and lights out was at 9:00 P.M. Jim recalled the graduation exercise as an impressive affair with thousands of recruits all gathered together on an expanse the size of ten football fields. For the parade of honor in front of all the Navy brass, each company of 100 men was led by one recruit, called a "grinder," whose job it was to keep time for the marching company. Jim was chosen for that honor.

All the recruits were given a ranking of SFC, seaman first class, and their assignment was GSD, general sea duty. Their assumption was they were all heading toward an invasion of Japan. When they boarded the troop train for San Francisco, they were issued marine gear and a new rifle caked with grease inside a clear wrapping. At the base at Treasure Island near San

Francisco, they boarded an old, rusted out troop ship for the 33-day voyage to the Philippines, which—to my amazement—I learned consists of more than 7,000 islands. Jim recalls his thought as the ship passed beneath the glorious Golden Gate bridge toward a beautiful setting sun: "What in the hell am I doing here, how did I get into this mess!" The naïve teenage patriotism he and all his buddies at Farmington Community High School had so strongly felt was now nothing more than a distant memory.

Seasickness was a most common malady aboard ship and nothing was done to help the victims. (Jim was thankful for not being one of them.) Each man had exactly one change of gear and no facilities for washing. Jim was assigned a bunk above a melancholy seaman from Kentucky, and found out he'd left five kids back home. Fortunately for that guy, Jim had studied naval regulations enough to know that with that many kids, the sailor had a right to not be assigned duty outside the United States. Together, they approached an officer and at the next port of call, the relieved and grateful father of five was headed back to America.

At this point in his storytelling—as we sat around his kitchen table—Jim pulled out a small well-worn photo album. He told me he bought it aboard ship, and that it was all that remained from his Navy experience. It was apparent from the way that he handled and talked about it that it was treasured. It was filled with numerous family snapshots sent to him by our mom, but there was more. While in the Philippines, Jim obtained an old, tiny box camera. Then he confiscated some photographic film used aboard fighter planes. Simply by trial and error he learned how to develop film and as a result, he had taken and preserved many photos of his Navy buddies.

Bear in mind, three weeks before Jim graduated from high school, on May 7, 1945, Germany had already surrendered. And while he was training at boot camp, Japan had surrendered the strategically important Philippine Islands on June 9, 1945. Now everyone thought the full force of all the allied powers would be brought to bear down upon Japan's evil empire. With Japan desperate and tenacious, the casualties on both sides were sure to be catastrophic. There was no reason for Jim and all the others on his ship to think their chances for survival were good.

But all that doomsday thinking took a dramatic change on August 6, 1945, when news reached them that a new "super bomb" had just been dropped on Japan, on a place called Hiroshima. That was followed a few days later by news of a second bomb being dropped on another large city called Nagasaki. Ever since that day, Jim has felt certain that "the atom bomb saved my life. Without the bomb, I think all of us in the Philippines would have invaded Japan and the results would have been monstrous, with casualties many times greater than those from the A-bombs." Finally came the news the whole free world had been waiting for. The war was ended on August 14, 1945, and the death toll of brave American men and women had finally come to an end at 405,500.

The Navy still had Philippines bases formerly held by Japan to secure, and with this assignment Jim's outfit headed for the island of Manicani. The night of their arrival would go down in weather annals as one of the worst typhoons in history. They disembarked quickly because the ship was nearly capsizing. The crew scrambled for the beaches; it was every young man for himself. Jim described it as chaos, not a thing like movies portraying well-organized efforts. When he landed, Jim found a piece of rope and lashed himself to a coconut tree. The storm roared through the night, but Jim's makeshift harness held tight. As the typhoon relented at break of day, the 18-year-old Jim looked around and saw dozens of limp bodies scattered like discarded rag dolls on the beach. So many men were just marked for death, combat or not.

On Manicani, Jim was assigned to the bakery detail along with 200 other seamen. But he was the only one who had ever worked in a bakery, so it was up to him to do a lot of teaching. There was a chief petty officer in charge, but he was a survivor of Pearl Harbor and had been so psychologically wounded he just sat in his tiny office doing nothing. The temperature on Manicani was usually about 120 degrees, so the bakery staff could only work in four-hour shifts and then had to take a day and a half off. Food wasn't rationed but there was a strict rule you had to eat everything put on your plate. And oddly enough, there were armed guards on duty to enforce the clean plate rule.

Jim recalled the closest he would come to combat action occurred "when an untrue rumor spread around camp that the cooking staff had been hiding food for ourselves. One night a few of the more disgruntled eaters decided to take matters into their own hands. After reveille, they positioned themselves close by the barracks of the cook staff and began firing into the barracks. I hit the floor quickly and stayed there quietly while some of the other guys were going nuts, screaming and shouting." The on-duty Shore Patrol showed up in a few minutes and the "food attack" was broken up without any of the cook staff being wounded. Of course, the truth had been that there simply wasn't enough food available to satisfy the disgruntled troops.

The torrential rains on the island were nothing like Jim had ever seen. They wore their raincoats all the time and the tradition was to write the name of your hometown on the back of your coat. One night as they were sitting on their coconuts watching a movie, it was raining so hard they couldn't see the show. Walking back to the barracks, a guy approached Jim from behind, saw his Farmington lettering and asked "do you know a Susan Jane Whitfield?" A shocked Jim replied "yea, she was a classmate of mine." But, strangely, the sailor didn't respond, he just walked away without a word. That was the end of that, until one night a few years later when Jim walked into Petrini's, the Farmington social spot for young folks, and there sat Susan Jane with the guy from Manicani. So Jim walked up to him and said " You were on Manicani!" And when the startled guy said yea, Jim just walked away. Fully forty years after that, Susan Jane showed up for the only class reunion she ever attended and sure enough, there was the guy again. Jim walked up to him and said again, "Did you ever serve on Manicani?"Stunned, the guy (obviously Susan Jane's husband of 40 years) said "yea," whereupon Jim just walked away again!

Jim holds his 19th birthday cake, 1946

Jim's fondest memory of the Philippines was when his bakery buddies violated the policy against birthday cakes and surprised him with a beauty of one on his 19th birthday, April 15, 1946. It remains one the most treasured photos in his collection. When Jim finally set shore on U.S. soil again, it was at Treasure Island at San Francisco. It so happened, his oldest friend from Farmington, Billy Max Thomas, was stationed there and they were able to meet up for a night on the town. Jim gorged himself with every seafood dish in sight… and within an hour allergies kicked in and he found himself in the hospital with a terrible outbreak of hives. Decidedly not a fond memory.

Jim returned to Farmington just in time to attend the wedding of our older sister, Barb to a young man from Milford, Il. named Phil "Flip" Osborn. Jim hadn't had time to acquire a nice suit for the occasion so he wore his dress Navy whites. While we all thought he looked great in them, Jim admitted that "I felt a little embarrassed because I had not been in combat like my brothers, Red and Hubert."

All the time Jim was in the service, he says he "never gave one thought to what the future might hold for me. My thoughts were just on getting by one day at a time." Fortunately, he had an older brother who was looking out for him. Red was ready to return to the University of Illinois and wanted Jim to join him. But there was one problem. Jim was still in the Philippines. Communication had been next to impossible during the war, with letters sometimes taking weeks or months to be exchanged. So Red simply went ahead and registered at school on Jim's behalf. On the line where it asked for your "major," Red decided to write "pre-medicine." That was the beginning of Jim's future.

Chapter 6: College Years

Family traditions are an important part of our lives. Some, like Christmas and birthday rituals, are just plain fun, but there are also those that are life changing. When our brother Red enrolled at the University of Illinois (U of I) at Champaign-Urbana in the fall of 1939, he became the first of ten brothers and sisters to attend college. When Red returned home from school for the first time, "we all saw him get off the Blue Star bus and start walking toward us," Jim recalled, "and we were all very proud."

Four of us—Jim, Phil, Harp and I—followed Red to the U of I, while Barb, Marcia and Alicia attended Western Illinois State Teachers College in Macomb. Sonny majored in education at Bradley in Peoria (after an ill-fated stint at mortuary school), and Greta Gay attended the Northern Baptist Theological Seminary in Chicago. Before all the Reeds left the hallowed halls of ivy, they'd earned a total of fifteen college degrees.

The unfortunate reality of American higher education is that desire and scholastic ability alone are not enough. Money is required (much more today, of course, than when the Reeds were matriculating). Since neither Red nor our parents had any money when he finished high school, he worked for a year as a handyman at Clayton's Dry Goods Store in Farmington. At college, part-time employment was plentiful and Red got a job as first floor desk manager at Newman Hall, a large Catholic dorm for men. Red's pay included room and board and the whopping sum of $0.25 per hour. After two years of school, Red served in WWII for three years. He reentered the U of I in 1945 and was a senior when Jim started his college career in 1946.

Jim and Red both benefited from one of the greatest pieces of federal legislation ever: the G.I. Bill, enacted into law in June, 1944. During the next 12 years (when the original bill expired) 7.8 million vets received education and training programs. The bill paid each veteran five years of free tuition plus a stipend of $62 per month. At the U of I admission applications were so numerous, additional campuses were opened at Galesburg, (just 30 miles northwest of Farmington) and Chicago. The Galesburg campus closed in 1949, by which time the main campus at Champaign-Urbana had added enough facilities to handle the demand. Of course, the Chicago campus remains.

Changes in colleges from 1946 to 2009 probably occurred more in the area of administration than academics. At the top of the list would be money, pure and simple.If Jim Reed hadn't been a GI when he finished the lengthy 16-hour registration process in Sept., 1946, he simply would've stepped to the window and plunked down his entire tuition payment. (For today's parents of college students, get ready to cringe, cuss and cry.) It was $40.00 for one semester! In the fall of 2009, any student majoring in chemistry had to come up with the tuition fee for one semester of $6,901.00. That's an increase of 17,200 %, or an average annual increase of 272% over the past 64 years. In the fall of 2009 my great niece, Hillary Osborn of Sterling, Ill., an entering UI freshman, plunked down $165.68 for one textbook, more than four times the amount of one semester's tuition in 1946!

While much of this book may be laced with references to the "good old days," it would be erroneous, I think, to conclude that the college students of today are not the equal of their grandparents. I say that because in 1946—and at least a couple of decades after that—any Illinois high school senior with a decent, but not outstanding academic record (such as yours truly for example) would be admitted into the U of I. That no longer is the case. The U of I is now much more selective about who it accepts because the numbers of applicants has risen sharply. For example, admissions in 2009 were limited to only one of every seven applicants.

I think there's little doubt that on the average, college students today at leading schools are more academically gifted than the average student in the 1940s and 50s. But I would quickly add that statistical averages are never directly applicable to specific individuals. Put another way, the average freshman entering the U of I in 2009 brought neither the work ethic of Jim Reed, nor the maturity of Jim Reed (15 months in WWII), nor the pure intellect of Jim Reed. Now let's go back to 1946 and see what college was like for Jim.

**Pictured on this old postcard is Newman Hall,
the college home for Jim and his brothers, Phil and Red**

Jim wasn't discharged from the Navy until just before the start of the 1946 school year, but Red had set him up with a job at Newman Hall as a 'monitor' of the dorm's third floor. He got the same deal as Red: room, board and $ 0.25 per hour. Jim's most taxing job duty as a dorm monitor was to keep the noise levels of students down to a minimum. "Here I was," he said with a laugh, "a young nineteen-year-old trying to give quiet orders to guys, some of whom were 23 or 24 and had been through heavy combat duty."

Now these vets were serious students, hell-bent on taking advantage of the GI Bill and getting a quality education as fast and as best they could. So they were inclined to take matters into their own hands rather than reporting disruptive behavior to Jim. For instance, one night Jim walked onto the third floor just in time to find an angry group of vets had wrapped some obnoxious New York kid in a sheet, and were about to throw him down the elevator shaft! Jim persuaded them to hold off on their plan for a while. Next day, the New York kid made a quick exit from Newman Hall.

On a lighter note, Red had a friend at Newman Hall named Ruck Steger, an All-American fullback on the Illini 1947 Rose Bowl Championship team. Ruck was a strapping, jovial kid from Chicago who always carried a guitar around. (After college, he became a successful insurance executive in Chicago.) Now Red knew that his little brother Jim, in spite of being a small fellow, was in great physical shape. So he arranged for Jim and Ruck to have a chin-up contest in Newman Hall. Then—with a crowd of rowdy bettors cheering on—Jim proceeded to defeat the bulky football star.

Newman Hall became a pipeline for kids from Farmington, and Red played a large part in that. After he was wounded in the war and recuperated at the Hines VA hospital near Chicago for a year, Red had a few weeks at home before returning to campus. He took that opportunity to talk up Newman Hall to kids in town. Back in school, Red was walking on campus one day when he ran into the Farmington High School principal, Russell Troxel and his freshman son Roger, who was looking for a place to live. Red suggested they come back to Newman Hall where Red promptly got Roger a room. Jim's younger brother, Phil, came to Newman Hall in 1947, along with his close high school friend, Bill Tuttle. (Having left his high school sweetheart behind in Farmington, "Tut", a future big league baseball player, became overwrought with homesickness and transferred to Bradley University after only a few weeks.) Phil, not eligible for the GI Bill, quickly ran out of money and left school to pursue a career in professional umpiring.

Farmington area native Art Pille, in his 1952 Army garb

After high school, Art Pille, valedictorian of the FCHS class following Jim, worked for two years at Caterpillar in Peoria to save money for school. Though he would come to the U of I two years after Jim, they were roommates in '48 and '49. In one of Jim's more inventive "harmless pranks," he was in a Champaign Italian restaurant and had his first ever whiff of parmesan cheese. That's when he hatched his plan. "I put some of the cheese into a napkin," Jim said "and carried it back to our room. When Art wasn't looking I put some of it inside his pillowcase. A little later, I told him I was so tired I was going to skip my shower and go on to bed. Then I stepped on his pillow to boost myself up into my bunk. Later, when Art turned in and laid his head on his pillow, he got a dose of the strong odor and let out with a scream, 'Dammit it Jim, you'd better take a shower!' "

**Jim's oldest living friend in Farmington, Dick Westerby,
with his wife, Helen, and daughter, Cindy, in 1949**

Art's closest high school friend, Dick Westerby, who skipped college and joined the work force, was a big sports fan and made frequent trips to Champaign to visit Art and Jim and attend football and basketball games. "Sometimes I'd even hitchhike down there in cold weather," he said, "and once, on the way back, I walked ten miles to Farmer City before I caught a ride."Now Dick had fallen in love with a Farmington High School girl named Helen Collins from nearby Glasford. They were planning to get married but kept it a secret from their parents, since Helen was only sixteen. A week before the wedding, they made a trip to Champaign and played a little trick on Art and Jim. They knocked on their Newman Hall door and when Jim opened it, they yelled, "Surprise, we just got married!" After the excitement and congrats quieted down, Dick told them it was just a joke. Art, normally a quiet guy, went berserk, cussing Dick, while Jim enjoyed a good belly laugh.

Dick and Helen returned home and actually were married the following Saturday. After a bare-bones ceremony, the newlyweds took off for Champaign and once more knocked on Art and Jim's door. When Art answered, Dick said the exact same thing he had said the week before. Art hollered and howled using language that can't be tastefully repeated in print form. After the ranting and raving subsided a little, Dick calmly pulled the marriage certificate out of his pocket. Then the real roars of congrats came out.

Chicagoan Russ Risdon

Jim made one other lifelong friend at Newman Hall, a very bright engineering student from Chicago named Russ Risdon. Their initial meeting was unusual: Jim was dressed in his robe headed to the community shower when he stopped at the water fountain. As he bent over, someone goosed him sharply. He jumped up, turned around and there stood Russ; mortified, Russ stammered an apology, saying he thought Jim was someone else. Despite the awkward introduction (or perhaps because of it) the two soon became fast friends. Before too many years, Risdon had made so many visits to the Reed home he began calling our parents Mom and Dad. A bachelor well into his forties, Russ surprised everyone when he suddenly married a multi-millionaire Chicago heiress. Twenty years later, after she passed away, Russ moved into a Chicago Loop apartment building where he and famed baseball broadcaster Harry Carey were the only residents.

At the high school level, academic work came so easily to Jim that he sometimes felt embarrassed about it. All of that ended when he entered the University of Illinois, where top students from around the world gathered. The bane of most freshmen was rhetoric (or learning how to write). The trouble arose mainly because the high schools had done little to prepare students for actually writing, focusing instead on grammar and readings. For example, our older brother Red was an honors student in high school and was shocked when his first college theme paper was returned to him with a grade of "C." Panicking, Red sought out a senior in his dorm for help with his next paper. The senior was very helpful, making many eloquent suggestions and grammatical corrections. Red was confident this time as the themes came back…and therefore astounded when he saw his grade of "D." (No more seniors after that for Red.) Jim managed to earn a "B" in his first course of rhetoric in his first semester of school but slipped to a "C" in his second rhet course.

In 1946, in order to have majored in any subject, a student was required to earn 20 hours (either 6 or 7 courses) of advanced coursework in his chosen field. (A requirement that's remained nearly unchanged for over 60 years.) Before he graduated, Jim amassed 27 hours of chemistry, the basic foundation of pre med students. Jim was fortunate because chemistry, along with physics, had been his favorite high school subject. His other stroke of luck was that he'd entered a university with a long history of having one of the very best chemistry departments in America. In 1946, one of its professors, Dr. Wendell Stanley, received the Nobel Prize for his work in the field of enzymes and virus proteins.

As a freshman pre med major in 1946, Jim was required to take trigonometry and two semesters each of rhetoric, zoology and chemistry. In his second year, he had to take two semesters each of chemistry, physics, and a foreign language (Jim chose German). The third year required two more courses of German, in chemistry and vertebrate embryology.

To the credit of the University of Illinois—and every other top-notch university—their goal was to produce 'well-rounded' graduates. Students majoring in one of the 'pure' sciences, like chemistry, botany, astronomy or geology, would come under the large umbrella of the College of Liberal Arts and Sciences (LAS). As such, those students majoring in one of the sciences had to take at least 14 hours (3 or 4 courses) of non-science courses. Jim opted to take one course each in the fields of economy, psychology and literature. He took two courses each in the fields of political science and history, for a total of 25 credit hours in non-science courses.

When I got my first look at Jim's grade transcript, I didn't see what I'd expected. I'd assumed I'd find a record dominated by "As" with a few

"Bs" scattered here and there in his non-science courses. But in fact, I had to scroll all the way down to his senior year before I saw his first "A." And I even found a dreaded "D" in his sophomore year German course. So once again I'd uncovered evidence my brilliant brother was fallible after all! I have to admit I had two immediate, opposing reactions when I reviewed Jim's transcript. The first was one of disappointment in Jim's lack of honor student status. But selfishly I felt glad that my own GPA (grade point average) of B- was nearly as good as his.

The truth, of course, is that frequently a student's scholastic record—at any level of schooling—is not an accurate reflection of his or her true intellectual ability. I think there were several factors which accounted for Jim's less-than-excellent academic achievements in college. First, his course work in high school had come so easy to him (he'd never taken a book home in high school) that he never developed any study habits. Also, the ease with which he'd earned straight "As" in high school may have made him a little complacent about education. Then, going straight from high school into WWII and living with the constant fear of impending death may have made him feel, subconsciously, that education wasn't that big a deal. Lastly, and perhaps most importantly, the necessity for Jim to work long evening hours at Newman Hall did not leave him sufficient time to pursue his course work with the necessary vigor.

There seems to be ample evidence however, that when Jim really wanted to attain high course marks—and had time to study—he got the job done. In a class called physical chemistry, the professor had a tedious habit of reading everyone's test scores aloud in front the entire class of nearly 200 students. After one particularly tough test, he was broadcasting the scores and nobody had surpassed even 80. Then he bellowed, "Would a Jim Reed please stand." As Jim rose from his chair, the professor announced that he'd achieved a perfect score! After that, other students would sometimes come to Jim for help and he was glad to tutor them. His abilities were recognized and rewarded when the school assigned him his own small private lab room. Said Jim, "I looked upon intelligence more as a gift I had been lucky to receive and not something I had earned."

To understand Jim's ability to function academically under pressure, I asked him for an example. "Once when I was on my way to a chemistry class," Jim responded, "I ran into a classmate who asked me if I was ready for the quiz. I had no idea what quiz he was talking about. He told me the test was to be on duplicating a series of complex chemical formulas called the 21 amino acids. So I had about ten minutes to prepare for it." He aced the test.

Jim and his brother Red in front of Newman Hall, April, 1947

Jim in trappings of a fantasy Big Man On Campus, in 1949

By the end of his junior year, Jim had matured to the point where he was thinking seriously about his future. Becoming a physician was now much more than the pipedream it seemed to be when he was on the Philippine Islands and his brother Red had chosen pre med for him. Now, Jim realized he needed to improve his scholastic record if he wanted a good chance of being admitted to medical school. Jim decided to quit the job he'd held at Newman Hall for three years to devote more time to his studies. He also moved out of the large, sometimes noisy Newman Hall to live in a small, quiet apartment.

Jim's strategy and renewed dedication paid off, big time. In the first semester of his senior year, he received all "As," including one in an advanced German class, after having received a "D" in his second German class during his sophomore year.

With his long work hours and tough class load throughout his four years at the U of I, Jim's time for social activities was very limited. There was no dating for him until 1947 when he met his future wife, Jan, whose older sister was a friend of our sister, Marcia Lou, when Jan's family lived in nearby Elmwood. Jan's family had moved to Kentucky while she was in high school, and so Jim's long distance courtship of her was limited to summers and school holidays. "I'd go to an occasional campus movie with some friends," Jim said, "and spend a few weekends a year back home with my buddies." Sadly, it was on one of those trips back home that Jim experienced his second encounter with the death of a good friend.

Jim went squirrel hunting with Chuck Thomas, the father of Jim's close friend, Billy Max Thomas. (Billy Max was not a hunter.) Jim and Chuck headed south toward Ipava. As hunters often do, they agreed to split up and meet again at a designated time. When that time arrived, Chuck never showed. After a half hour or so Jim suspected something was wrong and asked a farmer to phone Chuck's wife and have her send some of Chuck's friends down for a search. Meantime, Jim and the farmer decided to go out on their own instead of just waiting around. After half an hour, they came upon Chuck's body; apparently Chuck had come to a fence and leaned his loaded shotgun against it while he started to cross the fence. The gun then jarred loose and discharged, hitting Chuck squarely in the chest. He was almost certainly killed instantly. Jim and the farmer carried the body all the way back to the farm. Jim grieved over the loss of his oldest friend's father—a man who had treated him almost like a son. Nonetheless, the tragedy did little to lessen Jim's lifelong love of the outdoors, as the next story illustrates.

The Spoon River is best known for inspiring Lewistown resident Edgar Lee Masters' famous book of poetry, Spoon River Anthology, but it was also very important in the life of Jim Reed. By the fall of 1949, Jim's senior year at Illinois, he'd earned enough credit hours to choose an elective course. He picked a course designed for zoology PhD. candidates entitled Field Taxonomy. (Jim was the only non-zoology major in the class.) The course appealed to Jim because it involved completing a project by yourself out in nature. There was also some classwork involved and after the first six weeks, a test was given. Imagine Jim's surprise when the professor, Dr. Robertson, announced to all that "the kid sitting over there isn't even a zoology guy and he got the top score in class."

But the crux of the course was the field project, and when the professor noticed that Jim's home was in Fulton County, he asked his star pupil if he was familiar with the Spoon River. When Jim said he was, the professor informed him the river was one of the world's great fresh water sources of clam species, and that the last meaningful study done there went all the way back to 1891. (The study had in fact been done as a hobby by a Lewistown physician.) Jim immediately embraced the idea. His assignment would be to collect clams from the entire 50-mile length of the river, then dissect and identify each species and finish with a paper on the subject.

The project involved every weekend at the river during decent weather, wading into her every mile to hunt for the clam species. Since Jim didn't have a car, he had to enlist the help of his good buddies, Wayne Doubet and Bud Toft, both of whom shared Jim's love of the outdoors.

The job was a wet, muddy, foul one. During one of Jim's last collection weekends, the only car available was his brother Red's new 1949 blue Ford coupe. Now Red was more fastidious than any of the other Reeds, and that trait certainly extended to his new car—bad luck, because on that day, Wayne and Bud both slipped on a bank near Ipava, making a mudpie mess of themselves. There was no way Jim could allow them into Red's car in that condition so he insisted they strip off all their clothes, even though it was a chilly spring day. As Jim approached Ipava, he ordered Wayne and Bud into the trunk because he (allegedly) wanted to stop for an ice cream cone. Moments later, as they approached a bridge near London Mills, Jim decided to have a little fun. He stopped the car and told Wayne and Bud they could get out of the trunk. Just as they did, Jim took off, leaving them standing there completely naked! After a mile or so, he turned around and picked them up.

The collecting completed, Red took Jim and his gunnysack of clams to the bus station in Peoria for his trip back to school but the driver, smelling the mess, sagely refused to let Jim on the bus. Red was kind enough to haul Jim and his catch all the way to Champaign. When Jim finished the paper on his findings, his professor was so impressed he took Jim to meet the Department head, Dr. Adamstone, who suggested Jim "give up this idea of being a doctor and take up zoology." The class had the tradition of having one paper submitted for publication and Jim's was chosen. But Jim knew a classmate who was older, with a family, and so he asked the professor to grant him the honor. Jim's wish was granted but his collection was deemed to be of such quality that it was kept on display at the U of I Natural History Museum for many years.

Since Professor Adamstone could not persuade Jim to give up the idea of medicine, he suggested he apply to the prestigious McGill University School of Medicine at Montreal. At that point Jim had concerns about getting into med school anywhere, let alone at one of the world's best, which McGill surely was. (The U of I pre-med program had 900 students eligible for admission to the U of I med school, which could only accept one hundred.) But Jim decided to give McGill a shot; before long he received a letter telling him that unfortunately admissions had been filled for the year. He was disappointed as he told Dr. Adamstone the bad news… but much better news would soon be on its way. A few weeks later while Jim was in his lab, a friend came running in yelling that Jim had just received a telegraph and "it must be good news or else why would they bother." He was right. McGill had changed their mind about admitting Jim. Jim later learned that Dr. Adamstone himself was a graduate of McGill University and had written them a glowing letter on Jim's behalf. Jim left the U of I in June of 1950 with a B.S. degree in pre-medicine and was on his way to medical school.

Chapter 7: A Student of Medicine

Jim's guardian angel, and longtime Reed family friend, Cliff Perardi

In the summer of 1950 Jim Reed had two monumental concerns about beginning medical school—one was philosophical and the other practical. The philosophical one was not easy, especially for a 23-year-old. Frankly, he was daunted by the idea of becoming deeply enmeshed in the lives of other human beings. "I knew I would be involved in matters of life and death," Jim recalled, "and I wasn't sure I would be emotionally or psychologically able to handle the awesome responsibilities." It would be awhile before Jim resolved that all-important concern, but eventually it would come to him in a flash during his second year of school.

Jim's second concern was a very practical one. He needed money to attend medical school. Not in amounts anywhere near what he would need if he was in school today, but still it was an amount beyond his reach. The Great Depression made the Reed family—like millions of families all over the country—poor. Our father lost his postmaster's job and would never again be able to adequately support his large family.

Jim learned the meaning of hard work at an early age. First he worked through four years of high school to help support his family, then he worked through three years of college at the University of Illinois to help support himself. But those days were over. The huge demands placed upon his time, energy and emotions would not permit him to hold down a job while in medical school. He'd have to muster everything he had simply to meet the coming challenges of a medical education. And he would need outside help.

Jim's older brother by seven years, Red was the first of ten Reeds to attend college. After graduating from the U of I in 1947 with an accounting degree, Red got a good job at Caterpillar in Peoria. For a few years he remained single, and in 1950 was able to purchase a home for our family at 154 North West St. in Farmington. Then, he began a three-year pattern of helping Jim with medical school expenses. Red delayed his marriage to his fiancée, Lois Massey of Peoria, in order to help Jim. In addition to Red's help, after his schooling at the U of I, Jim was still eligible for one more year of the G.I. Bill, which paid tuition and $62 per month. But even with all that help, Jim required more assistance to get through that first year.

He needed a lucky break, needed Dame Fortune to smile down upon him. And smile she did. Dame Fortune had a name: Cliff Perardi, a local entrepreneur and close friend of our brother Red. Cliff's family had a large fur trading business; he also dabbled in oil wells in southern Illinois, some farm land, and a resort in Wisconsin. While he was still at the U of I, Red had begun to help Cliff with his bookkeeping needs. (Most likely, Red had done this without accepting any remuneration from Cliff, just as Red had received none from trekking over to Indiana University to tutor Allen Strong in accounting, as a gesture of friendship to Allen's father, a Farmington insurance man.)

Cliff, several years older than Red when drafted into WWII, was unaware of the law stipulating that older draftees were not to be sent overseas. So of course he was assigned overseas duty. As soon as Red found out about it, he did the paperwork to get Cliff properly reassigned to stateside duty.

Cliff was not an average guy. In fact, there was never another guy in Farmington quite like him. He was always upbeat, exuding more physical energy and zest for life than anyone Farmington had ever known. Jim told me that Cliff had never been sick a day in his life. He seemed to be living proof of a link between state of mind and state of health. When Cliff would play golf, not only would he refuse to use a golf cart, but he preferred to run from shot-to-shot, shouting as he went. Years later, when Cliff "would come to my home," Jim said "he would park in front of the house and instead of walking up the driveway, he would run and take a flying leap over the large drainage ditch."

In the summer of 1950, Cliff learned of Jim's financial need. One day, without being asked by Red or anyone else, he reached into his pocket, pulled out nine hundred-dollar bills, and handed them to Jim, no strings attached. Jim was speechless. It was an act of pure generosity and friendship that endeared Cliff to Jim from that day on until—and beyond—the day Cliff died, in November of 1992 at age eighty-eight.

So back in the late summer of 1950, finances now in hand, Jim packed his suitcase into Red's 1949 Ford and together they headed 1,100 miles northeast to Montreal. After quickly finding a rental room in the private home of a French couple at 3611 Hutchinson St., near the McGill campus, Jim moved in. The next day Red left for home and Jim readied for challenges the likes of which he'd never imagined. Formal medical education in the United States made dramatic strides during the first half of the twentieth century. According to a critical review of the profession conducted by Martin Gross and published in his 1966 book, "The Doctors":

> "During the 1800's, the majority of "doctors" were "graduates" of privately owned schools with incredibly low standards. The training was short. Even the most respectable schools required attendance only a few months a year. The proliferation of these medical diploma mills was staggering; Missouri alone had 42 so-called medical colleges. Scientific discipline and instruction were virtually unknown. Not until 1892 did Harvard lengthen its course to four years and require examinations for the M.D. degree."

The two most important names in American medical education in the early 1900's were Dr. William Osler and a non-physician, Abraham Flexnor. Osler, a Canadian, was an 1872 graduate of the McGill University School of Medicine. After serving on McGill's staff for 18 years, he became Chief of Staff at the newly created Johns Hopkins School of Medicine. Most famous for initiating the program of students learning through bedside contacts with patients, Osler is often referred to as the "Father of Modern Medicine." In 1910, Abraham Flexnor completed the most compelling study to that time on the shortcomings of America's medical education system, which lagged far behind its European counterpart. His report was credited with making scientific inquiry the basis of medicine, and moreover for putting the diploma mills out of business by 1930. By 1950, the basis for modern medical education was firmly established. Jim Reed was fortunate to come along at just the right time. (Not to mention his future patients!) The typical medical school education of 2009 differs little from the 1950 model.

The first class Jim attended would prove to be prophetic. He recalled entering a classroom that looked like something out of 19th century Europe lecture halls. "It was very old, wooden, built in a circle," he said, "with steeply tiered seats. When I looked around at the 95 guys and five gals I would be competing with during the next four years, I thought to myself, 'I don't see anyone here who looks that outstanding and able to handle anything that I can't handle.'"

About that time in walked the head of the Department of Anatomy. He began with a few welcoming remarks, which Jim still recalls: "Welcome to McGill. You must have some ability or you wouldn't be in that seat. We'll help you the best we can but you're going to have to work hard to stay in that seat. If you work hard, most of you will make it through the next four years. And maybe a few of you will be good enough to someday be an old fashioned country doctor and practice medicine the way it's meant to be practiced. That's what we're going to do for you here." That's the prophetic part because, at the time, Jim had no idea what his future in medicine would be.

With his greeting out of the way, the professor started right in on gross anatomy, the most important course in the first year of school. And he told them about the lab work they would begin right after the class. Jim will never forget that first experience. "We opened that lab door and were greeted with the overwhelming stench of formaldehyde. There were three long rows of marble slab tables with each slab holding a heavy canvas shroud soaked in said formaldehyde. Each shroud had a cadaver inside. We were divided into groups of five. Some students were overcome and overwhelmed and had to temporarily leave the room to regain their composure."

"We all felt it wasn't going to be a very pleasant experience but it was something we knew we were going to have to do and get used to." And they did. For the next nine months, they dissected their cadavers up one side and down the other until they became intimate with every muscle and every fiber, every nerve, every bone, every vessel and every organ, learning where each vital piece is supposed to be, what it is supposed to do and how each piece related to every other piece of the majestically, magically constructed human body.

At the end of that nine-month anatomy course, the presence of a human cadaver was second nature to all of them. Jim recalled one gorgeous spring day near the end of the year in the lab. "I glanced out the window and saw some young students laughing and shouting on their way to a soccer game. Just then, I turned to see one of my classmates walking down the isle of cadavers carrying a Milky Way candy bar in one hand and a human head in his other hand, as casually as if it was a loaf of bread. So, in the space of nine months, we had gone from viewing each cadaver as someone's parent, spouse or friend to simply thinking of them as homeless people who had been preserved in chemicals, waiting for the next batch of students to practice on them."

That system of schooling, however, was not uniformly applauded by everyone—to say the least. For example, the world renowned anthropologist, Ashley Montague, wrote in the 1963 issue of the Journal of the American Medical Association :

> "Instead of exposing the beginning student to health and vigorous life at its best, we expose him at the very outset of his medical training to the ravages of death and all that the preparation the anatomy morgue can do to render the very dead cadaver dissectible. The student is then supposed to reconstitute the cadaver as a living functioning organism. This is absurd. The future doctor should be prepared to minister to the needs of the living."

In the 60 years since Jim received his medical education, the curriculums of medical schools and practices of internships have not undergone significant changes. Well meaning critics can still be heard. Dr. Lewis Thomas, a research pathologist and former President and Chancellor of the famed Memorial Sloan-Kettering Cancer center in NYC, had this to say about medical education, in 1992, in the anthology book, "The Eloquent Essay":

> "The dilemma of modern medicine, and the underlying flaw in medical education, and most of all, in the training of interns, is the irresistible drive to do something, anything. It is expected by patients and too often agreed to by their doctor, in the face of ignorance. And, truth to tell, ignorance abounds side by side with neat blocks of precise scientific knowledge brought into medicine in recent years…My hope is for the removal of substantial parts of the curriculum in the first two years of schooling, making enough room for a few courses in medical ignorance, so that students can start out with a clear view of things medicine does not know."

But back in 1950, young Jim Reed considered it an honor to be in medical school, and he certainly wasn't there to question the system or the curriculum. As soon as school began, he realized the scholastic challenges at medical school were going to be much, much greater than anything he had encountered at the University of Illinois. "The amount of material they threw at us was unreal," he said. "You had to be highly skilled at memorizing or you would be lost real quickly."

In addition to the most important first year course, gross anatomy, other courses included physiology, the study of the make-up and function of all the body organs; histology, the microscopic study of normal body tissue cells; neuroanatomy, the study of the nervous system; embryology, the study of embryos and their development; and biochemistry, the study of chemical processes occurring in organisms. Jim was excused from the biochemistry course because he had majored in chemistry at one of the top-ranked undergrad chemistry departments in the world. But he was still required to take the final exam in that subject. All of the grades at McGill, like most medical schools, were simply pass-fail. If you failed a course, you were out: no second chances. The courses were usually taught by the department heads, while the lab work was usually handled by young doctors in their fellowship training program.

McGill was more progressive than most schools back then in that they would immediately begin allowing first year students to have contact with patients. "After studying a subject for a week," Jim recalled, "on each Friday the students would be exposed to a patient who was experiencing a problem which included elements of what we had just studied."

Medical school would also involve something subtly more important than (and just as difficult as) the class work. It would demand a drastic change in the way the young men and women approached their philosophies of life. They had to come to grips with the realization that doctors must be intimately involved with the lives of people. This would be a new experience for them, a daunting task filled with anxiety, soul-searching and self-doubting. While this adjustment to a new kind of life would take place gradually over a period of four years, some would have a defining moment, an epiphany. People who talk about being "called" into the ministry often mention such a moment. Jim Reed had his moment, and he clearly recalled the details.

"I got up one wintry morning in the second year of school and walked to my assigned hospital, about ten blocks away, in snow and zero degree weather. I got there early and had some time before I started duty. I was walking around and came to the doorway of a large patient ward filled with beds separated by cloth curtains. I just stood there and took in the sights and sounds. Patients were screaming and moaning and crying. Staff were hurrying about. I took in the medical smells. And suddenly I said to myself, 'What am I doing here? What have I gotten myself into? What can I do? What are my choices? If I don't turn around right now and leave, I am going to be in very deep with the care of human beings who are entrusting their care to a young student.' It was an extremely emotional moment. I knew that if I didn't get out of there at that time, I was going to be embroiled in something I wasn't sure I was strong enough emotionally to handle. Then, at that moment, I said to myself, 'I'm staying.' And I decided to apply myself even more than I had before. From that moment on, I never looked back. Nothing I ever saw, nothing I ever had to do, would ever make me doubt again that that's what I was going to do. I was not only going to do it but I was going to do it right. By applying myself, working hard and using common sense." At that moment, a supreme character trait was born in Jim's heart and soul: desire. That desire would in turn beget a lifetime thirst for medical knowledge and a total dedication to patient care.

The acclaimed German psychoanalyst, Erich Fromm, addressed this very matter in a 1943 article in the American Sociological Review:

> "In order that any society may function well, its members must acquire the kind of character which makes them 'want' to act in the way they 'have to act' as members of the society or of a special class within it. They have to 'desire' what objectively is necessary for them to do." 'Outer force' is replaced by 'inner compulsion,' and by the particular kind of human energy which is channeled into character traits."

No name in the history of medicine is more famous than Hippocrates, generally regarded as the "Father of Medicine." He established a written code of ethical behaviors for physicians when he penned his "Hippocratic Oath" about fifteen centuries ago. I'd assumed the oath was a solemn vow every medical student was required to memorize, or at least display on his or her apartment wall. My own image was a dignified medical school graduation ceremony in which the college dean led the newly minted physicians in a recitation, in unison, of the Oath. Imagine my dismay then when Jim told me "we never took the Oath at McGill, never studied it and no one ever read it to us." With his own personal epiphany, Jim had come up with his own oath. And by internalizing it as he did, he assured himself it would never abandon him.

Jim's second year of school included courses in bacteriology, the study of microscopic plants and their effect on the human body; pharmacology, the study of medications; microbiology, the study of microscopic forms of life; and immunology, the study of immunity and immune systems.

Patient contacts were more frequent in the second year of school. "We were allowed," Jim recalled, "to spend any free time we had, like on weekends, at the various teaching hospitals, looking over the shoulders of emergency room doctors. And the more time you spent there, the more the staff would let you perform minor procedures. Since I wasn't married and had no social life I had more time for this than did a lot of the other students. I think I ended up with about twice as much ER experience as the average student." One experience he never forgot happened when he was asked to drive the ambulance to the scene of a serious car accident. As Jim wheeled his way around the busy streets of Montreal, he ran right into the St. Patrick's Day Parade. Like a Hollywood stunt driver, Jim jumped the curb and used the sidewalk. What made it crazier still was that Jim didn't even have an ambulance drivers license!

"The third year of school was by far the most challenging one," Jim recollected. "Pathology received greater emphasis. Pathology, which is the study of disease, is generally recognized throughout the medical profession as the most important course in medical school. In fact, there is a saying among doctors that "you are only as good a doctor as you are a pathologist." Jim was fortunate to be at McGill because the Dean of the medical school, Dr. G. Lyman Duff, was one of the leading pathologists in the world and former President of the North American College of Pathologists. As a result of the Dean's commitment, students at McGill received more training in pathology than their counterparts at other schools. And contacts with patients became more frequent and more intensive. Groups of five or six would accompany young doctors in fellowship training through various wards of the hospital. Class work included, in addition to pathology, courses in surgery, psychology, obstetrics and internal medicine.

Since nearly all of a student's time was consumed with the arduous tasks of class work, study, and hospital rounds, every humorous incident was a welcome respite. Jim recalled the case of the inflatable feline: "One Saturday in pharmacology lab, four of us were working on an anesthetized cat. We were trying to learn how to insert a tube into the trachea and lung. As we were working on the cat, someone suddenly said, 'It looks like the cat might be pregnant. Her abdomen looks swollen.' Then, right before our eyes, her abdomen continued to swell. We all jumped back because we were afraid she was going to explode and splatter her innards all over us. Then, just in the nick of time, we realized that instead of inserting the tube into her lung, we had gotten it into her stomach. We quickly pulled it out, right before she exploded, and then she revived herself without catastrophe!"

During his first three years at McGill, Jim was completely on his own socially. (He was involved in a developing, serious, long distance, romantic relationship with his future wife, Janet Myers, but that's a subject for a later chapter.) Jim attended classes from 8 to 5. Then he'd take a hour break for dinner before hitting the books until midnight. There simply was no time to form, much less maintain new, close relationships. But illustrative of his bond with the friends he'd left behind, three of them made the long trek to Montreal just to spend a little time with him. One of them, Russ Risdon, was a competitive guy; it irked him, for example, that he was never able to beat our mother at Scrabble. But he couldn't get mad at her. She was too gracious to get mad at. (She never gloated. About anything. Ever.) Anyway, when Jim went to med school, Russ, a chemical engineer, took a good job in Texas with an oil company. As soon as he got some money, Russ bought a flashy, yellow Nash convertible. The next thing he did was to take some golf lessons—with a specific goal in mind. It just so happened that Jim was the best golfer among all his buddies. If he'd had more time to devote to his game, Jim could have been pretty darn good. Well, Russ' goal was to beat Jim. So, after a series of lessons, Russ jumped in his new car and headed for Montreal, a 2,000 mile drive, ostensibly to beat Jim in a game of golf. (Of course, the main reason was to visit his dear friend.)

When Russ and Jim made their way to a popular Montreal golf course, they found a large crowd of onlookers near the first tee. Jim, knowing how anxious Russ would be to begin with a bang, hoped to psych him out right at the start. Just as Russ was about to tee off, Jim sidled up to him, whispering in his ear, "Russ, for God's sake, whatever you do, don't miss the ball in front of all these people." Of course, after that perfectly timed psych-out job by Jim—and in spite of his expensive golf lessons—Russ swang with all his might and missed the ball! Psychologically, he was ruined for the rest of the match and tasted defeat once more at the hands of Jim. And to add insult to injury, the weather turned nasty and poor Russ wrecked his new Nash in Montreal; luckily, Russ was hurt less by the car accident than he was by his crushing golf loss.

Art Pille was another old friend of Jim's. After graduating from the U of I in 1952, Art was obligated to serve two years in the Armed Services, to fulfill his ROTC contract in return for the government paying for much of his education. But before he entered the service, Art had two things to do. One was to buy the new car he'd coveted for years. And the other was to visit his close buddy in Montreal one last time. They laughed and reminisced; no cars were crashed. After his tour of duty, Art returned to the Farmington area and remained closest of friends with Jim before passing away in June, 2003.

And then there's the story of the honeymoon detour. Jim recalled the knock on his door in early June of 1953. "When I opened it there stood my oldest Farmington friend, Bill Thomas, with his brand new bride, the former Virginia Manual." Jim had no idea they'd been married. "We were honeymooning on the east coast," Bill told Jim, "and since we were close we decided to drive on up and see you." As it happened, it was just a day before the end of the school term. Bill said they would stick around so Jim could ride back to Farmington with them. On the way home, they stopped in Buffalo, New York to watch Farmington's only (eventual) major league baseball player, Bill Tuttle."Tut" put on a show that night with a double, triple and home run.

Meanwhile, between Jim's first and second school years, he got a job at the ABC dishwasher company in Peoria. And after his second school year, he worked for a summer at Caterpillar in Peoria. But his best paying summer job came after his third school year. Our older brother, Hubert, was a supervisor of a large apartment complex in Chicago for many years, and he was able to get Jim a job substituting for all the janitors on summer vacation.

Shortly before the end of his third school year, Jim made inquiries with the Montreal school system about the possibility of a teaching job for his fiancée, and he received a positive response. With that in place, Jim and Jan set an August, 1953 wedding date. It was a beautiful outdoor affair in Beaver Dam, Ky. And, of course, their honeymoon trip was on to Montreal, where Jim was set to begin his final year of medical school, while Jan taught school and happily helped finance Jim's final school year.

"The fourth year of school was less stressful," Jim felt, "because by then each student realized they would be graduating, barring some strange happening." Since each of the four years had progressed from less class work to more hands on experience, the last year gave the students their most contact with patients (both the live ones and the dead ones.)Each student would spend a few weeks on each of the various Montreal hospital wards like pediatrics, obstetrics, psychiatry, ER, surgery and internal medicine.

Without question the most gut-wrenching personal experience a young medical student has is confronting and coming to grips with death. At all teaching hospitals, the rule was that autopsies had to be performed on 25% of deaths. "For me," Jim remembered, "the most difficult experience to cope with was to be talking with a living person one minute, and then a few minutes later, accompanying the same person to the morgue, and watching the body laid out on a slab, fully exposed, for the autopsy."

"You began to realize," Jim continued, "that no matter how hard you looked or how long you looked inside the body of the deceased, you could never see or hear or feel the source that had kept this body going for a lifetime: its very soul. Man is limited," he went on, "in our ability to understand the complicated functions of the human body. And it's very frustrating to try to understand more than we can understand. But, I never let that interfere with my determination to do better the next time."

Doctors don't have the luxury of lingering with death the way a poet might. Listen to the sad, soulful words of the renowned poet, Emily Dickenson:

> "The Dyings have been too deep for me,
> and before I could raise my heart from one
> another has come"

For doctors, especially busy family doctors like Jim, death is always lurking, refusing to call a cease-fire. With decades of experience, Jim would master the fine art of feeling great empathy for his dying patients and their families, while at the same time maintaining the high degree of calmness or equanimity which the "Father of Modern Medicine," Dr. William Osler, said was the most important trait of a true physician.

"I've always considered death to be my mortal enemy," Jim philosophized, choosing his words carefully and saying them slowly. "And I always felt a little defeated when I lost a patient, whatever the pathology." But in the decades to come, Jim would also resign himself to, and even become comfortable with, the concept of death being as natural as life itself. He learned when it was time to let go and time to help the patient let go with the least amount of pain as possible.

Jim concluded his thoughts on death saying he had one unforgettable experience as a student. It was one of his many exams, and he was shown to a table with the body of a person who had just died the night before. His task was to examine the corpse and determine the cause of death. As the professor looked on, Jim correctly diagnosed the cause of death as being lung cancer. He recalled what happened next. "The professor, as he was puffing away on a cigarette, leaned over and said to me, 'I think there might be something to this talk about a link between smoking and cancer.' Within a year, I learned that the professor had died of lung cancer."

The most stressful, grueling days Jim would ever experience were his final exams for medical school graduation. They went on for two weeks, with more than half the time spent just waiting for your turn to be grilled. The first day consisted entirely of written tests, tests that could include any subject they'd studied during their entire eight years of undergraduate and medical schooling. Another day of testing was spent at the bedsides of patients with professors firing all kinds of questions at them. This grilling didn't stop until the professors stumped the student, often with a question which had never been answered by anyone in the profession. Finally, three days were spent sitting around a large table while several distinguished specialists bombarded the students with what must've seemed like every obscure question in the books.

With the completion of final exams, Jim spent several of the most relaxing days of his life. His proud mother embarked on her first plane ride to attend graduation ceremonies. Then Jim drove her all the way back home in his old 1947 Chevy. It was the longest period of time he had ever spent alone with our mother (Jim's wife had to remain behind to finish her school year). They didn't say a lot but they didn't need to. Jim knew full well that everyone in his family had supported his endeavors and had shown confidence in what he could accomplish. He would never forget his debt of gratitude to his family and it eventually became the primary reason he returned to Farmington to practice medicine. As proud as our mother was to receive complimentary remarks from her neighbors and friends about her "doctor son," she kept it all in perspective. Evidence of that was witnessed by our brother Harp when he was walking with our mother downtown one day shortly after her return from Montreal. A friend stopped her and said how proud she must be of Jim. Harp said Mom's response was "I'm proud of all my children."

Jim had one more stop before he would finally return home for good. It would be two years of the most demanding work he'd ever do in his life.

Chapter 8: Tennessee Intern

St. Mary's Hospital, Jim's home-away-from-home from 1954-56

During the Christmas break in his fourth year of medical school, Jim and his wife, Jan, spent the holidays with her family in Kentucky. While there, he thought he would look around the hospitals in nearby Knoxville, Tenn. as a potential site for his internship. After his experiences in nothing but very large hospitals in Montreal, Jim found the idea of working in a smaller hospital to be appealing. He did a little sleuthing and heard good things about St. Mary's Hospital. The doctor who headed up their education department had a good reputation, and when Jim was given a tour of the facilities he was impressed. He submitted an application on the spot and it was quickly accepted.

The nature of an internship program did not vary much from one hospital to the next. The heart of it is often referred to as a "rotation" program. That means an intern will spend a set period of time working in each of the several hospital departments, such as pediatrics, obstetrics, internal medicine and surgery. The goal is to give the intern enough intensive experience to allow him to become at least minimally proficient in all of the areas. Another goal is to help the intern decide whether or not to pursue a medical specialty at the end of the internship. At the end of one year, every intern becomes eligible to begin the general practice of medicine, providing they can pass a state licensing examination. Or, at the end of that year, the intern might choose to stay on in the hospital to gain another year of specialized experience, called a residency. That's what most interns end up doing.

Jim's first rotation assignment as an intern was in the surgery, assisting fully qualified surgeons in major surgeries. He took to it immediately. He seemed to not only possess the physical skills, but also enjoyed the diagnostic aspects of the presenting problems that suggested the need for surgery. The rules of the internship program allowed an intern to trade a rotation with a fellow intern. That is to say, Jim was so interested in pursuing surgery that if another intern wanted more pediatric experience instead of surgery, they could trade. And that's what Jim did. The result was that by the end of the one-year internship, Jim estimated he'd had three times as much surgical experience as the other four interns combined.

Each intern was also required to gain experience in treating the wide range of problems that come through the emergency room as well as the family practice clinic setting. Not all of these experiences were performed under the close supervision of skilled, experienced doctors. A few case examples will illustrate some of the more unusual, educational situations to which Jim was exposed. For instance, interns were expected to take turns serving as the "on call" doctor at each University of Tennessee home football game. Each Saturday the gigantic stadium would be packed with 75,000 wildly screaming fans.(Football down south, of course, is akin to a religion. The old joke is that they have two sports down there. One is football and the other is Spring football.)

The key to believing what happened to Jim at his "on call" game is to understand the specifics of the seating arrangements. The long metal bleachers are adorned with little stripes of paint, designating where each person is supposed to sit. Nothing odd about that, right? The problem is that each space is really only wide enough to accommodate a fan who weighs about 110 pounds. Of course, none of them do, which means that they are all stuffed in tighter than the proverbial sardines in a can. Now, when the game gets going, the overexcited fans are jumping up and down on every other play. While they're doing that, they certainly aren't paying attention to any stranger sitting next to them.

As the game went on, Jim began not paying much attention to the action on the field—because he was, of course, a true Illini fan and therefore not really into the game. Now, something Jim had been trained to notice was changes in a person's behavioral patterns. And it suddenly dawned on him that the man sitting directly in front of him had stopped jumping up and down with the rest of the crowd. Instead, he was just sitting there without much movement. A few moments later, when the fans all rose to their feet once more, Jim noticed the man just slumped forward in his seat like a sack of potatoes.

Jim thought to himself that he'd better intervene to determine if the man was in distress. Turns out he was in great distress. Or rather, no distress at all; the poor man was dead. He'd had a massive heart attack. But no one had noticed, and he had not fallen completely over, because all the fans had been so squashed in together! Subsequent research determined that this was the only time in the history of "on call medicine" that a fan had expired less the two feet from the very person whose job had been to protect the health of the fans. While such an incident might have easily destroyed the self-confidence of a lesser young doctor, Jim recovered quickly from that traumatic event and continued to respond whenever and wherever he was needed, as this next case clearly shows.

Interns were routinely expected to substitute for vacationing staff physicians. On one such day, Jim was summoned out into the infamous "hill country," where the cabins were so isolated you couldn't even get close to them in a car. There'd be a dirt road that just ended all of a sudden, maybe at a stream, as much as a half-mile from the patient's cabin. Jim's assignment that day was to examine a lady experiencing a difficult pregnancy. After finally arriving at the tiny ramshackle cabin, Jim was met by three or four scruffy-looking men.

After introducing himself, Jim asked the men folk to leave the room so he could examine the lady. One of the men responded mildly that "I believe we'll just stay where we are." Jim was surprised and felt they hadn't heard him, so he politely repeated his request. That didn't make any impression on the husband who in turn just repeated what he had said. This time, Jim was a little more insistent with his request for privacy. But by now, the mountain man was losing his patience. He slowly left his chair and walked over to the bed. He reached down, pulled his shotgun from under the bed and told Jim, "you'd best get on with it Doc 'cause I ain't gunna be leavin'."

By this time Jim realized it would be advisable for him to compromise his medical ethics with regard to patient privacy. But there was still one more stumbling block. The husband would have nothing to do with Jim's plan to uncover his wife to conduct a proper examination of the essential bodily parts. So Jim had no alternative except to blindly do the best he could. As it turned out, while this kind of experience might not qualify as ideal training, it—and others like it—would help Jim prepare for many other unplanned situations he would find himself involved with in the years to come.

Jim understood intuitively that when you were up in the hills to provide service, you were in a different world, and to serve and survive you needed to play by their rules of the game. Unfortunately, not every physician was blessed with this understanding. Soon after his own interaction, Jim heard a story about one young "citified" doctor who was a little too full of himself. He'd gone up into the hills and found a seriously ill lady who needed to be hospitalized. When her husband told him that whatever it was that needed to be done would happen right there, the doctor exploded and recklessly said he was taking her out whether the husband liked it or not. He picked the woman up and started carrying her to his car. Suddenly a shot rang out and the doctor crumpled to the ground. He was dead. The story goes that the police never did anything because their policy was to just leave the hill people alone!

On a much, much lighter note, one of Jim's other cases involved an obstetrician known to be somewhat of a prankster. (We saw earlier that Jim also liked a good prank, so it wouldn't be easy for the OB-Gyny to get the best of him.) Seems this doctor had a female patient who was so large it was next to impossible to even examine her. So one time she made an appointment to be checked, thinking she might be pregnant. The doctor then conveniently planned to be gone for a few days and asked Jim to take his appointments. Of course, he failed to inform Jim of the lady's size. When she showed up, Jim was taken aback. "She was the biggest woman I had ever seen, weighing well over 450 pounds, but that was just an estimate because our scales wouldn't hold her. We called a nearby coal company to ask if we could use their scales but they told us they couldn't guarantee accuracy any closer than 50 pounds. By that time I knew I had been set up by her OB. She had so many rolls of fat covering every part of her body that it would have been a great accomplishment just to have been able to examine her. It was a Friday and I had had a long tough week, so I just told her I didn't think she was pregnant and that she should come back to see her OB if she missed another period."

That was the end of Jim's involvement, or so he thought. About eight months later, the patient was somehow even larger and about to give birth. Her OB pulled the same thing again. He asked Jim to take some on calls while he was out of town for a few days. Jim had forgotten about the lady until the hospital called him saying a woman was on her way in. He didn't even know who it was going to be until he arrived to find five men just holding her up so she could breathe. First they had to tie two hospital beds together just to hold her. Then Jim sent all the staff scurrying to find special instruments they would need for the delivery. "But lo and behold, when everyone reassembled in a few minutes, we approached the king sized bed to find that she had spontaneously delivered!" Mother and child made it through just fine—with no help whatsoever from her obstetrician, of course.

Jim recalled one other hill country experience fondly. "Every Friday was free clinic day. This one gentleman had walked two days down from the mountains just to be seen. When I saw him, he was very emaciated and weak. He told me he had been unable to eat because he couldn't lift his arm. What I found out was that he only ate what he could shoot and he had been unable to lift his gun. My diagnosis was that he was in severe pain from arthritis in his elbow. I gave him an injection of a steroidal compound and within a few days he was feeling much better. The next time he came into the clinic he handed me a gunnysack. When I opened it I found it stuffed with a lot of quail." In his two years of working close to the hills around Knoxville, Jim developed a fondness for the hill people. Ever since his youth, he'd always liked the outdoors. Maybe that's what drew him to them. He liked their directness and lack of pretense. And he liked their simplicity and ability to fend for themselves. It was as if the hill people were frozen in time, a relic of bygone centuries.

One extraordinary moment illustrates why it might be wise for doctors to take the time to know more about their patients' personal lives. This is a practice which has nearly disappeared with the past couple generations of doctors, who tend to show interest only in their patients medical problems. But that was never the case for Jim Reed. He wasn't in a hurry that day in 1954, when he saw his first-ever centenarian patient. It just so happened she was the mother of the hospital administrator, and in surprisingly good health, friendly and articulate. Jim wanted to take a few moments from his hectic schedule and so he was happy to listen to some childhood tales of life in the mid 1800's. She talked about attending a large political rally where the President was scheduled to appear. Jim could not believe what he was hearing when she described how excited she'd been to hear a speech given by Abraham Lincoln!

Jim successfully completed his year of internship in July of 1955 and had enjoyed his surgical experiences so much he decided to apply for a year of residency in the surgery department of St. Mary's Hospital in Knoxville. He felt honored when he was accepted and appointed First Assistant to the Chief of Surgery, Dr. Charles Chumley. Dr. Chumley was also Chief of Staff at the hospital and President of the Western Association Surgical Society, which covered all the states west of the Mississippi River.

Jim recalled thinking that "surgery was the most challenging of all the fields of medicine. Looking back now, I realize how mistaken I was. After fifty years as a family doctor, I'm certain that general practice is easily the most challenging of all the fields of medicine. And also the most rewarding. The great challenges result from never knowing what type of complex case might walk through the door at any time, from never knowing when an emergency might pop up, and from being deeply involved with your patients."

Jim's young wife, Jan, became pregnant in February of 1955, and as her November due date approached, Jim began feeling great pressure from trying to eke out an existence on the paltry residency salary of $125.00 a month. The culture in the medical profession in those days was that interns considered it a privilege merely to be selected as an intern and resident and to be allowed to learn under the supervision of highly respected physicians. Unbelievably long hours and little pay were the norms—which no one questioned. Years later all of that would change, to the point where now the average salary for a young doctor serving a residency is about $36,000 per year. In addition, the hours they are required to work have also been drastically reduced.

Twelve months of an internship, followed by twelve months of residency may not seem a very long period of time for young doctors to receive the hands-on training needed to strike out on their own. But keep in mind that during that time period they are were really working the equivalent of four years, because their typical workday was about sixteen hours.

During Jim's year of surgical residency, he was assigned more responsibility and was involved in more difficult operations. However, he always functioned as an assistant, a resident in training. Toward the very end of his residency, Jim was thrilled to be allowed to perform his most complex surgical procedure, an open-heart operation. This was not an arterial bypass operation, which is now a common procedure but in 1956 was just in its infancy. Instead, Jim successfully went into the patient's left arterial appendage with his hand and manually opened the mitral valve.

Seven months after the birth of Jim and Jan's first child, Cynthia, in November of 1955, Jan became pregnant again in May of 1956. The pressure on Jim now mounted to support his family and clearly the time had arrived to end his formal training and get out into the real world. His leaning all along had been to enter the field of family medicine. Now, he weighed the pros and cons of returning to his hometown of Farmington. He felt a natural inclination to come home. "I told Jan I felt I should go back to Farmington because my parents and family deserved to have what I could offer them. I wanted to put back into their lives what they had put into mine. They had done so much to help me become what I had become that I felt a strong urge to go back and provide for them the highest level of care I could. I had become familiar enough with what was available in Farmington that I felt confident I could give the community a more modern and comprehensive quality of care than they had been receiving."

At the same time Jim was not without doubts and fears about what lay ahead. He hadn't experienced treating family members, and close friends; he wondered how he'd handle the layered emotions of that. Another concern was that he'd now be practicing medicine solo for the very first time. There'd be no supervision or handy consultation. Added to those anxieties was the fact that he would be located in a rural area, which meant his patients would have to travel to get hospital service. Lastly, Jim knew he would be faced with serious emergency situations. He was aware of the medical research which indicated that the two most dangerous occupations in America were farming and coal mining—both of those at the heart of where he would be going. Again, he knew he'd have to face those emergencies alone, something he had never done before.

In retrospect, what we know now is that Jim Reed had more of the "right stuff" inside him than he was aware of. Six of the seven key ingredients for an outstanding family doctor were in place in 1956, just waiting to be served up to an eager hometown. We previously identified six of them. First of all, Jim had the good fortune of being born with a high degree of native intelligence. Every doctor has to have it to withstand the great challenges of their schooling. Secondly, Jim had a childhood free of serious trauma. That ingredient permits a quality doctor to practice without being emotionally crippled by his past. Next, the type of physical demands which would soon be placed upon Jim's time could only be successfully handled by a person with a very strong work ethic. There can be no question that characteristic was firmly ingrained in Jim by the time he returned to Farmington. Fourthly, at least ten years of quality higher education and training are of course essential in the making of an outstanding physician.

We've seen how Jim got that. Also, a total commitment to both the medical profession and the patient is an absolute essential part to the ideal doctor. We've covered Jim's epiphany at McGill when he resolved to always be the best he could possibly be, and furthermore to always secure the best level of care possible for his patients. Sixthly, the doctor small town folks prefer needs to have a certain personality; he'd tend to share their background and beliefs; he'd be more like one of them, not some rich kid from New York or California. He would always be sympathetic and understanding, and would really know who you were, not just what he read about you in his medical file. And lastly there is the trait the "Father of Modern Medicine," Dr. William Osler, felt was the most important of all: the ability to always remain calm, cool and collected. Would Jim have the seventh and final ingredient?

Before heading out for Chicago and the Illinois Licensing Examination, Jim stopped in Farmington for a brief family visit. As he was pulling out of the driveway to head for Chicago, everyone was wishing him good luck. Everyone but teenager me. Our mother noticed and asked why I had remained quiet. I remember my exact words. "Because he doesn't need any luck."

The state exam was three days long. It included one day of written questions, one day of questions while they were at the bedsides of patients, and one day of sitting around a table being grilled by specialists. Still, the ordeal was not nearly as taxing as the medical school finals. Jim felt confident but in his words, "you can never be sure." He was not pleased when they told him it might take as long as three months before he'd get his test results. He'd already emotionally severed his ties to St. Mary's and was anxious to move on. After two months of waiting for his test results, he abruptly told Jan to pack their belongings: they were moving to Farmington before he even knew if he'd be allowed to practice in the state of Ilinois. Ironically, one day after arriving back home, Jim received a letter from the state advising him he had passed the exam. He was ready and willing to enter the real world. Little did he know how real it would get!

Part III

The Doctor Is In

"The woods are lovely, dark and deep
But I have promises to keep
And miles to go before I sleep
And miles to go before I sleep"
--Robert Frost

Chapter 9: Farmington, Over Time

The biggest difference between small towns like Farmington (pop. 2,500) and larger cities like Decatur (my current home, pop. 80,000) is that, well, small towns have a lot fewer people. That in turn defines the major life style difference between large and small towns: personal closeness. Large towns tend to be defined by 'things.' For decades, Decatur was known for big factories: Caterpillar, Firestone, Staleys and ADM. The identity of small towns is determined more by its people.

The trademark of small towns was personal familiarity, a feeling of security and self-sufficiency. It was impossible not to feel connected with everything going on in Farmington. People walked all over town. Women walked to stores. Kids walked to school. And while you walked, you talked to all the passer-bys and neighbors in their yards. There were no strangers.

**Farmington's "main drag," Fort Street,
looking east from the site of Jim Reed's first office**

All the stores were small businesses, and all the employees, including the owners, were local folks, well known to everyone. Michela's Grocer—one of five grocers in town—was where we shopped. It was the largest grocer but had only three employees. Louie Michela was the owner and butcher. His son, Johnny, was the cashier, and Bob Clark was the stock man and made deliveries. Louie was also our landlord. Johnny's beautiful little daughter, Peggy, was in our mother's day care center, and Bob Clark's son, Dick, spent a lot of time playing sandlot football with me. Louie also owned the downtown apartment building where our family lived for eight years.

The Reed home from 1942-1950 was this downtown, second story apartment, the width of which matched that of the awning on the right

**The Reed family home from 1950-1973,
when the matriarch of the family died**

But even the smallest towns weren't immune from national trends. The great fear of child sexual abuse began to grip the country in the late 1960s. Even in tiny Farmington, that led to adults admonishing all children not to talk to strangers. Eventually, that led to kids simply not talking to adults. When I was a kid, I had a close relationship with four men: Jim Fresia, Walt Grebe, Jim Perelli and Dee Massingale. They were all like fathers to me. But those wonderful days are gone, thanks to fear and isolation.

Much of the closeness we experienced was forced by circumstances upon us. There were no computers and no TV, so we all played together outdoors. There was no special education for handicapped children, so we all mixed together. Dickie Wilson was a severely handicapped boy who was tiny, frail and could barely talk, but he played baseball with us every day.

Farmington City Park, site of ballgames and carnivals

In the summer, when I was a kid, I loved to go right into the sweltering bakery and watch the men make doughnuts and bread. No one objected or paid any attention to me. I was mesmerized by the bread-cutting and wrapping machine. In the 1990's, I was a volunteer big brother in a Decatur elementary school and called a local bakery to set up a tour for some kids. No could do. The bakery advised me their insurance policy wouldn't allow it.

Since this book is a story of close relationships as much as it is a story of medicine, it had to take place in a small town. It could not have happened in Decatur or Peoria. The lives of older folks who've spent their entire existence in their small hometowns cannot be separated from the life of the town itself. The people and the town have been so interwoven—back and forth, over and under, around and through—that to talk about one without talking about the other does an injustice to both. To separate them would be to present a less clear, accurate, meaningful picture of their lives. We'll meet the people of Farmington a little later. For now, let's meet Farmington.

The first settler was a man named Jonah Marchant, in 1837. The community was incorporated as a town in 1857, one year before a politician named Lincoln came to town to deliver a stump speech in his bid for a seat in the U.S. Senate. He stayed the night with his old friend, Rev. John Williams, an Episcopalian minister, at the Reverend's home on East Fort Street before continuing in his quest for the seat he eventually lost to Stephen Douglas.

In action that most certainly would have made Pres. Lincoln proud, Farmington was heavily involved in the organized efforts to provide safe passage for the movement of American slaves into Canada. Private homes served as safe houses for the slaves—a system a system better known, of course, as the "underground railroad." The available historical records indicate there were as many as ten such homes in Farmington.

The state of Illinois—and central Illinois in particular—was blessed centuries ago by Mother Nature with rich, fertile farm land. And the icing below much of that land was a mammoth deposit of coal. Those two very fortunate geological conditions provided much of the impetus for the birth and growth of many communities such as Farmington.

The first form of coal mining practiced by individual settlers in the early 1800's was simply a matter of ore being found on the surface of river banks. These were areas—called "dog holes"—where erosion had exposed the coal. To this day, Jim Reed, who has a strong interest in the history of the area, can point out the location of some dog holes located on farmland west of Farmington owned long ago by our maternal great grandfather, Jacob Martin. Area residents were allowed to retrieve coal from Martin's dog holes without charge.

The real coal boom was born in Illinois around 1864 when dangerous deep shaft mining was instituted; the first such mine near Farmington was probably the Chapman mine in 1876. Of course, health and safety standards were non-existent. The work was dirty, back-breaking and low-paying. The first step in improved working conditions took place when ponies and small mules replaced men to pull the coal cars in the shafts. Many of those animals never saw the light of day (and some were more valued by the mine owners than the workers.) But even with the free labor of horseflesh, the deplorable work conditions didn't truly become bearable until the formation of the United Mine Workers of America union in 1890.

From the opening of the first mine in the Farmington area in 1876 until the closing of the last mine in 1996, no fewer than twelve mines were active in Fulton County, including the Chapman, Old Jerkwater, Pond Lily, Nickel Plate, George Westerby, Sr., Maplewood #1 and #2, Gilchrist, National Mine, #8, Silver Creek and the Westerby Brothers. It was one of the largest coal producing counties in the United States.

After the Great Depression, deep shaft mining was superseded by much more productive strip mining operations. In this system, instead of tunneling down into the coal seams, the land was simply stripped away, in many cases hundreds of feet, down to the seams. This of course required the use of huge earthmoving equipment. The work remained very tough and dirty and would come to produce numerous cases of black lung disease.

The enormous earthmoving shovels were so massive they became tourist attractions themselves, subjects of photos and postcards picturing people posed inside the buckets of the shovels. Such was their size that a mere six buckets full were enough to fill a house basement of 24 x 36 feet proportions. The strip mines were capable of producing more coal in one week than most deep shaft mines could produce in one month.

In 1956, when Jim Reed opened his office in Farmington, there were still five active mines in the area, with a total work force of about 1,000 people. Mining remained a very dangerous occupation, and one accident involving the collapse of a huge wall of wet earth onto a massive shovel, burying two men in the cab, provided the setting for one of the most heroic medical feats of Jim Reed's career. (That story will be covered in another chapter.) The coal mining industry served as a magnet drawing workers from other coal-rich states like Missouri and Pennsylvania. By virtue of that attraction, during the early decades of the twentieth century, Farmington became a final destination for what would become its largest ethnic, non-Anglican population: Italians. The largest migration of Italians into the area occurred between 1890 and 1920, and there was a pipeline of sorts to assist them in relocating. The Bernardi family of Farmington had relatives in Tonica Il., 60 miles northeast, who owned a hotel. Many Italians would stay there until they secured a job in the mines, then they would move into temporary, private housing in Farmington. Jim Perelli's paternal grandmother had three tiny rental homes in an area west of the cemetery called Puff Up. Other Italians settled in areas called Forty Acres and Diamond Point.

Before long, there were many local businesses owned by Italians. The Politos owned a small fruit market, with bushel baskets lining the sidewalk in front of the store. Petrini and Pozzi, a confectionary, was the local hangout for kids. There were two Italian taverns, Columbia's and Bigliazzi's. Jim Fresia—later to become mayor—had a clothing store and Elmer Guidi owned a photography studio. The Italians cornered the market on grocery stores, with Michela's, Scapecchi's, Viara's, Barnabee's and Contenuto's.

Teens of Italian heritage became some of the best athletes ever seen in Farmington. Bruno Tattini won a European 100 meter sprint championship during WWII. One of the Lenzi's was a lightweight boxing champion. Some of the many high school football standouts included John Baudino, Gino Muzzerelli, Joe Polazzi, Fred Balagna and R. Scapecchi. Of course, among the older Italians, bocci ball was the most popular game. Some of the renowned players were Nardo Scapecchi and the Morotti brothers, "Dink" and "Taters."

A favorite gathering spot for the senior Italians was just outside Columbia's Tap, at the corner of Fort and Main. They would sit right on the hard concrete curb by the road, in their old gray work shirts and well-worn dark felt hats. They had names like Patarazzi and Agnoletti. They all had deeply lined faces and dark complexions and never spoke English. To kids passing them by, they all looked to be about 100 years old.

Jim Reed—and nearly everyone else in town—knew all these good Italians, by sight if not by name. Language excepted, they acted no differently and thought and behaved no differently than anyone else. They were not foreigners from outside Farmington. They were Farmington. Before describing how Farmington has changed over the decades, a bit more background is probably in order. Farmington is located 20 miles due west of Peoria at the intersections of state routes 116 and 78. Inside the city limits, those two roads become Fort Street, which is the main street of town, running east and west. Main Street itself runs north and south. Farmington reached a population of 2,500 in 1970 and peaked out at 3,100 in 1980. The last census established the population at 2,600. There has never been a stoplight in the town. Violent crime is nearly non-existent, and a murder hasn't been committed in the city for more than half a century.

The changes in Farmington were much more pronounced during the twenty years after Jim Reed returned in 1956 than they were in the twenty years before 1956. The most obvious change was the disappearance of small, family-owned businesses. In 1956, three blocks of Fort Street and two blocks of Main Street were dotted with Smith's Jewelry, Slagel Shoe repair, Clayton's Dry Goods, two men's clothing stores (Pages and Fresia's), three hardware stores (Negley's, Elliot's and Bigliazzi's), a Ben Franklin dimestore, two confectionaries (Petrinis and Jacksons), Guidi's photography shop, three taverns (Sonny's, Columbia's and Thomas'), three barber shops, three gas stations (Reid's, Lane's and Schyler's), Massingale's Cream Station, a bank, a pool hall, three restaurants, and the Farmington Bugle, a tri-weekly (our brother Sonny worked there awhile and explained that tri-weekly meant they tried like hell to come out once a week), two law offices (Baudino and Toohill), Melgreen's furniture store, four groceries, the Princess Theater, four doctor's offices and, last but not least, the amazing Betty Anne Bakery. By 1976, nearly all those stores were gone.

The Princess Theater, one of only a handful of social outlets in Farmington, closed its doors in the early 1960's, the victim of the TV revolution.

Unquestionably the two most famous products to ever come out of Farmington (excluding Jim Reed's brand of medicine) were doughnuts and potato chips. The chip company, named Kitchen Cooked, spent its early years in what had once been a church, very near the cemetery. It was a low-key operation, started by Flossie Howard during the Depression. (One of the ways kids could make a nickel was to find a clean box in one of the towns two back alleys and sell it to the chip factory for their use in distributing their well-known product throughout the area). Every self-respecting chip connoisseur knew that, prior to the food patrol's ban of fat in chips, there was never a better chip made anywhere in the country than Farmington's Kitchen Cooked chips. In the early 21st century, the national magazine, Esquire, voted them the second best regional chip in the country. So, in the post-fat era, they were still terrific, but not as scrumptious as before.

The other food product which area old timers will never forget were the raised doughnuts carefully hand crafted by the staff of the Betty Anne Bakery. We simply called them glazed doughnuts. Cloud-soft and cotton candy sweet, they rivaled the Farmington potato chips for sheer, out-of-this world delectability. The Reed family had strong ties to the bakery-- Jim, Phil, Hubert and Barbara Jeanne all worked there. Then for good measure, the Reed family actually lived above the production part of it from 1940 until 1950. Sadly, the bakery produced its last mouth-watering delight in 1976. With apologies to no one, if anyone ever asks you to name the best doughnut ever made, just say Betty Anne's in Farmington.

Betty Anne's, though, like sooo many others is long gone. In fact, in 2010, there are only three establishments in downtown Farmington that were there in 1956, when Jim Reed came home. One is Melgreens Furniture Store. Another is the Toohill Law Office. And the last is Dr. Jim Reed.

In keeping with the theme of stability that characterized rural life from 1900 up to about the mid 1960s, Farmington was served by several doctors who were raised in the area and remained to practice medicine. The Plummer family of nearby Trivoli produced three doctors. Dr. Frank Jacobs was born on a farm near Trivoli. Farmington produced Dr. Victor Williams, Dr. R.P. Grimm, and most notably, Dr. E. K. Dimmitt. Ironically, Dr. Dimmitt began his medical career in London Mills (Jim Reed's birthplace). Dr. Dimmitt returned to Farmington around 1904, and along with Jim Reed, provided Farmington with more than 100 consecutive years of medical care. The last physician to graduate from Farmington High School and practice locally was Dr. Mark Baylor, who went into practice with Jim in 1986. When Mark was in high school and beginning to develop an interest in medicine Jim allowed him to "shadow" him around for a few days. Then, while in college, Jim helped Mark secure a summer job at the nursing home. Mark practiced with Jim for a couple of years before deciding to strike out on his own.

Chapter 10: The Shingle is Hung

In June of 1956, Jim Reed drove into Farmington in his new blue Ford sedan—his old car died—pregnant wife Jan, their seven-months old daughter, Cynthia, and their red Doberman Pinscher, whose name they've forgotten. They moved into a small, log-cabin-like rental home in Farmington's west end. Jim's six years of medical education and training were over. It was time for him to enter the real world.

In 1956, a new Ford sold for from $1,750. to $3,150. Stamps cost three cents. Gas was $.23 per gal and bread was $.18 a loaf. Eggs were $.45 per dozen, spareribs were $.39 lb. and a can of beer was a quarter.

In the world of entertainment, the top-rated TV shows were Ed Sullivan, The $64,000 Question, Perry Como, and I Love Lucy. Two classics opened on Broadway, My Fair Lady and Auntie Mame. The biggest hit song, "Mack the Knife," was recorded by no fewer than seventeen different artists, including Bobby Darin, Ella Fitzgerald and Louie Armstrong. But all those stars were about to be overshadowed by a young southern kid whose favorite pastime was riding bumper cars at amusement parks. "The King" burst onto the scene with a #1 song called "Heartbreak Hotel." "The Ten Commandments" was a box-office smash but lost out in the Oscar race for best picture to "Around the World in 80 Days."

In the sports world, it was a summer Olympic year, and a young man named Bill Russell led the USA team to an 89-55 rout of Russia in the basketball gold medal game. In the Sport of Kings, Nashua had received all the publicity but was upset by Swaps in the Kentucky Derby. Baseball was still America's Pastime and in the Fall Classic, the Yanks met the Bums for the fourth time in five years. The Bronx Bombers triumphed in seven games, and game five became a classic when Don Larsen became the only pitcher in World Series history to hurl a perfect game, retiring all twenty seven batters he faced.

In July, free elections were scheduled in Viet Nam on the question of forming one country. But the South's president announced he would not abide by what he said would be a rigged election. Meanwhile, in Cuba, a young rebel named Castro shouted "Liberty or death in 1956", and over in Russia, party chief Nakita Khrushchev taunted the West with four infamous words: "We will bury you."

On the U.S. political scene, 1956 was a presidential election year. A junior senator named John Kennedy lost out to Estes Kefauver in a battle for the VP slot along side Illinois' favorite son, Adlai Stevenson, who in turn lost the election to the incumbent war hero, Dwight Eisenhower. In a notable race-related development that presaged the 1960's Civil Rights movement, a blue ribbon panel appointed by Eisenhower in 1952 issued their report on the state of Negro education. The report concluded that in failing to educate Negroes, our country was guilty of perpetrating the "greatest waste of human resources in the U.S."

But in 1956, Jim Reed did not follow sports, politics or international affairs. And he didn't go to many movies or watch much TV. He hadn't had a chance to do any of that in the six years prior to his arrival in Farmington. And he still wouldn't in Farmington. He had only two concerns, his family and his job. He simply couldn't do all the things an average Joe did. Not if he was to have any chance of attaining his lofty goal, which was set six years earlier. His cause was very clear and his commitment total. He was anxious and ready to go to work, but before he could do that, he needed a couple of things.

The entire focus of Jim's strenuous six years of medical education and training had been on one goal and one goal only: learning to provide high quality medical care to suffering people. At no time during those six years had he received any training at all in the area of how to administer the provision of medical services. But whether he realized it or not, Jim was about to become the administrator of an office. What that meant was he would have to do things like find an office, find a way to pay for office space, hire assistants, train and coordinate them.

On the day Dr. R. P. Grimm had died in 1954, his widow locked the door to his office, located up a long flight of old, creaky, wooden stairs above the aged post office on West Fort Street in Farmington, and she never went back. Jim talked with Mrs. Grimm in the late spring of 1956 and she agreed to sell the office contents to him for $2,400. Lacking any funds, Jim was able to secure the $2,400 loan from an area bank.

Dr. Grimm's office space and everything in it had been gathering dust for a long time and was in dire need of a good cleaning. One advantage of living close to your large family is that there is always someone around to help out. All the Reeds knew the meaning of hard work, and in no time Jim's office was put in spic and span shape by our mother, our brother, Harp, our youngest sister, Alicia, and me. I was all of eighteen at the time and still very wet behind the ears. I can recall not fully grasping the reality that my brother would soon be practicing medicine in this space. But it all began to feel more real when we saw the painter carefully lettering the door and windows with the words, "J.M. Reed, M.D., Physician and Surgeon."

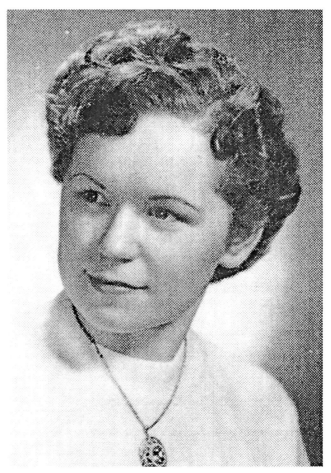

Jean Fidler Locke in 1956

The most important job Jim had before he could open his door was the hiring of four women to assist him in his practice. He placed a small ad in the Farmington Bugle newspaper and waited for applicants. The very first person he hired was a young Trivoli gal named Jean Fidler, who had just graduated from Farmington High School. "I was working at a Peoria loan company right after graduation," Jean told me. "One day when I came home, your brother Phil was there. He was an old family friend. He told me his brother was setting up a medical practice and suggested I might apply for a job. The idea of working in a medical environment appealed to me, so I applied. I was very happy when I got the job."

Jean Fidler was the first person in Jim Reed's long career to develop a deep, enduring admiration for his medical skills, his dedication to his profession and, most of all, his devotion to, and compassion for, his patients. Nearly fifty years have passed since Jean, now Mrs. Jean Larke of Peoria, has seen or spoken to Jim Reed. But such was the impression that he made upon her that she still vividly recalls many details about their close working relationship. Her memories needed no paraphrasing or filtering:

"I started out being a receptionist but after a few weeks, I told Doctor I wanted to learn everything he was willing to teach me. And he was willing. He began by teaching me how to clean an exam room and the instruments. Then he hired Goldie Negley to take over my front desk job so that I could assist him in the exam rooms. He taught me how to collect patient information, how to take pulse rates and blood pressures, and how to prep patients. I can still recall the first time I went into a room with him and a patient. It was a tiny baby and I think my heart was beating faster than the baby's. Right after that, an accident victim came in and I assisted with the suturing. I remember wanting to learn anything Dr. Reed was willing to teach me. I am still amazed at his willingness to teach and train me. He was always teaching me by using the actual situation at hand. You could never, in a million years, learn from a book what he could teach you in just a few minutes. When you were taught something, you would remember it forever. That's just how he taught you. I know because I still use his teaching to this day. Every time he bought a new piece of equipment, he taught me how to use it. First there was the EKG machine, then a physio-therapy machine. Next, there was the BMR (an air-capacity lung test machine). Then he sent me to a crash course at the hospital on operating lab equipment like a centrifuge and a microscope. Next was learning how to give shots. He had hired my sister-in-law, Shirley Bennett Fidler, an RN, and she was my guinea pig. After that, I started to make house calls alone to give shots. All that learning had taken place in seven months. Then, in January, 1957, Dr. Reed moved to Trivoli, into Dr. McKnight's vacated home. It had an attached office with an X-ray machine, and so Doctor sent me to a crash course on how to use it and develop film. It was a pleasure to get up in the morning and go to work. Even with all the sickness and all the patients, the office never had a negative word or atmosphere. Around that time I got married and then pregnant. Dr. Reed delivered our healthy son. But his office was so busy that he had to hire someone to take my place. That was a sad day for me. Later, I took a job with a doctor in nearby Creve Couer. After a while, I went back to school and became a licensed LPN. And here I am, still working full-time, fifty-two years after I started with Dr.Reed. I so enjoyed helping patients and it was all due to Dr. Reed's teaching and willingness to allow me to learn and develop and grow in something that I loved so much. I have never forgotten his loving patient care and compassion. I owe him so much and I will never forget him."

Mary Louise Cline Wilson   **Goldie Negley**   **Barbara "Babs" Hedden**

In addition to Jean Fidler, the other three women Jim hired early on were Mary Louise Cline Wilson, the daughter of the local photographer, Goldie Negley and Barbara Hedden, the young wife of Jim's close childhood friend, Virgil Hedden. None of these first three staff had any background at all in the field of medicine. Jim actually preferred that because it allowed him to teach them what he wanted them to know and do without them having formed any previous bad habits. In those days, he could proceed in that manner because there were no state regulations overseeing staff qualifications.

Graham Hospital, Canton, Il.

Jim realized another immediate need was to have some sort of emergency vehicle (it would be 6 years before a Rescue Unit was formed) available on short notice to transport seriously injured patients in need of hospitalization. The closest facility was Graham Hospital, 10 miles south of Farmington. Peoria hospitals were 20 miles away. There was only one vehicle in Farmington that fit the bill. Unfortunately, it was a hearse. Jim knew that from a psychological view, it would not be ideal to transport ill people in a vehicle designed and used to carry deceased people to a cemetery. But he was—and always would be—a realist and he knew it was the only choice.

Tom Anderson

As luck would have it, Jim had been a childhood friend and classmate of Tom Anderson, whose parents owned the local funeral home, which still stands, right across the street from the old Chapman School. Tom, who was working there when Jim came to town, was a bit of a live wire. Betty Tolf, another classmate, recalled that on their senior prom night, "Tom confiscated his father's hearse and eight of us piled in and headed for Peoria." So, Jim thought Tom might go for the excitement of being a makeshift ambulance driver. And he was right.

Jim and Tom did encounter one problem with the hearse-ambulance. "Since it had no flashing bubble," Jim recalled while laughing, "oncoming drivers at night had no way of knowing that they should get out of the way. Tom came up with a quick, but dangerous, solution. He simply drove right down the middle of the road, sending all the cars in his way scrambling off to the side of the road!"

 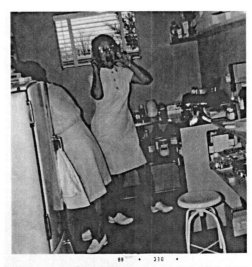

Maxine Unsicker, RN   **Minnie Locke**

As Jim's patient caseload began to grow, he added three more staff: the two ladies pictured above and Virginia Thomas. The first Registered Nurse Jim hired was Maxine Unsicker, who had previously worked for Dr. Dimmitt. She'd been retired for several years before Jim came to town, but was happy to get back to work. Virginia Manual Thomas, the wife of Jim's oldest Farmington friend, Bill Thomas, came on board in 1959. Earlier that year, Jim had delivered their son Karl. "I went into labor early on a Sunday," Virginia recalled, "and Dr. Jim stayed with me the entire day until I delivered." She remembered his joking that "it would give him a chance to catch up on his paperwork."

Beginning in 1904, the two hometown doctors pictured here, E. K. Dimmitt, on the left, and J. M. Reed, provided 107 consecutive years of medical care to their hometown. Above, Dr. Dimmitt holds Clark Thomas, born 6-17-54, and Dr. Reed holds Karl Thomas, born 3-3-57. The children's father, Bill Thomas, was the first person Jim befriended in Farmington, in 1933, and they remained lifelong friends.

Virginia worked for Jim for twelve years before her family moved out West. Now widowed, she lives in Elmwood. She's Jim's patient now and was recently in the office when some staff were talking about their hectic pace. "I just laughed and told them they should have seen the old days." She remembered patients lining up outdoors before the office opened and when the waiting room was full. "One day Dr. Jim returned back at the office from supper," she laughingly recalled, "he came through the door and hollered for us to get the examining rooms filled up because the bank president was sitting on the steps outside."

All of Jim's patients eventually became aware of his remarkable recall, his memory for every detail of their long medical histories. So it's no shock to them that he still remembers his very first patient contact of fifty-two years ago. Her name was Mrs. James Perelli, Sr. Her husband was a salesman for over forty years in the Page Clothing Store. Her schoolteacher son, Jim, now 86, and one of Farmington's most beloved citizens of the past 60 years told me, "My mother remained proud the rest of her life that she had been Dr. Reed's first patient." Jim remembered that office visit. "She had a sore throat, and when she got up to leave she asked me how much she owed me. That's when it dawned on me that we had not set up a patient fee schedule." Not knowing what else to do, Jim asked one of the office gals to call Dr. Jacobs' office to find out what they charged for an office visit. They learned it was $2.00. Mrs. Perelli, who had been patiently waiting for the results of the financial research, said that seemed reasonable to her. Another patient on that first day was a teenager named Charlene Reid, whose father was Charlie Reid, the owner of a local gas station. She had a dog bite, and Jim lacked what he needed to treat her, so what did he do? "Jim called me at home," our brother Harp said, "and asked me to run to the drugstore for a medicine for her." Young Miss Reid was then promptly treated, and recovered just fine.

Now I had just assumed that Jim must've been pretty confident in his abilities when he opened his practice. But he quickly corrected me. "Oh God no!" he said loudly with feeling, "You'd be a fool to be very confident. I think every new doctor has the feeling of 'what makes me think that anyone would come to see me.' They don't know anything about me, where I studied, how I studied, how I managed. It's often difficult for me to understand how people choose which doctor to see." When we returned to that topic a bit later, Jim did grant that "Maybe after about twenty years I started feeling pretty comfortable and secure about what I was doing."

One of the most remarkable tales Jim would ever hear from a patient happened early in his practice when he was called to the home of Frank Switzer's mother. (Frank owned a local gas station.) Mrs. Switzer told Jim she was 100 years old, which put her birth in 1856. She went on to say"We were living out West during my childhood, and when I was eight our family decided to move east and so we packed our belongings into a covered wagon and started out on the long, tough, perilous journey." What she told Jim next rendered him speechless. "We hadn't gotten too far along in our journey when we came under attack from a small party of Indians. I remember my parents quickly hiding me in one of those large quilt trunks which were attached to the sides of the wagons." She was pleased to report to Jim that her family managed to hold off the brief attack and escape the harrowing experiencing without harm.

By the end of his first few weeks Jim was seeing about ten patients a day. He recalled going home one night and telling his wife, "if we can begin seeing about fifteen patients a day, I think we'll be okay financially." As it turned out he would reach and far surpass that goal pretty quickly. Meanwhile, by September 1956, our brother Harp was ready to begin his final year at the University of Illinois and this writer, a naive 18-year-old would enter his first year there. "This would be the point in time," Jim recalled, "when I would be able to take great satisfaction in starting to pay back my family for everything they had done for me for so long." The cost of school in the mid-fifties would stay at a constant $1,000 per year. Quite affordable by today's standards, but back then I definitely needed help from Jim. And he gave it. The catch was, Jim's generosity began a regular four-year embarrassing moment for me every time I cashed the checks he made out to me. Because by a strange coincidence, the only place on the U of I campus that cashed checks was a jewelry store named M. J. Reed's. And so for four years, every time they saw Jim's check, they would give me a very long, strange look—because Jim just signed his checks, J.M. Reed, without the title of M.D. In 1957, the youngest of the 14 Reeds, Alicia, graduated from high school and with the sole help of Jim, she enrolled at Illinois Western University.

The commonly accepted medical ethic in the mid-1950's was that no patient would be denied treatment because of an inability to pay for services rendered. It never occurred to Jim to consider payment as a prerequisite to treatment. His early patients quickly learned that and respected him for it. He would regularly be "paid in kind" with freshly killed and frozen meats, as well as desserts, vegetables, etc. Even with that, at the end of his first year of practice, there was still about $20,000 worth of patient debts on his books. No effort would ever be made on his part to collect on those debts. When Jim received his medical degree, he pledged to provide medical care to those in need, without regard to ability to pay. Like every part of his profession's sacred oath, he would always faithfully abide by it. The fact is, Jim never had much interest in the financial record-keeping aspects of his practice since he viewed that as unrelated to the practice of medicine. Eventually, Jim turned over those important duties to our brother Red, a trained accountant and Treasurer of the Illinois Mutual Life Insurance Company in Peoria. Red once confided to me that he was in complete shock at Jim's record keeping. "His idea of a responsible system was to just throw everything into a shoebox and let it all lie there!"

In small rural communities like Farmington, the news—good or bad—spread quickly by word of mouth. Unsurprisingly then, Jim's excellent reputation got around fast, among both patients and his fellow doctors. Dr. Dimmitt had known Jim since he was a kid, and when Dimmitt's health began to deteriorate rapidly around 1956, he began referring his patients to Jim. Moreover, since Jim sent all his patients to the same hospital, in nearby Canton, the largest town (about 11,000) in the area, his reputation began to spread there, too. Carolyn Armstrong said she can still remember her father, Dr. David Bennett of Canton, "always speaking so highly of the young Dr. Reed."

Shortly after beginning his practice, Jim became acquainted with the most experienced surgeon in Canton, Dr. J. P. Coleman, who headed up the local Coleman Medical Clinic. As soon as Dr. Coleman learned that Jim had completed his residency training in surgery, he approached Jim about assisting him with some of his surgical work. Because Jim had become accustomed to a heavy work load during his internship and residency, he didn't like the idea of having time on his hands. So he gladly accepted Dr. Coleman's offer and began traveling on Thursdays to Rushville and Kewanee, where, Jim said, "We performed all kinds of procedures except brain and heart surgeries." Dr. Coleman must have been pretty impressed with Jim's abilities because "He offered me a full-time job after the first day I assisted him," Jim said. "I appreciated his offer but I liked the idea of working independently."

"When I began my practice in 1956," Jim recalled, "I was surprised at the number of patients I started seeing who had been living with serious problems which had never been diagnosed. Problems like coronary heart disease, diabetes and thyroid trouble. We gradually got some of the older patients on the road to recovery." I could see that Jim was taking pains not to point fingers at the quality of care the patients had been receiving before he came to town. "That situation," he continued, "wasn't due at all to a lack of concern or dedication on the part of the older doctors in town. They were all well-meaning, compassionate men who were doing the best they could. But they had been hampered by a combination of a lack of quality education, a lack of available specialist consultation and perhaps most importantly, a lack of appropriate drug medications." Jim was glad he had the chance to get to know a lot of the older doctors in Farmington and Canton. "It's sort of amazing what they could do," he said, "given the conditions they had to work under. Prior to 1936, there was only one medicine available for any serious problem. That was digitalis for congestive heart failure. After that, the sulfur drugs were developed for the treatment of infections."

A few years after Jim opened his practice, a series of events unfolded which were destined to change his life. First, in December, 1956, Dr. Clinton Mc Knight decided to leave Farmington to return to his native southern Illinois. Then, Dr. E. K. Dimmitt's health took a sharp decline and he passed away in July, 1958. Lastly, Dr. Frank Jacobs was killed in a tragic car accident in 1961. When Jim returned to his hometown in 1956, there was a fourth physician in town: Mrs. Elizabeth Henderson. The wife of a long-time popular Farmington High School math teacher and mother of several young children, Mrs. Henderson never had an active practice. However, she always commanded the respect of Jim because for many summers, she returned to her native Kentucky, donating her services to a health clinic for the needy. She was cared for by Jim until her death in 2008.

The powerful work ethic, the professional skill and the physical stamina Dr. Jim Reed developed during his arduous medical school internship and residency, as well as his strong sense of personal dedication, were about to be put to tests he couldn't have imagined. His budding reputation was soon greatly enhanced by the best means possible: providing quality medical care for all; whenever and wherever needed.

Jim Reed and Janet Myers were wed on August 22, 1953 in Beaver Dam, Ky.

The Trivoli home, 5 miles east of Farmington,
where Jim's family has lived since Jan. 1957

Young Reed cowhands, in 1961. From left to right, Bryan, 4, Cynthia,
6 and Bruce, 3

The cowhands as city slickers, joined by their baby brother, Brent, in 1964. From left to right, Cindy, 9, Bryan, 7 and Bruce, 6

On the right, Janet, with her close friend, Virginia Thomas

Janet with her granddaughter, Josie Reed,
one month before Janet's death in November, 2008

Chapter 11: Silent Partner

Any human endeavor, be it a mega corporation business like Caterpillar Tractor Company or a small medical clinic, can succeed only through the efforts of a team of people who share common goals, passions and work ethics. With the hiring of his nursing and secretarial staff, Jim felt everything was in order; but he was wrong. No one realized it at the time, but a key ingredient of his medical team was missing—and it would take a few months to fill the job.

It was a position Jim wouldn't have to advertise to fill. In fact, there wouldn't even be a salary involved. It would be a 'silent partner' job, a person largely unseen and unheard. She wouldn't even have to come into the office to work. It would all be done out of her home—their home. Jim's wife Jan took the job willingly and held it for more than 55 years.

Must've been fate: Two days after I started writing this chapter, my wife came home from the library with videos of one of history's most beloved TV series, "All Creatures Great and Small." The similarities between my brother and the show's vet, Dr. James Herriot jumped out at me. Both practiced in rural areas, both were passionate about relieving suffering, both were compassionate, humble and worked 24-7.

I call it fate because just as I was beginning to write about Jim's wife, I watched two episodes of 'Creatures' that focused on the budding relationship between Dr. Herriot and Helen, the young lady who'd caught his fancy. The shows were beautifully done and delivered a message that reverberates for all time, everywhere. The message was about what makes people good and attracts them to each other. It was more about the romancing of the soul than the allure of the body.

To be sure, Dr. Herriot was captivated by Helen's good looks as surely as an unexpected rainbow attracts our eye. But for Helen, the appeal of young Dr. Herriot was the nature of his heart and soul, which, when the surface beauty fades, (as it always does) is the only basis for a long-lasting loving relationship. She was drawn to his great passion for a noble calling, to the kind way he related not only to animals but to their owners, and finally, to his sense of humor. Her love for him was total and she gladly shared everything in his life, including his practice of veterinary medicine. So it would also be with Janet Myers Reed.

If Jim had taken the advice of his childhood friend Bud Toft, he might have married Janet Myers long before his 27th birthday. You see, shortly after graduating from high school in 1946, Bud took a part-time job at one of the area coal mines. There he met Daniel "Mike" Myers, a grizzled man with a no-nonsense, tough nosed reputation. In spite of that, Bud managed to befriend the man he called "Pops." Bud told me, "Sometimes his (Pops') wife would drive out and pick him up after work, and a couple of times she brought their teenage daughter along. She was really pretty, so I told Jim he ought to come out to the mine around closing time just to catch a glimpse of her." For whatever reason, Jim failed to take Bud up on his offer.

The funny thing about that story was that when I was relating it to Jim and Janet, she told me she had never heard her dad called "Pops" before. Of course, Bud was right, Jan was a really attractive girl. I thought she bore a striking resemblance to a movie actress named Jan Sterling and, to a lesser degree, a young Rosemary Clooney.

Except for those rare couples who grew up knowing each other, there are always fortuitous circumstances bringing people together. For Janet Myers and Jim Reed it was coal mining and Girls State. Had the Farmington area not been a hotbed for mining, the Myers family would never have migrated to nearby Elmwood from Pennsylvania. And if Jim's younger sister, Marcia Lou, had not been an outstanding student in high school, Jim would have never met Janet.

Girls State, sponsored by the State of Illinois, was a week-long summer educational camp for high school girls who'd completed their junior year with a record of outstanding citizenship and scholarship. The camp's purpose was to teach the girls about how government operates. Each school selected one student. In 1946, that student was Marcia Lou in Farmington, and in nearby Elmwood, it was Barbara Myers, Jan's older sister. Marcia and Barbara became good friends at Girls State, but before Jim even met Jan, the Myers family moved to Beaver Dam, Kentucky in 1947, when Jan was fifteen.

Fortunately, the Myers sisters returned to Elmwood from time-to-time to visit old friends. On one such occasion, Barb and Jan came to visit Marcia Lou, and Jan happened to see a photo of Jim on display in our living room. Without any prodding, she just blurted out that she'd like to meet Jim. Meanwhile, Jim was in the next room and overheard what Jan had said. Remembering what Bud Toft had told him a couple of years earlier, Jim popped out from behind the door. After a few minutes of social niceties, he asked Jan if she'd like to see a movie, and off they went to the Princess (Jan recalled it was a revival of "Gone With the Wind). The rest is history.

Jim and Jan's courtship was neither typical nor ideal; in fact it was largely long distance and it lasted six years. Jim was in college while Jan was graduating from the tiny high school in Beaver Dam. From there, she enrolled at Western Kentucky University with a major in elementary education. Their face-to-face wooing would be limited to summers and school breaks.

After four years of a long-distance courtship, Jim and Jan announced their engagement in June of 1951. Jan was 19 and Jim was 24. In the spring of 1953, as Jim was successfully completing his third year of medical school, he knew that the most grinding and exhausting part of his education was behind him. Tiring of his six year, long distance romancing, he seized upon his window of opportunity. He and Jan set an August 22, 1953 wedding date. With family and friends looking on that gorgeous summer day, Jim and Jan were married in a beautiful outdoor ceremony in Beaver Dam, Ky. Their brief honeymoon consisted of a leisurely, scenic drive to Montreal, surely one of the most wonderful times of their lives. But the day following their arrival, Jan would receive her first experience of what was destined to be a lifetime of sharing a large part her husband's life with his medical career.

Jim began his final year of medical school the day after their arrival in Montreal with a hands-on hospital rotation assignment on a hospital obstetrics ward. He was required to spend both his nights and days there, not the ideal way to start a marriage. After nine straight days and nights at the hospital, Jim couldn't take the separation from his new bride any longer. He went AWOL, sneaking out of the hospital in the middle of the night to spend a few precious hours with his bride. He was found out, of course, called on the carpet and received a reprimand. By now, Jim was a mature 27-year-old and he knew he was going to graduate, so he just let the criticism roll off his back.

That nine-day separation was 21-year-old Janet's initiation into what became a 55-year pattern of sharing her beloved husband with the profession and patients he'd dedicated his life to. For the next three years Jan had a lot of practice in learning to spend time alone, as Jim's schedule in his internship and residency was much more hectic than it had been in medical school; by the time they arrived in Farmington, in the summer of 1956, Jan, still a youthful 24, had become accustomed to Jim's absences. But another major factor was about to be added to the equation.

For the first three years of their marriage, Jim's medical duties didn't impact Janet in her home, but that was about to dramatically change. With

Jim out on his own in private practice, and given his commitment to being on call 24-7, his practice was about to enter both his and Jan's private lives.

One night just a few months after Jim' practice had opened, he and Jan were spending a quiet evening in their small rental home in Farmington's west end when there was a knock at the door. There stood a female patient who said she needed to see Jim. Jan led her into the living room and then she (Jan) sat down next to Jim. (Jim hadn't known this lady very long, but he did know she was a little obsessed and very emotional about her non-serious problem, which was female in nature.) Meanwhile, the patient, without uttering a word, walked right over to Jim and standing very close to both him and Jan,suddenly pulled up her dress, exposing everything she owned, and asked Jim to check over her female anatomy. "Jan immediately leapt to her feet," Jim recalled, while trying to suppress a grin, "let out a loud scream and ran out of the room." Meanwhile, back at the scene of the action, Jim said it was all he could do to keep from laughing at his patient as he explained to her that he'd just seen her recently and nothing had changed since that time.

After that rocky beginning, Jan quickly adjusted to all kinds of interruptions and strange happenings at her home. More importantly, she quickly gained a goodly amount of basic medical knowledge from Jim, as well as a growing familiarity with Jim's patients and their medical histories. After a few years, Jan became a most reliable assistant to Jim. After Jim's regular office hours, Jan screened all incoming calls to their home. Over the years, she also developed the essential calmness under stress that characterized Jim's demeanor.

I think the primary reason Jan was able to develop into an absolutely essential part of Jim's career is that she daily absorbed, almost by osmosis, much of Jim's relentless passion and dedication. This allowed her to be totally comfortable with, and accepting of, Jim's unusual commitment of time and effort in serving his patients. Had Jan not been able to do that, their marriage, as well as Jim's career, couldn't have succeeded like it did. Jan would no more have asked Jim to cut back the time he gave his patients than Carl Sandburg's wife would have asked him to cut back on his writing.

Jan's hectic lifestyle helping Jim while raising four children didn't permit her to become well acquainted with many of Jim's patients, but that didn't prevent their being touched by her kindness and concern. Nancy Dikeman, a 50-year patient of Jim's said she barely knew Jan. Yet Nancy recalled what happened when she experienced some mysterious bleeding one Sunday afternoon. She phoned Jim's house and as usual, Jan took the call. Once on the line, Jim directed Nancy to go straight to the hospital for testing. Fortunately, the test results were negative and Nancy returned home. "A couple of days later," Nancy recounted, "Jan called me just to see how I was feeling. I assumed Doctor had asked her to call, but a few days later when I saw Doctor and told him I'd spoken with Jan, he didn't even know she had called me. I thought that was a really nice thing for her to do." Another longtime patient, Mrs. Barbara Frank surely expressed sentiments shared by many when she said that she and her husband "always felt that Dr. Reed and Jan always worked together as a team."

Many of us make life more complicated than it need be, perhaps because we don't have our life priorities in order. Jim and Jan did. Compared to their priorities of family and service to patients, everything else was relatively unimportant. That included, for example, such things as fine food.

Mind you, Jan never aspired to be Julia Child, never trained to be Julia Child. She tried her best, but before very long, word of Jan's non-expertise in the kitchen spread throughout the area. That means it's okay to relate a couple of stories without talking out of school. It seems that one evening when the family gathered for supper, mashed potatoes were on the menu. Like many harried mothers do, Jan remained over the hot stove as her family began to dine. The potatoes elicited a loud, disrespectful comment from Jim. At that point, Jan lost control, scooped up a glop of taters, and sent them flying in Jim's direction. Well, not being Bob Gibson, Jan's throw was off target. The starchy missile flew by Jim and landed high on the kitchen wall. Then, ever so slowly, it started its long descent down the wall as the entire family watched in stunned silence.

And then there was the meatloaf incident. Now, most dogs I've known have ravenous appetites and are more than willing to gobble anything that's not nailed down. However, there are exceptions. One evening, Jim's clan was seated at the kitchen table eagerly awaiting Jan's version of the American favorite; meatloaf. As usual, their Doberman was hovering nearby, ready to leap on anything that might fall to the floor. Well, on this night, as Jan carried the plate to the table, she slipped and the entire meatloaf went flying off the plate. Their dobie raced to the scene, took one sniff… turned and walked away!

Of course it's a given that most women want to look their best whenever they're out in public. That just seems to be a natural law; in fact, my wife puts on lipstick every morning even though we're not going anywhere. Now, from what I've learned about women—which isn't all that much—there's no part of their appearance they fret over more than their hair. And so the next episode, referred to as the "case of the runaway wig," has become Reed family lore.

Unassuming women like Jan (and my wife is another one) always imagine they appear less appealing than they really are. That's likely the underlying reason Jan decided, while still only 56, to take the big leap and begin wearing a wig. Jan saw follicle flaws, like thinning hair, that no one else would ever notice. Recounting this story, Jan's only daughter, Cynthia, began by saying, "You remember that awful wig Mom used to wear don't you?" Actually, I'd forgotten about it long ago. Until Cindy reminded me.

It was about twice the size of her real head of hair and no harder to spot than a man on stilts. Anyway, Cindy said the whole family secretly wished one of their Dobermans would kidnap it and chew it to shreds. But that never happened. It did however come close once to flying the coop.

One day in 1971, following extensive planning, the family took off on one of their rare vacations, a summer car trip out West. Halfway through their trip, one early morning, Jan was so harried trying to get everyone and everything into their long station wagon that she forgot to pin down her wig. Well, as the day wore on, the temperature rose and all the car windows came down. Jan, sitting in the front seat next to Jim, moved her head a little too close to the window to catch the refreshing breeze and before she could say "gimme a perm," the wind sucked the wig right off her head like an industrial vacuum. It went flying out the window as Jan screamed bloody murder. Of course, in that moment everyone else in the car was thinking that their wish had finally come true. Everyone except the youngest, 7-year-old Brent. With cat like reflexes, Brent, who was sitting in the third row of seats, on the same side of the wagon as his mother, shot his arm out the window just as the wig flew past him. With all the grace of Willie Mays, he snagged the much-maligned wig right out of mid air. In the end, Janet, a lady of sense and sensibility, apparently took this whole wild experience as some sort of sign because shortly thereafter, she voluntarily retired her beloved head-blanket!

Chapter 12: Testing Young Mettle

In a rural area like the farmlands and coal mines around Farmington, the best way for any newcomer to town to establish a reputation, whatever their particular field of endeavor, was to provide a quality product, then let the news spread by word of mouth—which it always did. As for Jim Reed, soon after his arrival in town, there was a platinum opportunity to prove that maxim with Mrs. Robert Ronk, the wife of the Middlegrove coal mine superintendent.

Mrs. Ronk, in her early seventies when Jim came to town, had been suffering many years from the effects of asthma, a misunderstood affliction which had nevertheless been written about for centuries. Early treatments spoke of a change of climate, moderation in sleep and sexual activity, avoiding polluted city environments and eating chicken soup. Some treatments proceeded from the premise that asthma was caused by psychological problems. The asthmatic wheeze was interpreted as the child's suppressed cry for his or her mother.

Two developments in the middle of the twentieth century forever changed the understanding and treatment of asthma. One was the discovery of the inflammatory nature of asthma, obstructing the flow of air in and out of the lungs. And the other was the development of cortisone, which won the 1950 Nobel Prize in medicine for its three researchers. Coincidentally, one of the researchers was a professor at the University of Montreal while Jim was in medical school at McGill University, and Jim had the opportunity to be at one of his lectures when the researcher discussed the topic. Little did Jim know that what he learned at the lecture about controlling asthma with medications would eventually be the salvation of Mrs.Ronk.

Year after painful year, Mrs. Ronk had been unable to secure any meaningful relief from her asthmatic condition; she'd lived for decades with the real and rational fear that one of her attacks might someday prove fatal. Since the Ronks fortunately had the financial resources to pursue all possible avenues of treatment, that's what they did. Pursuing alternative treatments is not an uncommon course when patients don't receive relief for their conditions. Of course this often results in rather bizarre developments, as it did for Mrs. Ronk.

Somewhere along the way, someone recommended Mrs Ronk might be helped by a much colder environment. The pursuit of this pipe dream led to the building of a special room in a Canton ice house just for her! Then someone suggested she consult with a so-called expert in Arizona, and so she temporarily relocated there, lived in a hotel next door to the provider. But again her hopes went unfulfilled. Shortly after her Arizona experiment, the Ronks heard about the arrival of a new young doctor in Farmington. And so, as Mrs. Ronk was suffering another onset of her dangerous attacks, Mr. Ronk decided to give the new doctor a chance.

He placed his frantic phone call to Jim, briefly told him what was happening and asked him to come to their home as soon as possible. Jim arrived to find Mrs. Ronk still enduring her asthma attack. With a few quick questions, Jim surmised that no one who'd treated Mrs. Ronk had kept up to date with developments in the field; namely, the use of cortosteroids which Jim had studied in medical school. He administered an intravenous dosage of the drug and within a few minutes Mrs. Ronk was relieved from her asthma attack. After a few days, she was feeling much better than she had in years. In fact, she was so elated and appreciative, she told Jim she was going to call all her friends and tell them what he'd done for her.

To illustrate how far the field of medicine has advanced during the 50 years since Jim was in training, he said, "I don't think I've had to hospitalize a patient for asthma for at least fifteen years, due largely to advances in the field of pharmacology and preventive medicine." This does not mean, however, that tragedies can always be averted. And the most difficult of all tragedies are those involving the loss of lives of children and young adults. Jim still vividly recalls the night he received a phone call from the frantic mother of an eleven-year-old boy. The boy, in addition to being plagued with polio, was a severe asthmatic and was in the middle of a terrible attack. Jim told her to rush her son to his home. Jim met them in his driveway, only to discover the boy had died in the car just before they arrived.

It might be a stretch to describe this next case as Jim's "worst nightmare," but it would come very close. It's the type of scenario Jim worried about during his internship, while contemplating setting up practice in his hometown. He was leery of handling a serious farm or mine accident on his own, something he'd never done before. He was about to be tested.

It was a cool rainy night when the phone next to Jim's bed rang. As always, Jim's wife Jan took the call; after a moment, she handed the phone to Jim with the awful news that there'd been a mine accident. (Jan knew about the fears miners and their families had to live with on a daily basis since her father had worked the mines in Pennsylvania, Illinois and Kentucky.) Since I had never seen one of the huge mining shovels, I asked an old classmate of mine, Bob Gilstrap, to put it into perspective for me. Bob spent his adult work life in the mining business, working his way up to general manager of several mines. He said the shovel Jim was about to encounter "weighed about 300 tons, with a bucket capacity of 65 cubic yards. The frame was so massive, NASA used one very similar to it to move the space shuttle around Cape Canaveral. Under any circumstances," Bob added, "it would be tough for anyone unfamiliar with the machine to climb up to its cab in the dark."

The massive type of mine shovel Jim had to scale to save a life

The rest of this story is in Jim's own words. "The guy on the phone said it looked like a bad accident with a couple of guys trapped in the cabin of a big shovel. He said it was at the Peabody Coal Company pit #3. I knew where that was because of all the traveling I'd done over the years out in the country. I told him I'd be there in a few minutes."

"When I arrived it was pitch dark," Jim continued, "because the generators had blown and they had lost their electricity. I couldn't see anything except what was right in front of me. At first glance, it looked to me like the shovel might have gotten too close to the high wall where they had been digging, and the wall collapsed on them. The miner who met me there said he thought the two guys in the cabin were trapped in there. I immediately called Tom Anderson at the funeral home and asked him to get the hearse out here as fast as he could and bring a couple of flashlights with him."

"Then I began to search around the huge shovel to find a way to climb up to the cabin. I saw some steps and platforms and started up in the rain and pitch dark. But when I got about half way there, the rest of the steps had been buried in mud. The wet dirt had fallen in such massive amounts that it was impenetrable, almost like concrete. So I had to come back down and look for another way up. I finally managed to reach what had been the cabin only to find it had been smashed and crushed by the collapse of the hill of dirt. There was only one small window. The dirt seemed as hard as concrete and couldn't be budged. I could just barely see the two men, who were still alive at that point. They were in wrenching pain and agony. I told them who I was and asked them to hold on while I got my bag and a flashlight. I went back down and by that time Tom Anderson had arrived. A couple of other miners had arrived and I asked them to call CILCO, the power company and ask them to get a "cherry picker" (a lift bucket) out here. I knew I couldn't do much up there if I had to stand on the ladder rungs and hold on with one hand, leaving only one free hand to work with."

"I went back up and since the door to the cabin was crushed and immoveable, my only access would be through the small window. Only my head and one hand would fit through the window. I could see that the man closest to me was in worse shape than the guy on the other side of him who was in an upright position but could not move. The man next to the window was badly crushed and looked like he had been bleeding profusely. I could tell he would be dead before long and so all I could do was to give him a massive dose of morphine to lessen his suffering. He died in a few minutes. He was a middle-aged man named Holly Wynn."

"I went back down and by that time the cherry picker lift had arrived. We went back up and I managed to extricate the dead man, thereby allowing us to reach the man who was still alive. He said his name was George Long. He told me he saw the collapse coming and shouted for his partner to jump out but he didn't have time."

"I then managed to pull Long out of the window and into the cherry picker. We got him down and into the hearse. I could see he had both legs broken, both arms broken and both shoulders broken. The whole rescue mission took several hours. Mr. Long's recovery in the hospital took many months and he was never able to return to work. The United Mine Workers Union spread word of the accident and rescue effort all over the country, and I got a phone call from their national headquarters thanking me for what I had done. And of course word spread all over town about what had happened."

A few years after the deadly mine accident Jim came face-to-face with his first farm emergency. He recalled "just having been laid up with a bad back for two or three days and finally getting back to the office, hoping my first day might be a quiet one—but it wasn't in the cards. A man came running up the office stairs screaming that he thought he saw a farmer in a bad accident south of town, hollering, like maybe he was caught in his cornpicker. After he told me where the farm was, I jumped in my car and took off."

"When I got there I saw the guy out in the field. There was a fence separating us and when I started to climb over it, it collapsed on me, throwing me to the ground, re-injuring my back. After I managed to pick myself up, I rushed toward the farmer, who I recognized as Chippy Oldfield. He was screaming and hollering in agony. I could see immediately his arm had been badly crushed and mangled by the cornpicker. He was bleeding profusely and I knew he would bleed to death if something wasn't done quickly. I didn't have my surgical bag with me, so I didn't have anything to operate with."

"About that time, a guy drove by and hollered out if he could help. I asked if he had a pocketknife. Luckily he did and threw it to me. I told him to rush to my office and tell the girls to grab all the bandages they could and bring them out here. And I asked him to call Tom Anderson and the hearse out here. I took off my belt and tried to make a t⸱⸱ didn't work because his arm was too mangled. I h⸱⸱ arm off or he would bleed to death. I'⸱ I was in my surgical residency, but o⸱ working with a team of staff and had ⸱

"I told Chippy what I had to do ⸱ was going to hurt. He was already scr⸱ anything for the pain. It didn't take long elbow, maybe five minutes. Actually the ı so badly by the corn picker it made it e⸱ wasn't much bone to cut through."

124

"About that time one of my nurses showed up, along with Tom Anderson, and we started an IV. By this time, Chippy was in shock. The hospital had been called and told to have the surgical team ready to go. Chippy came through the ordeal in pretty good shape. Here again, word about the 'pocket knife surgery' spread quickly throughout the area. Of course, Chippy had to give up farming but he lived for many more years."

Over the years, Jim would become known as a prodigious work horse. That reputation likely began one bitterly cold day in the winter of 1957-58; a day the likes of which Jim had never seen before—and would never see again. The 1957-58 Asian Flu pandemic would eventually result in the deaths of about two million people world wide, making it the second most deadly flu outbreak in modern history. (The 1918 pandemic had killed more people than WWI.)

The Asian Flu started in China in February, 1957, and by June of that year had spread to the United States. It would kill 70,000 Americans before being brought under control in 1958. It's a good thing Jim Reed had worked long, tough hours during his internship because he would need all the strength he could muster when the flu hit the Farmington area.

"As I recall," Jim said, "I started to work at about 5:00A.M. and didn't quit seeing patients until about midnight. The office was packed the whole time. Patients were waiting outside to get in and they were lying on the floors. I ended up seeing 212 patients." I was flabbergasted and told Jim I didn't understand how he could do it.

"Since everyone there had the same problem," he said, "I was able to move pretty quickly from one patient to the next. And I also did something I would not normally do. I saw entire families at the same time. And I was lucky to have a very skilled, dedicated staff who worked together smoothly and quickly."

After a pause, Jim added "it was the only day I ever felt like I was rushing through my patient contacts. It's not a good way to practice medicine." When I reminded him that he didn't appear to have had much choice that day, he seemed to be a little more accepting of his actions. While impossible to verify, it's hard to imagine that any other family doctor America has ever seen more patients in one day than Jim's two hundred twelve.

With young Jim Reed's reputation now firmly and forever planted, he for the patient explosion that was about to go off.

Part IV

Service

"I don't know what your destiny
will be, but one thing I do know:
the only ones among you who will
be really happy are those who have
sought and found how to serve."

--Dr. Albert Schweitzer
Theologian, philosopher, musician, physician
1952 Nobel Prize for Peace
1875-1965

Chapter 13: The Practice Explodes

An eerie, unfortunate set of circumstances began developing shortly after Jim arrived back in his hometown in 1956. Within the next five years the local medical community of four practicing doctors was reduced to just one. (How that happened was detailed in a previous chapter.) The other three doctors had overseen rather small practices, each treating about 15 patients a day. Naturally, nearly all of those patients began seeing Jim, since he was now the only practicing doctor in town. Added to his own 30 a day, it meant he began seeing about 75 patients a day. The only way for Jim to provide quality care to that many patients was to begin working long hours.

His typical day began at about 5:00 A.M. when he headed for Graham Hospital to check on his patients there. He usually arrived at his office at about 7:30. After a full morning of seeing patients, he might make a couple of house calls before stopping at our mother's home—just a couple of blocks from his office—for lunch and a thirty minute nap. Then, after a full afternoon at his office, he'd head to Trivoli for supper. On his way back to the office for evening hours he might make a couple of more house calls. His day didn't end "until patients stopped coming," he said, which was usually about 10:00 P.M.

It wasn't long before Jim averaged a staggering 100 patients a day. When he happened to mention this to a couple of his colleagues at the hospital, they had difficulty believing him. They didn't understand how he could do it. At the time, Jim estimated that among his peers the average daily patient load was about thirty. Unsurprisingly, he also felt there might have been a bit of professional jealousy involved. For those reasons, Jim decided to never again discuss his workload with any colleagues.

Jim's guesstimate of thirty as the average size of doctor's patient load was right on target. In his 1966 book entitled "The Doctors," respected health care writer Martin Gross reported that in the 1930's, the average patient load size for general practitioners was only ten per day. By 1965, it had jumped to 34 per day. This meant that in 1965 Jim's patient load was incredibly about triple the national average. Of course, the heavy workload also necessitated additional staff.

Betsy Fogliana Kimbrell was fresh out of St. John's School of Nursing in Springfield when she hired by Jim in 1975. "I'll never forget my first day of work," Betsy told me. "Things were moving so fast I didn't know what was going on. We saw 92 patients that day. I was lost. I told Doctor that someone was going to have to show me where everything was." Jim smiled when he recalled that, "the next day Betsy came in and told me she was exhausted. She soon learned to keep up and she's been keeping up now for 35 years."

For many years, some doctors have expressed concern about the lessening amount of time primary physicians are spending with their patients. One of them, Dr. Kenneth Ludmerer, is a professor of both medicine and history at Washington University in St. Louis. In his acclaimed 1999 book, "Time To Heal," he opined that the significant decline in the amount of time doctors were spending with each patient was the major problem facing the medical profession. When managed care became a dominant player in the health care industry, it was estimated the average amount of time a doctor spent with each patient dropped from sixteen to eight minutes.

Jim was never one for detailed record keeping and said he really didn't know how much time he was spending with each patient during the two decades when he was seeing about 100 patients each day. Then and now, he's always felt he spends exactly as much time as each patient needs. But, let's assume for a moment that he was spending a little less time per visit than the average doctor. There were likely a couple of factors in play that offset any concerns.

One was his uncanny familiarity with each patient's history, on top of the fact that he had all that information stored in his head, available to him more quickly than the fastest supercomputer. So he didn't need time to review charts or ask his patients personal medical history questions. Another factor was Jim's around-the-clock availability to his patients. They knew from experience that if they needed to get in touch with him about any type of follow-up question, it would be done easily.

For the most part, Jim's patients were very understanding of the enormous time demands placed upon him. They could see his jam-packed waiting room every time they visited. There's no question some of his patients felt they were being a little rushed. And some weren't the least bit shy in expressing their concern.

"I was in the examining room," Diane Burgess told me. "He came in, listened to my chest, then my back, and he was gone. The next time I came in, he started to do the same thing but I grabbed his white coat and said, 'wait a minute, just sit your butt down. I'm paying the bill and I'll tell you when I'm done.' The next few times he took more time with me!" This was all just good-natured ribbing, and illustrates the comfort level that existed between Jim and his patients.

Other patients figured out ways to slow Jim down a little. "In Dr. Reed's younger years," Gerald Buckman said, "when you went to see him you had to have your questions ready, as he would zip in, check you out and then he was gone. My dad and I would always ask him about his race horses. That was a good way to get him to sit down and visit for a few minutes." Decades later, Bob Gilstrap still recalls being shocked that "on one office visit, Doc spent 55 minutes talking with me about coal mining. I felt guilty because I knew he had a roomful of patients waiting to see him."

Early in his career (in fact while he was still in medical school) Jim had made a commitment to himself to, whenever possible, always be present when a patient was in the process of dying. "It had never felt right to me to not do that," he revealed. That compassionate practice was one of several reasons why he earned the respect and admiration of his patients, who didn't hesitate to express their gratitude, as a pair of examples illustrate. "Thanks for always being there for Mom and Dad, and for coming when she wanted no one but you, there at the end. We knew you had been up all night but you came anyway," wrote Mrs. Mabel Doubet Van Dusen. And from Jo Ann Huffman Smith came this expression of deep gratitude. "Dr. Reed cared for my husband's parents like they were his own parents. I know it was hard for him to tell my mother-in-law she had macular degeneration. Later, as they were dying, he even drove to their home and doctored and visited them there. They both thought the world of him, and for good reason. What a nice commitment for a doctor to care that much and we were all grateful to him."

No one spoke more movingly about Jim's help with the death of a loved one than Jim Unsicker. His mother, Maxine, had been the first RN to ever practice in Farmington. After having worked for Dr. Dimmitt, she worked in Jim's office for 25 years before she retired to care for her ailing husband. After he passed away in 1998, her own health deteriorated and she died in 2007. Jim Unsicker had felt deeply indebted to Jim Reed since 1964 for helping save his life when he was only eighteen and got himself pinned beneath a car. But it was what Jim did at his mother's funeral that Unsicker will treasure forever. "When Dr. Reed came through the condolence line, he whispered in my ear that I should always feel free to call him whenever I needed someone to talk to." Unsicker, who lives 30 miles from Farmington, went through a very emotionally difficult divorce. He said he's reached out to Jim for emotional support and guidance many times and Jim never let him down.

Balancing the sorrow of losing patients was the pleasure Jim realized in helping bring new life into the world. His maternity practice grew to the point of delivering about 100 babies a year, more than any other doctor in the area. Jim made the same pledge to his expectant mothers as he had to his dying patients: to always be there at the crucial time. He recalled that of the hundreds of maternity cases he'd served, he had missed out on the actual delivery of only a couple. Like every aspect of his practice, Jim had some unusual tales about his maternity patients.

He remembered one terrible wintry day, blizzard-like conditions. Unfortunately, babies waiting to be born don't care about such things, which was why Jim found himself sequestered in the hospital with five— yes five—expectant mothers at the same time. But meanwhile, out in the country near Elmwood (about 7 miles from Farmington), a mother-to-be was ready to give birth in her home, when she got a phone call from her elderly doctor telling her the weather was too bad for him to get to her house. Frantic, the very, very pregnant woman could think of nothing else to do but call the home of a doctor she'd heard about but never met.

She telephoned Jim's home and related her predicament to Jim's wife, Jan. Feeling very sorry for the lady's circumstances, Jan told her she'd try to reach Jim at the hospital where he was waiting to deliver the first of those other five babies. Luckily, by this point in his career, Jim was able to prioritize his emergencies in a matter of seconds, so he headed out for the Elmwood countryside, after telling hospital staff to get hold of another doctor if things there began to happen before he returned. Capitalizing on back-of-his-hand familiarity with the countryside, Jim weathered the blizzard, arriving at his new patient's home in the narrowest of time. And no sooner had he led that baby into the world, he hopped into his car and sped back to the hospital barely in time to begin his five deliveries there!

For pure devotion to their maternity doctor, none of Jim's patients rival Mary Jean Wilcoxen Hunter. "I was raised in Farmington," Mary Jean said, "and I was a senior in high school in 1957 when I first went to Dr. Reed. Shortly after graduation, I married a career Air Force serviceman and we moved to Oklahoma. Then I got pregnant—and camed came back home to Dr. Reed until our Valerie was born. In 1960, I left Oklahoma again with my second pregnancy to return to Dr. Reed until our Dorothy was born." By 1962, Mary Jean continued, "we were stationed in Alaska, and I came home again and to Dr. Reed for our third child, Bill. Four years later, in 1966, we were stationed in Texas when I got pregnant. Then my husband was assigned to France. But I returned home and to Dr. Reed for the last time, for our Norina!" How many doctors of your acquaintance can claim that kind of loyalty?

Soon after that a specialist in obstetrics located in Canton. This was perfect timing for Jim because the growing demands on his schedule would've prevented his serving obstetrical patients with the same level of dedication he'd previously provided. He was therefore pleased to give up that part of his practice in 1968. Linda Barclay, one of Jim's many Canton patients, had begun seeing Jim when she was only eleven. She told me that for the past 41 years, she's been proud to say that her son, James, was the last baby Jim personally delivered. In a rare lapse of Jim's memory, he said he truthfully did not remember that. But, he added, "It was complicated because you wouldn't believe the number of people who've made the same claim as Mrs. Barclay." (Jim's assertion was borne out when I visited John Higgs about the development of Farmington's emergency response system, and he happened to mention his son Joe was the last baby Jim delivered, on Oct. 19, 1966.)

Very early in his career, Jim received a lot of favorable publicity from his unusual work on three cases recounted in the earlier chapter, "Testing Young Mettle." Later, two more emergency situations brought him additional notoriety. One involved another terrible farm accident; a patient of Jim's had become entangled in a large auger. By the time Jim reached him, the young man had become so mangled, Jim couldn't even recognize him. Jim's immediate focus was on taking action to stop the massive bleeding from the face and arms until they could reach the ER. He was rushed to the hospital, his life saved by two full days of emergency surgery by Jim's colleagues. News of this somehow reached all the way to Chicago, and a TV station dispatched a crew downstate to do a story with the lead-in headline of, "What a Country Doctor Can Accomplish." But after a gut-wrenching 48 hours of surgery, Jim said he and his colleagues were in no mood to talk with the media about the experience, (and that subsequently, the young man had to undergo a great many plastic surgical procedures).

The other situation happened on Jim's 50th birthday in 1977. He had the day off, but remembered getting a little bored "so I decided to stop by the office. I was back at my desk when I heard one of the nurses scream out that a woman had fainted in the waiting room. That's a fairly common occurrence. As soon as I went out I recognized the patient as being Alice Dilts and I could tell she was already dead. We always try resuscitation," he continued, "but I knew it would be tough because she weighed between 350-400 pounds. It took five of us to drag her back to the exam room and get her up on the table. Then we tried to resuscitate her several times," he went on, "but with no luck. We were about to give up when I said we'd try it once more and to my amazement, on the last try we brought her back to life. We rushed her to the hospital," he concluded, "where she underwent emergency heart bypass surgery, and went on to live about twenty-five more years. That story spread all over town."

After keeping late evening office hours for several years, Jim had an experience that encouraged him to make a change. He was working at about 9:00 PM and during a rare breather, he stood at his window looking down at the Princess Theater flashing marquee lights. The first showing had just let out and he noticed a woman walking in the general direction of his office. A few minutes later, he was surprised to see her enter his office. He thought to himself, "if that patient is well enough to go to the movies, then she can certainly wait until the next day to see me." Thus ended his regular evening office hours.

Not that that ended his well-known practice of seeing patients any time, any day. If one thing stands out above all others in his patient's comments, it's his willingness to always be available whenever and wherever needed. Bonnie Bach, a highly respected cardiac unit nurse for many years at Peoria Methodist Hospital described this to me in an unusual way: "Dr. Reed always had the knack at showing up for a patient just at the right time, just as the patient needed him, like Superman used to do."

In my initial book interview with Jim, he hit me with the first of what became—before this book was completed—an arsenal of shocks. In that wondering interview I told him that I had a lot of friends who seemed to rather nonchalantly "blow off" their doctor's orders. So I wanted to know what percentage of his patients he thought followed his orders. "About 95%," was his response. "About the only ones who don't," he went on, "are those where dietary changes are important. I wouldn't trust any patient in that area, even our own mother." I understood what Jim meant after hearing from JoAnn Huffman Smith. "My husband Paul thought the world of Dr. Reed. He'd take any medicine, go for any test, see any specialist and follow any orders Dr. Reed gave him. But he couldn't, wouldn't and didn't change some of his bad habits over the years. He just couldn't make himself lose weight or exercise and eat properly for anything, even though Dr. Reed tried his best to help, time after time." To punctuate his point about non-compliant dietary patients, Jim asked me if I remembered John Baudino, a Farmington native. I sure did.

John became close friends of our brother Red when they attended the U of I. (John, several years older than Red, was in law school while Red was an undergrad.) John became a local celebrity after WWII when word got around that he'd secretly served as a bodyguard to atomic bomb scientist Enrico Fermi, and been an eyewitness to the very first bomb test in White Sands, New Mexico. In 1950, when our family moved just two houses south of the Baudinos on North West St., I didn't know anything about his war experience. I was twelve years old, and all I cared about was that he had one of the first TV sets, and my sister, Alicia, and I watched Howdy Doody at John's house along with his two young daughters, Jeannie and Becky.

John practiced law in Farmington and was a highly respected and well-liked member of the community. He was also, however, one of the most nervous people in town; not a good trait for someone with sugar diabetes. Of course, the control of one's diet is vital to every diabetic, and John didn't have much, especially during late-night hours. It seems he regularly engaged in midnight food binges, long after his sweet and unsuspecting wife Chris was fast asleep. Immediately following his enjoyable sprees, John's anxieties about his blood sugar levels would overcome him, and he would resort to the only thing he could think of: calling Jim. All the while Jim was relating this story he was laughing. "John called me out of bed more than any patient I ever had, and all he truly needed was reassurance."

Of course, most people—including doctors—would've been irate over a patient like John. But not Jim. He simply said things like that didn't bother him. Then again, it would've been hard for anyone to be upset with John, who, although a hulk of a man, was a kind, gentle soul. Even though 60 years have passed, I still remember that every afternoon when John walked into his home while my sister and I were there watching Howdy Doody with his daughters, he always greeted us warmly, calling us by name.

After Jim's story about dietetic desperados, he provided shock #2 of this initial interview. "I doubt if there have been more than 15 nights during the past 53 years when I wasn't awakened from my sleep by a call about a patient." Perhaps even more amazing is that when I repeated that fact to many of Jim's fifty-year patients, none of them seemed surprised!

After more than five decades, it's unsurprising that Jim's office doesn't have complete records of everything he's done. The sheer volume is overwhelming; he saw about 100 patients a day for 25 years. The rarity of that accomplishment was recognized in the mid-1970's by the Physicians Desk Reference, (PDR) which annually publishes prescription medicine definitions. Based upon their records of doctors all over the country, they told Jim's staff that they thought he had the largest solo family practice in Illinois, if not the entire country. That story was also written up in an area newspaper.

Jim's medical office from 1964-2010

The only patient caseload count Jim's staff ever did was in 1964 when they moved all their records from his second story office above the post office to his new office right across the street from the city park. Starting from scratch in 1956, by 1964 his practice had grown to the staggering total of 16,000 regular patients. If every man, woman and child in Farmington was a patient of Jim's, that would account for only 2,500 patients. Jim estimated that about one-third of his patient load has always come from Canton, (which at 12,000 was by far the largest town in a twenty mile radius of Farmington). So that would be another 5,300 patients. That still left 8,200 patients unaccounted for.

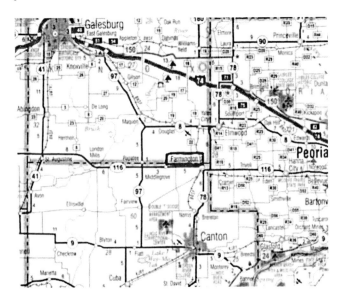

To get some feel as to where those other 8,200 folks were coming from, I looked at the map and began reading to Jim the name of every little town in the area. North and west of Farmington were Middlegrove, Rapatee, Gilson, Maquon, Knoxville, Douglas, London Mills and Abingdon. In the southwest quadrant were Ellisville, Avon, Norris, Little America and Dumferline. In the southeast, Brereton, Breeds, Glasford, Lancaster, Eden, Cramer, Smithville, Hanna City and Trivoli. Finally, in the less populated northeast quadrant were Yates City, Elmwood, Southport and Oak Hill. Not only did Jim confirm he'd always had patients from all of those 26 hamlets, but his detailed knowledge of each of the towns amazed me. "A few of them aren't really towns," he added, "they just have a few homes."

It's difficult to imagine that any other family doctor in American history has ever had more patient contacts than Jim. A bold claim—but think about it. First, during the time that the average doctor was seeing about 35 patients a day, Jim was seeing 100. Second, he kept up that furious pace for at least 25 years. Third, he seldom took a vacation from work, and in fact, has continued that practice throughout his career. And lastly, very few doctors have ever surpassed Jim's record of longevity. Jim's records do not go back 54 years, but based on what we know, a fair estimate of the total patient visits he's had in his career would be 1,000,000. A good estimate for the number of different patients he's cared for would be 25,000.

One clue as to whether or not you have a highly skilled, dedicated family doctor is his or her willingness to take a position that varies from mainstream medical thinking. For example, a vaccine for shingles debuted several years ago and was highly touted in the media. So I was surprised when Jim told me he wasn't recommending it for his patients. Firstly, he said shingles is not as bad as many people think; lots of his patients have had it without even knowing it. In addition, when diagnosed in its early stages, shingles is treatable with drugs. Plus, he's always felt a conservative approach is the best practice when responding to new products. Lastly, the vaccine was quite expensive--and Jim has always considered the costs to his patients.

Easily the most important area where Jim parted ways with convention was in the treatment of URIs (upper respiratory illnesses). The three most common forms of URIs are colds, sore throats and influenza. Because URIs occur so frequently and start out so innocently, most of us tend to not take them very seriously. But a good doctor takes everything as potentially dangerous.

When presented with a patient experiencing URI symptoms, the primary concern of a doctor is preventing complications from developing.

(The more serious of those are bronchitis, pneumonia and rheumatic fever.) Two types of germs cause URIs: viral germs and bacterial germs. The former are relatively harmless, but the bacterial-caused URIs are the potentially dangerous ones. Fortunately, about 70% of all URIs are caused by viruses.

The problem for doctors is that when they are first presented with a URI patient, there is no way to tell whether the culprit germs are viral or bacterial. Only lab analysis can reveal that key element. The mainstream medical thinking on how a doctor should treat URIs is represented by this entry taken from the WebMD website:

> "Because viral illnesses are the most common cause of URIs, it is important not to use antibiotics to treat them. Antibiotics do not alter the course of viral infections and their unnecessary use exposes patients to the risks of allergic reactions and side effects such as nausea, vomiting, diarrhea, rashes and yeast infections. Antibiotics may also kill the beneficial bacteria and encourage the development of antibiotic resistant bacteria."

Jim's thinking has however always run counter to that mainstream outlook. Here's how, in his own words. "For the sake of argument, let's say I have a day when I see ten patients with URI symptoms. I know the chances are that seven of them are going to have non-serious viral infections. But the important thing is that three of them are going to have the potentially serious bacterial infections. I can't know which is which without lab work. The problem is that it can take up to 36 hours to get the definitive results from the lab. If I waited around for the lab results, those three patients with bacterial infections could be in serious danger of having their conditions worsen, with untold harm being done on their immune systems, their lungs and their hearts. Why should I take that chance? Why not treat all ten of the URIs aggressively with antibiotics as soon as I see them? The side effects on the seven who didn't need the antibiotics are minimal compared with the possible serious damage done if the three patients were left untreated."

When I mentioned Jim's approach to one of his long-time nurses, Debbie Bozoski, said she supports Jim's strategy whole-heartedly. She emphasized that Jim monitors the type and amount of antibiotics to each patient very carefully.

The average person might guess that what's brought Jim the most satisfaction over his long career was the heroic, life-saving acts. But no. Most of those incidents were emergencies requiring instinctual reactions.

What he derives most satisfaction from is having NEVER lost a child to the flu or rheumatic fever or Bright's Disease (a kidney disorder). He attributes that to his consistent practice of aggressive treatment.

At this late stage of his long career, Jim is confident in what he knows and does not know. He pointed out that most of the medical literature is written by academicians, not clinicians like himself, and that sometimes theoretical science-based medicine has to take a back seat to evidence-based medicine. We left this conversation with Jim describing a night many years ago when an acclaimed professor of medicine from the east coast was in nearby Canton giving a lecture. In the course of his remarks, he proclaimed his support for the type of aggressive treatment Jim had been practicing. Comforting confirmation never hurts.

Chapter 14: The Clinician

When I began working on this book early in 2008, I started with a little "googling." I ran across a new book intriguingly titled, "How Doctors Think," by Harvard University Medical School professor Dr. Jerome Groopman. From Dr. Groopman's website, I downloaded a long, detailed excerpt that chronicled the gut-wrenching story of a young woman who went to a score of doctors over fifteen years, trying to get an accurate diagnosis of her serious mystery illness. During those years, she heard a lot of medical opinions. All of them were wrong.

All that time the unfortunate, misdiagnosed lady suffered needlessly from severe eating disorders, cramping, vomiting and diarrhea. She saw endocrinologists, orthopedists, hemotologists, infectious diseases specialists, even psychologists and psychiatrists. She changed family doctors several times in her search for help, but her condition only worsened. She experienced infections, including meningitis. She was on four anti-depressants. (who could blame her?) Hospitalized several times, her weight dropped to eighty-two pounds; she was dying a slow death from malnutrition. Finally, in 2004, she visited a doctor who saw something none of the others had seen, and she was on her way to health.

I couldn't wait to get my brother's opinion of this case study. Remember, this was one of my first interviews with Jim, before I'd learned what to expect from him. I gave it to him to read and a week later when I asked him about it, I was stunned at his response. "That was a joke," he said, in his straight-forward manner, throwing the article back at me. "What do you mean?" I responded. "I would have had that case diagnosed in about thirty minutes. The lady should've sued them, she would have been a millionaire." He was clearly angered by both the inferior service the lady had received and the needless suffering she had experienced

My first reaction to Jim's comment was disbelief, in spite of the fact he's my own brother. It was simply hard to believe a case that'd stumped numerous specialists for fifteen years had just been so quickly and easily dismissed by Jim. "I see three or four of these cases every year," he said.

"In fact," he added, "one of them was one of my own nurses." So I actually had a way to verify what Jim was telling me; I couldn't wait to talk with this nurse, to get her version of the story.

Debbie Bozoski has worked in Jim's office for 32 years, since she was only 16 and a high school intern. She also happened to be Jim's daughter-in-law for ten years. While working full time, she attended nursing school part time, all while rearing three children. She is only 48, but her work ethic is 'old school.' "I was raised that if you had a job to do, you did it," Debbie told me, "and if you didn't feel well, it didn't matter, you still did your job." And that's what she did, even though it made her life a living hell for about two years.

When Debbie was 36, she developed the same "mystery" ailment that plagued the long-suffering patient described in Dr. Groopman's book. "At first," Debbie said, "I thought it was just a bad case of fatigue and it would get better on its own." But it didn't. "I began having digestive problems, diarrhea and vomiting. I was able to do my job, but that's all. When I got home at night I collapsed. Not one other person knew what I was going through. I never mentioned it to anyone."

Debbie's experience, while demonstrating her inner toughness, also illustrated the folly of someone trying to self-diagnose and treat their own problems. It is one thing for an ailing person to indulge in short-term self-diagnosis and self-treatment for a non-critical condition like a back problem. But it is something entirely different to try to cope with a serious ailment like Debbie's for a couple years without seeking medical advice. "It's a dangerous practice," Jim said, "because during that time permanent internal damage could be taking place without the patient even being aware of it."

"I thought the problems I was having," Debbie said, "might be due to my diet. So I cut out all the so-called 'bad foods' and went to natural foods." She later learned that change, which for most people would make good sense, actually worsened her condition. "It began to affect my mind too," said Debbie. "I remember thinking that someone might be trying to poison me. Once, I was in a convenience store and I remember thinking to myself that maybe their recycled paper cups were poisoned."

"Finally, I couldn't take it any longer," she continued. "I felt so bad I just wanted to die. That's just how I felt." She easily recalled that night. It was New Year's Eve in 1998. In the depths of her despair, Debbie did one of the smartest things in her life—and one she now knows she should have done two years earlier—she picked up the phone and called her boss of two decades, Jim Reed. It was the first time she'd ever discussed her problem with anyone.

"Doctor came out to my house immediately," Debbie went on. "After I described the history of my problems with him, he said he felt like the culprit was in my upper, not my lower, intestines." Jim immediately suspected the cause: celiac disease. He had Debbie undergo an endoscopy, to confirm his diagnosis. In the procedure, a thin, lighted, camera-like tube is snaked down the throat to provide the doctor a clear picture of the small intestine. At the same time, the gastroenterologist Jim had referred her to for the endoscopy also took a small sample of tissue for a biopsy. The two tests indeed confirmed Jim's initial diagnosis.

Celiac disease is a problem with digesting gluten, a protein found in foods like bread, crackers and pasta. With celiac disease, your immune system harms your small intestine when you eat those kinds of food. Gluten comes from grains like wheat, barley and rye. Doctors don't really know what causes the disease. Treatment involves not eating any foods that have gluten. By no means is it a rare disease, occurring about once in every 300 people.

Celiac disease was in fact the mystery ailment that nearly killed the patient in Dr. Groopman's book. It stymied doctor after doctor after doctor for fifteen years. It made Debbie Bozoski feel like she wanted to die. But Jim had it diagnosed in thirty minutes. "Two weeks after I went on the restrictive diet," said Debbie, "I felt like a new woman. Because of my problem, I had also developed a severe iron deficiency and my hemoglobin count was very low. I had been starving myself. Normally, I'd have gone into the hospital to receive IV's for that, but Doctor arranged to have it done in our office."

Now, two years into this book and many patient and colleague interviews later, it appears to me Jim Reed may stand apart from other doctors as a diagnostician, as much as he stands apart in the art of medicine. Dr. Thanad Shay, a prominent Peoria cadiologist for more than thirty years, has worked closely with hundreds of physicians. He and Jim have collaborated on several hundred of Jim's patients. Jim has developed the utmost respect for Dr. Shay's skills. Jim told me "he could thread a needle in the middle of a windstorm." While that was indeed a very high compliment, it did not compare to the one paid to Jim by Dr. Shay, who proclaimed that Jim has "the sharpest medical eye I've ever seen." One has to wonder how Jim got that way.

What likely first occurs to lay people like you and me is that Jim is probably just smarter than the average doctor. "Not so," said Jim. "All doctors are smart. They wouldn't have made it through med school if they weren't." He's probably right, however, a review of some medical literature leads one to conclude that not all doctors are created equal. In a famous 1960's study conducted by Dr.Osler Peterson (later a professor of public health at Harvard Medical School) 44% of the nearly 100 practitioners were graded below average in diagnostic skill.

Jim Reed couldn't have asked for a better opportunity to learn the basics of disease symptomatology than at McGill University, because the Dean of the Medical school was a renowned pathologist. As a result, McGill students received more training in that area than students at other medical schools. Of course, there is more to diagnosing than mere book learning.

Jim related an early incident to me that was revealing about both his personality and his diagnostic approach. While he was interning, a nationally renown professor happened to be visiting their hospital and agreed to spend some time on 'rounds' with the interns. They stopped at the bedside of one patient when the professor decided to test the five interns. After reviewing the patient's chart and reiterating the symptoms to the interns, he asked each of them to offer a diagnosis. The first four interns were wrong.

Jim said the other interns had assumed that the professor wouldn't have chosen this patient to discuss unless some exotic disease was involved, not wanting to waste his time on a simple problem. So one by one, the four interns offered different unusual disease diagnostic impressions. The visiting scholar dismissed them all. Then it was Jim's turn. He suggested the problem seemed like a simple case of appendicitis—and the professor agreed

Jim said there were several important points to that story. One was to never try to impress anyone. Another was to never jump to conclusions. A third lesson was to first rule out the most obvious possibilities before considering the more unusual ones. Lastly, he said when caring for a patient, focus on nothing but the problem at hand.

One young medical educator, quoted anonymously in Martin Gross' book, "Doctors," felt "the inferior state of diagnosing stemmed from a lack of thoroughness and dedication." Jim on the other hand, has had those two qualities in abundance from day one of his practice. Debbie Bozoski witnessed them firsthand again a few years after her battle with celiac disease.

"I began having pains in my ankles," Debbie said. "Then a couple of weeks later I developed some lumps on my leg and after that, I started to have pain while I was walking." Having learned her lesson the hard way, this time she went to Jim after a few weeks. He had one of the lumps biopsied and found nothing conclusive. Then Debbie developed a lump on her knee. That's when Jim said something she'd never heard him say: "I've never seen anything like this before." While Debbie was taken aback by one of Jim's few diagnostic quandaries, by all rights she shouldn't have been.

Throughout the long history of medicine, some 30,000 diseases have been identified which can prey upon our fragile bodies. That fact alone is enough to conclude that the practice of family medicine is the most complex and challenging aspect in the medical profession. Since family practitioners are the first line of defense in keeping illness at bay from patients, they have to be highly skilled at first recognizing an unlimited number of symptoms, then matching those symptoms up with a long laundry list of possible diseases.

Of course, a great number of those 30,000 diseases are of the 'common garden' variety which many lay people can diagnose. But on the other hand, there are hundreds which are so rare that a doctor may never encounter them. A rare disease—or as they're called in the profession, 'orphan diseases'—is one which has been reported no more than 200,000 times in U.S. history.

Now, getting back to the time when Jim told Debbie she had a condition he'd never seen. At that point, Jim did something Debbie said sets him apart from a lot of doctors. "He asked me to give him a week to investigate, since I'd had the condition for a few weeks and it wasn't an emergency. He has a dogged determination to never back down from a tough problem until he figures out what it is. He studied medical books and talked with some other doctors and sure enough, in a week he had the answer." She was suffering from mastocytosis, a rare autoimmune condition in which the body has too many mast cells (a type of immune system cell found in many parts of the body), producing multiple, non life-threatening, symptoms in various parts of the body. Jim treated Debbie's condition with the steroid, cortisone. She responded well and while the problem can flare up from time-to-time, it's well controlled with the medication. Jim felt the condition was under-reported in the medical literature.

A respected British study categorized the four parts of successful diagnoses, with some surprising findings. Only 5% of the patient information came from costly invasive tests, and another 5% came from routine tests. Ten percent came from a thorough physical exam. A whopping 75% came from a detailed patient history. And 5% went undiagnosed. All of Jim's patients testify to his complete knowledge of their medical histories. It's one of the key reasons they have total trust in him. And it's one of the main reasons Jim insists on following through with his patients, no matter what specialists they might see. He knows the specialist won't have all the information on a patient that he has—and his and his patients know it too.

In order to produce optimum health benefits for his patients, a family practice doctor has to have a good working relationship with the aforementioned medical specialists. It's a two way street; they each have to assess the other's abilities before they can begin to develop a high level of trust. This step does not always come easily, as the following example illustrates.

When the first pediatric surgeon came to the Peoria area, Jim's initial referral was an infant he was certain was suffering from pyloric stenosis—a malfunctioning of the valve between the stomach and the intestines, making normal food intake and digestion impossible. (The only treatment for this rather common malady is surgery to repair the valve.) After examining the infant, the surgeon told Jim he wasn't sure of the diagnosis and he wanted to practice 'watchful waiting.' So Jim waited. The symptoms persisted and Jim re-referred the baby back to the surgeon in a few weeks. Surprisingly, the surgeon's response was exactly the same as before; namely, more 'watchful waiting.' So Jim waited again. The infant continued to suffer. Jim made his third referral back to the surgeon. This time the surgeon decided Jim's original diagnosis was correct. He proceeded with the surgery.

Wouldn't you know, a couple of months later Jim had another newborn he was certain had the same problem: pyloric stenosis. He referred the baby to the same surgeon (the only one available). His response was the same as it was for Jim's first referral. And so the exact same chain of events was repeated, with the end result being the surgeon agreeing with Jim's initial recommendation.

Unreal as it sounds, soon after that incident, Jim had a third infant with the same problem. But by this time the surgeon had learned his lesson. He advised his nurse that "the next time we get a referral from Dr. Reed, just go ahead and call my surgical team together." And that's not the only surgeon who learned to listen to Jim.

Dr. Jack Gibbs was a general surgeon in Canton. At the ceremony in 2004 celebrating Jim's 50th year in practice, Dr. Gibbs was one of the speakers and told this story about getting to know Jim. "My customary procedure whenever I received a referral for surgery from a doctor was to examine the patient to determine for myself the need for the surgery. But after working with Jim for a few months and always finding his diagnoses to be correct, I felt so comfortable when receiving an emergency referral from him for things like appendectomies; I would just call my nurse and tell her to get the surgery team together."

Experienced doctors of high ability—be they specialists or family practitioners—don't become upset whenever a disagreement occurs. For instance, there could not be a stronger working relationship than the one between Jim and Dr. Thanad Shay, the aforementioned Peoria cardiologist. They have complete trust in each other's abilities. Dr. Shay has been closely involved in saving Jim's life on more than one occasion, and has also provided excellent care to several other members of the Reed family. Yet, I know for a fact they don't always agree—but Jim says that has no effect whatsoever on their close working relationship. Moreover, the trust Jim has in other doctors like Shay is transferred from him to his patients, because of the complete trust the patients have in anything Jim recommends. But that same trust and devotion Jim's patients place in him does present a problem at times with those specialists Jim doesn't know very well.

"Specialists I refer my patients to," Jim said, "sometimes get upset with them because after seeing them and making recommendations, the patient will say to the specialist, 'thank you very much for your help and I appreciate what you did for me but now I want to go back to Dr. Reed and talk with him about what he thinks is best.' " Jim has as much if not more respect for specialists as anyone. But he also knows that even specialists can sometimes make mistakes just like anyone else, and that's why he wants to review their reports. Debbie Bozoski had a good example of that.

While in nursing school, Debbie was in the hospital one day talking to a radiologist when they saw Jim walking toward them down the hallway. "I wonder which one of us screwed up this time," he said to Debbie. The assumption was that if Jim was coming, he had caught an error. (I found that story a little hard to believe until I read a research report on radiologists conducted at Michigan State University in which 100 radiologists were shown a chest x-ray. They disagreed 20% of the time on the question of whether the x-ray was normal.)

According to various research studies which the medical profession is not inclined to publicize, serious medical misdiagnoses are much more common than the unsuspecting public realizes. This alone is reason enough to always obtain a second opinion. Listen to some of the reasons for misdiagnoses listed in the book, "Doctors," by Martin Gross:

> "Some physicians are not bright enough; some do not give enough time or concern to the art; others do not have sufficient experience to have seen a breadth of disease; some diagnose everything to relate to their particular medical interests; others insist on diagnosing cases of 'this year's ailment'; some diagnose by habit or prejudice; others let economic factors dictate what they do; some have a low index of suspicion; some stop looking after they find one problem."

From that exhausting list, I challenge anyone to find a colleague or patient of Jim's who feels he demonstrates any of those troubling characteristics. I know from talking with Don Zessin that he and his wife have never questioned Jim's diagnostic skills since their first encounter with him many years ago as a young couple.

"My wife," Zessin told me, "had a regular babysitting job for a new doctor in town. So when we got pregnant, she naturally felt she had to go to him. Our baby, Ronald, was sick almost from the day he was born, crying and irritable all the time. The doctor just told us it was colic and Ronald would have to outgrow it. Well, it got worse and when we went back to the doctor, he just told us the same thing again. But it still kept getting worse. Finally, when Ronald was 4 or 5 weeks old we got so worried, we decided to call Dr. Reed at his home, even though we didn't know him. We were frantic and we called him late at night at his home. After a brief phone conversation with me telling him what was going on, he told us to bring our baby right out to his house. We did just that and were glad we did. After examining Ronald, Dr Reed told us he thought the problem was a double hernia. He admitted him to the hospital the next day. Testing confirmed Dr. Reed's diagnosis and surgery was performed. Dr. Reed was a god-send and from that day on, he was our doctor."

There's one way only for a doctor to keep abreast of the latest developments in the field: constant reading and study. Jim reads at his office whenever he gets a free minute but mostly his book learning is done at home in the evening. Testimony to his efforts was offered by Rev. Larry Kirk, a Chaplin at Methodist Hospital for 25 years, most of it spent on the cardiac care ward. "I think Dr. Reed kept up with developments in the field of cardiology better than any other doctor I ever knew." Jim's bedside reading material is the huge two-volume, 2,500 page Textbook of Medicine, now in it's 22nd edition, plus several medical journals.

The wonderful thing about good family doctors is that they really improve with age, and more experience with every patient. The payoff for that is most profound when a patient's life is at stake. "I went into the hospital with a bad back in 1984," said Minnie Locke, (at a community-wide 70th birthday party for Jim in 1997). Minnie, an RN from Scotland who had worked in Jim's office, was 74 at the time. "After a few days, Doctor Jim came in and said he guessed I could go home. Then after a minute, he said that on second thought he didn't like my color and would I mind staying another day for some tests. I told him that would be okay. That afternoon I had some pictures taken and the next morning I was in surgery having a malignant mass the size of a grapefruit removed from my colon. I had had no symptoms except my 'color' that Doctor didn't like. I'll always be indebted to Doctor for his insight." Minnie went on to live for another fifteen years.

As we proceed with this book, we'll hear from many other patients about Jim's diagnostic abilities. While I've attempted in this chapter to isolate Jim's diagnostic skills from his other abilities, the truth is it's impossible to separate Jim Reed the clinician from Jim Reed the artist, just as it's impossible to separate the science of medicine from the art. To do so does a grave disservice to doctors, the medical profession and most importantly, to the patients.

146

Chapter 15: Q. and A. With the Doc

RR---We're going to get down and dirty in this session so let's get right to it. Like millions of other guys, I'm carrying about 20 pounds of excess blubber around my midsection. I know it and you know it. So here's the question: at age 72, is it medically worth the effort and stress on my psyche to take off—and keep off—those 20 pounds?

Doc---Yes it is. In general, your ideal weight is what you weighed when you were 25. Maintaining that weight is very essential for reducing the risks of strokes and heart attacks. Of course, that doesn't guarantee you won't have a stroke or a heart attack.

RR---I'm kind of sorry I asked that question. Moving on, in our newspaper, there's an article every day in which a doctor answers write-in questions from readers. How much do you think that kind of advice is worth ?

Doc---How much do you pay for the paper?

RR---Fifty cents.

Doc---That's about what the advice is worth because that doctor has never seen you, hasn't examined you and doesn't know your history

RR---You and I have both had bypass heart surgery. I'll never forget the day a few years ago when our families were over in Ellisville having lunch and you ordered high-fat food. When my wife and I got back home, she told me she was shocked by you. She watches my diet closer than Warren Buffett watches the stock market. How do you explain your actions?

Doc (laughing)—I don't eat like that very often. If you just do it occasionally, it's okay.

RR---Awhile back I went with my wife to the specialist she sees for her rotator cuff injury. We're waiting in the examining room. First a nurse comes in and stands off to the side in front of a computer, while asking my wife questions, without once looking at her. Then the specialist comes in and sits right in front of us—but there's a laptop computer screen between him and us, and he barely gives us a glance. Then another nurse comes in and she stands before the computer without saying a word. By now, I'm starting to think my wife is not being treated by human beings. How do you feel about that?

Doc.---If I'd been your wife, I'd have gotten up and left and found a new doctor. When I'm with a patient, I want to give all my attention to the patient. After I see four or five patients, then I go to my office and dictate on the cases.

RR---Once in awhile, I'll see something on TV or in the papers about some strange thing that happened to a patient while he or she was in the hospital. Have you ever been involved in any situation like that?

Doc---Once I was in the hospital room of one of my patients who was recuperating from a heart attack, and while I was there her son happened to stop in to visit her. While we were talking, sitting there next to her bed, he had a heart attack. The other strange situation I recall is that on three separate occasions, I had a patient standing at the check out desk ready to leave the hospital when suddenly they collapsed and died of a brain aneurism.

RR---What is your medical opinion about when life begins?

Doc---It's not an opinion, it's a fact. Life begins at the moment of conception.

RR---So does that mean you're opposed to abortion?

Doc---I sure am, always have been, always will be. If a patient comes to me and asks for help in obtaining an abortion, I won't help her. To the best of my knowledge, I've never personally known a doctor who's performed an abortion.

RR---Gastric bypass surgery for grossly obese people has become more common place during recent years. Of the hundreds of such patients you've seen over the years, how many have you recommended for that kind of drastic surgery?

Doc—None.

RR—Why is that?

Doc—Because it's not the answer. The benefits from gastric bypass procedures are short term. Medically, dietary change is the answer, and my patients soon learn to (at least try to) change diets.

RR---Every time I'm at my doctor's there are always drug representatives coming and going. Do they have appointments?

Doc---Most of the time, yes.

RR---How do you handle them?

Doc---They're nice people and they have good information. They all have a prepared speech about their meds. If I feel like having a little fun with them, I'll interrupt them. That confuses them so that they have to go back to the start of their speech. We don't get as many as we once did because of all the advertising the drug companies are doing on TV. If the drug reps are pushing a new medication, I don't believe anything they say.

RR---Have you ever treated any Christian Scientists?

Doc---Yes I have, just a couple. Both of them lay at home with broken hips for two weeks. Both of them of course suffered needlessly. I don't have any argument with them using their relationship with the Almighty for healing purposes, but in the event that they don't show some improvement, I think it's a good idea that you try to convince them that it's not anti-Christian to take medicine.

RR---I thought they didn't believe in doctors and medicine.

DOC---They seem to when they get really sick.

RR---Of all the dying patients you've cared for, about what percentage do you wonder if there was something else you might have done to help them?

Doc---About 99%

RR---You've seen more of the "human condition" than just about anyone during the past half century. Few subjects seem to stir up people more than the phenomenon of homosexual behavior. Some Christians are convinced it's a chosen lifestyle, while many feel it's a biological, genetic condition. Where do you stand?

DOC—I tend to think it's a genetic condition. Once I had a long, one-on-one private talk with a 12 or 13-year-old boy, and after he honestly and sincerely discussed his history and behaviors and feelings with me, I was pretty convinced he was born that way.

RR---I started jogging 37 years ago. Since then, my pulse has been 20 beats per minute slower than the average Joe. I did the math. Over 37 years, that means my heart has beaten 39 million fewer times than the average Joe. Does that mean my heart will last a lot longer than the average Joe?

DOC---Unfortunately, no it doesn't. You're looking for a guarantee that doesn't exist. The only guarantee you're ever going to get out of me is that you're going to die. But regular exercising is very important. By the way, I'd recommend against long distance running. I think it's too hard on the body. Brisk walking would be better.

RR---I'll never forget that day I had a waiver form to be signed by a doctor as a requirement to enter a road race; a doctor had to verify I was in good health. You took the form, signed it, and handed it back to me. I asked if you weren't going to examine me. Your response was, "I already did." What did you mean by that?

DOC---I can tell quite a bit just from looking and listening to a patient. I looked at your posture, your body build, your color, your fingernails, your eyes, your tongue, your gait, your skin. And I knew your medical history.

RR---Tell me something about seriously overweight people that might surprise folks.

DOC---If a grossly obese person loses a hundred pounds, it's not very important because most of the medical damage was done when they gained all that weight in the first place.

RR---Drug makers have been trying to come up with an effective diet pill for decades. They know if they succeed it will probably sell better than all other meds combined. They thought they had one in 'fen-phen' but it was pulled off the market in 1997 because of serious side effects. My question is what has been your practice with regard to diet pills?

Doc---I haven't prescribed diet pills much at all. For those patients I have, they're supervised closely. They have to agree to come in every 6-8 weeks for weighing and if they're not losing, they don't get any more pills. I never prescribed 'fen-phen' or amphetamines. They're only good for taking off a few pounds for about six weeks. After that, all the patient might get is a feeling of euphoria, which they can get with a bottle of beer.

RR---I know this isn't a strictly medical question but could you give me a rough idea of the level of your self-confidence during your career?

DOC—Well, of course, when I first started out, I didn't have a lot of confidence because of my inexperience. I'd say it took me about twenty years before I began feeling real confident. If you ever feel totally self-confident, you're a damn fool.

RR---We've all heard horror stories about patients who were misdiagnosed and mistreated due to factors like errors on lab reports, mistakes in reading X-rays and lapses in judgment by physicians. When your patients are placed in the hands of other doctors—some of whom you've never met—are there any specific steps you take to help assure that those kind of mistakes don't happen?

DOC---I choose my referrals very, very carefully and of course I review all the reports closely. If my patient's not happy with a specialist and I'm not pleased with the results of the referral, then I'll look for another resource. Fortunately, that hasn't happened very often during my career.

RR---You told me once that your little black bag had seldom ever left your side and even though they're made of leather, you'd been through four or five of them. For a long time I've wondered exactly what you've been carrying around in that little black bag. Can you open it up right now and show me what's in there and tell me what the stuff is for.

DOC---There's a stethoscope, blood pressure kit, heavy surgical bandage, scissors, needles, alcohol swabs, sterile water and bandage. And there were 21 small doses of various medications, including 3 steroids, 4 antibiotics, 2 anti-inflammatories, 1 to induce vomiting, 1 for blood clots, 1 diuretic, 2 for hypertension, 1 for heart arrythmia. (Later during this visit, Jim examined my foot for what might have been a neuroma. He thought an injection of an anti-inflammatory was called for, so he opened up his black bag. He searched around in their for the med for what seemed like several minutes. So I laughed and told him I was sure glad this wasn't an emergency. He said if it was he would've dumped everything out and quickly found what he needed.)

RR---Stan Musial is one of baseball's all-time greats and yet—as he was fond of saying—he only got a hit once every three times at bat, so he failed 66% of the time. I know you'd have been a big bust if your success average was 66%. So, here's the question. What do you think your diagnostic batting average has been?

DOC---Well I never kept track of things like that but I've taken satisfaction in knowing that during the past 54 years, I've referred about one patient a month to the Mayo Clinic for consultation and of those 650 patients, not once has Mayo's ever disagreed with one of my diagnostic impressions.

RR---I think you'd agree that since the time you entered med school in 1950, one of the most important advancements in the field of medicine has been the development of hundreds of very beneficial drug medications. But having said that, it seems like now every night when I watch TV, the airwaves are bombarded with ads for new drugs to treat everything from baldness to backaches, colds to cancer and heartburn to hemorrhoids. I was just wondering how you react to all that.

DOC---Most of the new medications are of no value to me and are put out strictly for commercial gain.

RR---We read a lot about how computer technology will revolutionize the practice of medicine, in terms of things like immediate access to the sharing of records between doctors, educating providers with the latest research, defining symptoms, diseases and treatment options, patient visits conducted via computer, etc. How do you feel about the changes taking place?
DOC---Like most clinicians, I see very little benefit to the patient. The technology is of some benefit to the management functions of an office.

RR---Who are the better patients, men or women?
DOC---Well, I've never thought in terms of some people being better patients than others, but my experience has been that women tend to come in for medical care more than men do. The reluctance of men to seek medical attention makes it more difficult to manage their medical conditions. I think women are also more cooperative with treatment regimens than men.

RR---Given that you never received any formal training in marriage counseling, how much of it did you do over the years and how comfortable did you feel doing it?
DOC---It wasn't difficult for me to attempt but I never did very much for the simple reason that I don't have much faith in counseling.

RR---For years, America was the only industrialized country in the world without some form of national health plan for all its citizens. Now, we appear on our way to national coverage. What are your thoughts?
DOC---Can you name me one successfully run government program? Socialized medicine will never be accepted in America. Doctors will refuse to be dictated to by people such as our recent state governors.

RR---Imagine for a moment that a family doctor with ten years of experience applies to become a partner with you. How long do you think it'd take you to determine whether he or she would be a good doctor and what are some of the tell-tell signs you'd look for?
DOC---It wouldn't take me very long, maybe a half hour. You can pretty much rule out any doctor who tells you that he'd wanted to be a doctor ever since he was five years old. Then, how quickly he'd ask about salary and vacation. The sooner he asks, the lesser the doctor.

RR---In the debate about overhauling our health care system, I've heard many medical professionals express the opinion that "Americans die badly," by which they mean that they die suffering and connected to machines. 75% of Americans die in hospitals or nursing homes. Nearly 20% die in hospital intensive care units, at a cost of about $10,000 per day. We spend about 55 billion dollars a year on the last two months of life of dying patients. How do you feel about hospitals and doctors keeping terminal patients alive as long as possible, regardless of cost or quality of life?

DOC---You're raising one of the most complex issues facing the medical profession. Speaking just for myself, I would never feel comfortable in giving less than everything I have to offer to every patient. That's what I was trained to do and that's what I've always tried to do. When you try to make a life or death decision for someone else, you're coming very close to playing God, and that's something I think doctors should stay away from. I would like to see a health care system in which doctors help patients think about the end of life, and let the patients, perhaps along with the counsel of family members, make decisions for themselves, while they're still in possession of their faculties.

Chapter 16: Small Town Surprises

The Red Foxx Gang

Jim's professional habit of responding to every call for help—whether or not he knew the person—was bound to get him into a delicate situation every once in awhile.Recalling these incidents usually brings a smile to his face, but that was likely not his reaction at the time.

One night in 1975, Jim got a call from a lady he'd never met. She said she was too sick to come into his office and wondered if he might come out to her country home. She added that they were new to the area. Of course, Jim obliged her. When he pulled into her driveway, he noticed something strange. There were maybe ten cars in the yard. Then, when he went inside, he noticed another strange thing. There were about a dozen women there, but not a man in sight. Never having met his prospective patient, he didn't feel comfortable asking her about all the cars... or the peculiar absence of men.

The woman introduced herself—Jim doesn't recall the name she gave him—before he proceeded to examine her. Eventually, he prescribed a medication for her non-serious condition and turned to leave. As he did, she handed him a hundred dollar bill."Ten dollars would be plenty," a startled Jim told her.She told him to keep the whole hundred to show they would always settle their debt. "Besides," she went on, "we might need you in an emergency sometime and this will show you we're good for the bill."

Sure enough, a couple of weeks later Jim got a call from her saying they were leaving the area the next morning, and asking could she come by now and get a prescription for some meds to take with her. Of course, Jim agreed to accommodate. So this time she came out to his house. They talked for a few moments, then she suddenly asked, "You know who I am don't you?" Jim said sure he did and repeated the name she had given him before. "No," she responded, "that's not my real name." Then she just blurted out, "I'm part of the Red Foxx bank robbery gang." Jim immediately recognized the name because the felonious females had received publicity in the Peoria newspaper. "I jumped up out of my seat and my first thought was the gang might come back sometime to rub me out. She actually told me they'd be out robbing a bank that night, and they were hightailing it out of here after that. So I asked her to just leave and not mention her contacts with me to anyone." The saga ended a couple of weeks later, when Jim heard on the news that the gang had all been captured somewhere near Indianapolis.

Drive-by Delivery

This next tale was recounted by Karen Riccioni Petersen, now a wily veteran with over thirty years nursing experience with Jim. But she was young and brand new at Jim's office when this wild patient experience happened in 1975:

> "One day this guy we had never seen before comes running into the office screaming 'my wife's outside in the car having a baby.' Our first thought was that he was just another hysterical husband unable to cope with his wife's labor pains. So Babs (Hedden) and I went out to the car with him. His wife was stretched out in the back of their station wagon and sure enough. We could see the baby's head coming out of the birth canal. At that point, Babs and I got pretty excited and ran back in the office hollering for Dr. Reed. He told us to call the emergency trauma unit and then gather all the instruments we had to help with a delivery. By the time we got back out to the car, the trauma unit had arrived but all they could do now was stand around peering through all the car windows as Dr. Reed delivered the baby. Then we got the baby and the mother into the office and cleaned them up. Of course, Dr. Reed wanted them to go on to the hospital but the mother refused. She told us this was her ninth child and she could tell she didn't need further care. Doctor finally agreed but said he wanted to see her and the baby the next day. So they all drove off and we never saw them again. Afterwards we figured they had planned the whole thing this way to avoid paying any bills. The strange thing is that nine years later, we got a call one day and it was the mother. She said they were living in Brazil and needed a copy of the baby's birth certificate."

I think this next experience illustrates a couple of things about Jim. For one, it exemplifies how he's never very far away from his patients, either in his thoughts or his actions. And it also shows just how easily and quickly he moves from his "non-work" frame of mind into his medical frame of mind.

A Hearty Menu

One particularly lovely Spring day a few years ago—a day when Jim was supposedly off work—he and Jan were treating my wife and I to a tour of the countryside in search of Reed family roots. We decided to stop at a small town diner Jim and his wife knew quite well. After the waitress took our order we visited for a few minutes. Then, right out of the blue, Jim said to me, "Do you see that guy over there? Would you like to see his heart?" Now, since I have a hearing loss, I often ask people to repeat what they say. I was pretty sure I'd misunderstood what Jim had said, so I asked him to repeat it. "Would you like to see his heart, he's wearing an artificial heart just under his shirt." I told him I'd pass. "He won't mind at all," was Jim's comeback. I said I wouldn't feel comfortable doing that in a restaurant in front of other people. Plus, I thought I wouldn't be able to eat my lunch afterward.

About that time, the woman who owned the restaurant came over. Turned out, the guy with the exterior hanging heart was her husband. Jim told her he'd look in on her husband after lunch. (They lived right next door to the restaurant.) Later, as we were leaving the restaurant, Jim asked me again if I'd like to go in with him to see the guy's heart. Again, I passed on his generous but odd invitation. My cop out this time was that I thought that I would lose my lunch if I went with him. (I should close by saying that this incident happened a few years before the idea for this book had been hatched. If it'd happened after the book was under way, I probably would have accepted Jim's offer, in the interest of research. Honest.)

The Face of Neglect

A few months after he arrived in Farmington, Jim got a call from a woman who said her family had a bad problem, and needed him to come out to their home. Jim headed to the rather isolated area outside of town. "When I stepped into the house I saw a mess like I'd never seen before or since. There was a large hole, maybe six feet square right in the middle of the living room which went all the way down to the ground. And it was filled with the decaying bones of about fifty cats and dogs. Then I noticed a man lying on the couch. I knew right away that he was dead and that he had been dead for several days. The rest of the small house was completely filthy, with messes and junk all over. I think there were three generations living there and they all seemed to be mentally retarded. As I recall there were two adults and two kids in the house."

Being young and never having encountered anything like this before, Jim was at a loss about where to turn. There were no agencies in Farmington to serve such families. So Jim asked his staff to see what they could do to find someone to help the family. The Women of the Moose Club agreed to help, cleaning the house and getting the two kids enrolled in special education classes in Canton.

What became of that family? Well, five years passed without contact when one day, one of the ladies in the home walked into Jim's office about ready to deliver. "When I delivered her I recall telling the nursing staff that I hoped the baby was retarded because a baby with normal intelligence would be ruined in that family." The child turned out to be normal.

Then another ten years passed before Jim had his interaction with the family. He got a call asking him to come out to their house; when he got there he found the situation to be almost exactly as it had been fifteen years earlier. "As I entered the house I saw a man on the couch who had obviously been dead for several days. He was the son of the dead man from fifteen year earlier. The large hole in the middle of the room was gone but when I opened the door to another room I found it was filled with animal bones. I learned the deceased man had worked at an animal pound in Peoria and was sneaking cats out of there all the time and taking them home under his coat on his bus rides home. The house was just as messy and filthy as it had ever been. The door was off the fridge and there was no food in the house."

Jim was irate. "I proceeded to call the Mayor, the schools, the states attorney, the minister and a court judge. I insisted they all come out to the house at once and told them I would not leave and would not sign the death certificate allowing the body to be removed from the premises until they did." The family was removed from the house that day and placed temporarily in the local nursing home. From there they were eventually all relocated to live in the State Soldier's and Sailor's Home in Quincy.

Destination Unknown

"This next situation was the strangest medical experience I was ever involved in," said Jim. "In fact, it was so strange I suggested to the nurse with me that it might be best if we never talked about it with anyone." But that was many years ago, and now Jim—at age 84—is much less inhibited about talking about such matters.

It was a quiet Saturday evening at the Graham Hospital when one of Jim's patients, 75 year-old Ross Jackson, was admitted with chest pains, the most common symptom of someone experiencing a heart attack. Mr. Jackson was in the process of dying from heart-related problems. I pointedly used the word "process" because a review of some literature on the subject of death suggests it is more of a "process" than an "event." Technically, clinical death does occur when breathing stops, the heart stops and brain activity stops. All of that happens during a cardiac arrest. But, there also follows a period of time—up to about an hour—during which efforts at resuscitation may be successful at reversing the dying process.

"That evening," Jim said, "I got a call from the nurse on the Intensive Care Unit (ICU) who told me that Mr. Jackson was beginning to show signs of increasing complications, including abnormal rhythms of the heart that often leads to cardiac arrest and death. I decided the best thing I could do was to return to the hospital to re-evaluate Mr. Jackson's status. It was 8:00 P.M. when I got there and the lights were dimmed all over the unit. Mr. Jackson was the only patient on the unit at the time so there was only one nurse on duty, the same one who'd called me at home. I'd worked with her many times in the past and had a lot of respect for her. After arriving, I approached Mr. Jackson as quietly as possible, trying not to make him aware of the fact that things were not going as well as we would like. Right above the headboard of the patient's bed, we keep a series of monitors that continuously give us information on the vital signs of the patient. It was quite obvious on the monitors that cardiac arrhythmias leading to sudden cardiac death were beginning to be present, so I mentioned to the nurse that she should bring in what we call the 'crash cart,' which contains everything necessary to manage cardiac arrest problems. We tried to make casual conversation with Mr. Jackson but he gradually became more aware that something abnormal was going on. Then he went into full cardiac pulmonary arrest."

"It only took one electric pericardium shock to start the cardiac function again," Jim continued. " Mr. Jackson gained consciousness but was not satisfied with the usual small talk. He was aware something different was going on and asked for details, which we provided. A few minutes later, he suffered another cardiac arrest and this time it took two administrations of pericardium shock to get the cardiac contractions to return. Mr. Jackson seemed very anxious, spoke rapidly and wanted answers to his questions about what we were doing. Then, because he was just barely whispering, I leaned over close to him. That's when Jackson dropped the bombshell, saying, "I was floating up around the ceiling and not understanding what was happening and I was watching you work on my body.'

At this point Jim's own delivery of this story slowed down and he became more emotional. "A strange feeling came over me that there was something very different going on in the room. It wasn't anything I could point to or see, but just a strange feeling." A few moments later, Jackson went into cardiac arrest for the third time. This time none of the methods used in the protocol were successful so Jim deemed it medically inadvisable to continue any further life saving actions.

At that point, Jim was so shook up by what had taken place that he approached his trusted nurse. "By any chance," he asked her, "did you happen to have a feeling that something different had happened in the room?" And to Jim's amazement, she reported having the same reaction as him. Jim was so upset that he suggested to the nurse "it might be best if we never mention this to anyone." Jim reminded me this was years before various so-called 'end of life experiences' were being written about.

If this tale had ended at that point, it would have been eerie enough. But the tale of Mr. Jackson got spookier. As soon as Jim regained his composure, he did what he always had to do. He went to the patient's home to break the terrible news to his widow.

When Mrs. Jackson answered the door, before Jim said a word, she told him that,"just a few minutes ago, there was a knock at the door and when I opened it, my husband was standing there with a red coat on. My first words to him were why on earth are you wearing that ugly red coat. But his only response was that he had to leave and he had just come to say goodbye." That was installment #2 of this strange story. The third and last chapter occurred the next day when Mrs. Jackson called Jim to tell him her son just arrived at her home that morning—and was wearing the exact same ugly red coat her husband had worn the night before. Jim ended this tale by saying that this was the only such experience he'd ever been involved in during his long career.

Things that go Bump on the Road

In a much lighter vein, Jim's closest friend in the area, Dick Westerby, had laughingly told me Jim was "the world's worst driver." Without admitting or denying that serious allegation, Jim told me a story about the time his helter-skelter, high-speed style of driving had a surprisingly beneficial effect on one of his patients. It all happened one late afternoon after Jim had closed up shop and was on his way to a Norris restaurant with his wife to have dinner.

As often was the case, he decided to stop off on the way to see a patient in-home. (This particular man had complained earlier in the day of an upper respiratory illness.) After Jim looked at him he gave him a shot of penicillin. But then he did something he didn't usually do, and he would soon regret it. His usual practice was to wait with the patient for a few minutes after an injection to see if the patient had an adverse reaction. But Jim had had a long, tiring day, his wife was waiting in the car, and they were both famished. So, a rarity, he left without waiting.

A mile down the road, Jim heard an ambulance siren go off behind him and he immediately knew what had happened. He turned his car around and sped back to his patient's home to find him in shock with a serious reaction to the shot. Jim knew there was no time to waste, so he loaded the patient in his car and headed to Graham Hospital, about five miles away. At speeds approaching 100 miles an hour, and with his wife holding on for dear life, Jim flew over several oversized potholes, some bad bumps, and a ditch or two.

Meanwhile, in the back seat, his patient was speechless and—like Jim's wife—in fear for his life. When they reached the hospital, Jim was amazed to find the patient had come out of his drug-induced shock. The only thing Jim could think of was that the emotional trauma of the car ride had set off such a strong chemical reaction in his patient that it had self-corrected the penicillin. Regardless of the positive results of Jim's exciting automotive "treatment," he never "prescribed it" again. Nor did he ever again immediately leave a patient after giving him or her a shot of penicillin.

Hawaiian Heartache

Vic and Dorothy Venturi

I can't remember ever not knowing Vic Venturi. I spent a lot of time with Vic when I was a kid, even though he was five years older than I. Back in those days in small towns, it was common for kids of different ages to hang out together. Some of my happiest autumnal childhood days were spent playing touch football on crisp Saturday mornings with older guys on the east side of Chapman School. Then, in the spring we'd all play basketball on Dr. Jacobs' driveway court.

I was the youngest of a clubhouse gang with headquarters in a small room at the back of Jim Fresia's Clothing Store. The other club members were Jim Dudley (Fresia's nephew), Tom Elias, my brother, Harp, Willie Wilcoxen, and Vic. Harp was a part-time salesman at Fresia's and a close friend of Vic. Jim Fresia, the hairiest man I ever knew, was a bachelor who gave a lot of his time to kids. He'd take us all fishing at the strip mines near Rapatee on hot summer evenings. The very first major league baseball game I ever attended was courtesy of Jim Fresia. In 1950, all the guys piled into his baby-blue 1949 Chrysler sedan and motored to Wrigley Field. Later in life, Fresia became a county probation officer and Mayor of Farmington.

All the Fresia clubhouse members grew up and moved away from Farmington. All except Vic Venturi. He followed his older brother, Leno, "Lemon," into work at the CILCO electric office in Farmington, and married the petite and pretty Dorothy Butler, who was one year ahead of me in school. Dorothy—a talented musician who taught piano privately—and Vic remained childless, leaving them time for their favorite activity: long distance running. They were often seen around the surrounding countryside and became veterans of many grueling marathon races.

In the late 1990s, Vic and Dorothy were able to take their dream vacation to Hawaii. Unknown to them—and most people—was that visitors to the islands are more susceptible to infections than they are on the mainland. Sure enough, shortly after arriving, Vic started experiencing cold symptoms. Vic and Dorothy weren't too concerned—until the symptoms worsened. By the time they returned home, Vic felt quite ill, so he sought out "Old Doc," as he liked to call Jim.

After Jim examined Vic, he felt something serious might be going on so he ordered some scans. "When I saw the pictures, I was stunned," Jim said. "Vic's heart was swollen to the size of a volleyball." The normal heart is about the size of a fist. "Vic's heart filled his entire chest cavity," Jim went on, "and I felt he would die soon if he didn't have a heart transplant. So I told him to go home and do nothing except wait by the phone for a call about an available transplant."

Of course body organs for transplant are at a premium, with the demand far exceeding the supply. So patients are subjected to the anxiety-filled experience of weeks or months of waiting, followed by more waiting. After a few weeks passed Vic returned to Jim for a checkup. Jim was shocked at what he saw on a new scan. Vic's heart had begun to shrink. While writing this book I only heard Jim use the word "miracle" a couple of times. This was one of them. After a few more weeks of hopeful waiting Vic returned to Jim for another checkup. Incredibly, his heart had returned to normal size. "Vic probably had contracted an infection which infiltrated his heart wall muscle, causing the inflammation and swelling," Jim concluded.

Several years of healthy living passed when Vic and Dorothy decided to return to Hawaii. Vic suffered no symptoms while he was there but shortly after his return home, he became deathly ill. "It was really strange," Jim said, "a very complicated neurological condition. His brain just sorted of melted away on us. It reminded me a lot of West Nile virus." In a few weeks Vic was gone.

One of the things that living 100 miles from my hometown has meant is that I lost touch with people who meant a lot to me when I was a child. There are six people in Farmington who've died whose funerals I would have attended. But for all of them, it was too late when I learned of their deaths. Dee Massingale, Walter Grebe, Jim Fresia, John Baudino and Cliff Perardi were all like father figures to me, and Vic Venturi was like a big brother to me. There would have been much sadness for me in attending those six services. But there would have been more happiness in recalling the many days of my youth I spent with each of them, including Vic Venturi.

Dying Four Times

The lady who refused to die, Wilma Deushane, seated with her daughter, Vicki, and granddaughter, Tanya Bolger

For sheer medical mystery and intrigue, nothing Jim ever encountered would top his experience with Ross Jackson. But running a close second would be Wilma Deushane. Wilma had battled vascular and heart disease for 15 years, but in 2004, at age 86, everyone knew the end was near. Throughout her long battle the people by her side had been her daughter, Vicki, Vicki's husband, Wilbur, and Jim Reed

Vicki told me that at one point she stayed at the hospital 24 hours a day for 14 straight weeks. She said at one point Jim ordered her husband to "get Vicki out of here for a few hours." During part of that time, Jim was also hospitalized with his fractured pelvis, and Vicki visited him every day. "Even though he was flat on his back in a hospital bed," Vicki said, "he kept abreast of Mom's condition, getting reports from nurses and giving orders to staff."

When it finally became clear that further hospitalization of Mrs. Deushane would be of no benefit, the family was grateful Jim suggested she spend her final few days at Vicki and Wilbur's home. The family knew that Jim would always be available to them anytime at a moment's notice, even on those rare occasions when he was enjoying a little time off. So it was that on Wednesday, July 28th, 2004, Jim was on the golf course when he received a call from a distraught Vicki who thought her mother was fading fast. Jim was at her bedside in 30 minutes.

Now, very early that day, Vicki had called her younger brother, John, who happened to be on a golf course near his California home. She asked him to come back home as fast as he could. John was fortunate to land a seat on a flight immediately after talking to his sister.

After examining Wilma, Jim advised the family that their mother was close to death. Vicki asked Jim if her brother would have time to make it back. At that time John was in the air from Ohio; Jim had to tell Vicki he was afraid John wouldn't be able to make it. At that point, Vicki and Jim went into Wilma's room for Vicki to say goodbye to her mother. Five minutes later Jim pronounced Wilma dead.

A distraught Vicki sat next to her deceased mother on one side of the bed, Jim right across from her on the other side. Vicki held her mother's hand for several minutes; then suddenly Vicki shot straight up in her chair, hollering out to Jim that she felt a very faint pulse in her Mom's wrist. Jim immediately checked Wilma's vital signs carefully. Then he turned to Vicki. "While I don't believe in miracles, that's pretty much what we just witnessed," Jim said. "By God she wants to live and we're going to help her." He went into his black bag and came out with an injection of adrenalin for Wilma.

Vicki added at that point she thought her brother was about four hours away. Bear in mind, Wilma was still comatose, barely clinging to life—and after another ten minutes, she passed away—for the second time. The family gathered around their mother one last time, or so they thought. But after a few moments, Wilma shocked everyone again. She opened her eyes and was obviously more alive than after her first return from death. (Meanwhile, Wilma's son, John, —unaware of what was transpiring— continued to inch closer and closer to home.) Vicki's daughter, Tammy Overcash, on the phone from her home in Florida, told Vicki to "Tell Gram that John was on his way." Vicki did, and said Wilma opened her eyes and smiled. Still, in her severely weakened state, she couldn't last much longer. After an additional 60 minutes of life, Jim pronounced Wilma dead for the third time. But the bizarre chain of events hadn't ended.

After yet another family huddle around Wilma, she regained consciousness for the third time! And now she was stronger than ever! By this time, Jim Reed was baffled and bewildered like he'd never experienced in his half-century medical career. After administering another dose of adrenalin to Wilma, and feeling hungry, exhausted and grimy (having made the house call straight from the golf course), Jim told the family he needed to rush home to freshen up, and grab a bite to eat.

When Jim returned sixty minutes later, he was stunned to find Wilma out of her bed, sitting up in a recliner, carrying on an animated conversation! Wilma's grandson, Chance Rickard—whom Wilma had babysat since he was born—ran to her side and they expressed their love for each other. And there was an extraordinary bonus: with Jim and all the family members sitting there, Wilma's son John walked through the door. Mother and son had a tearful reunion. After a few minutes, Jim asked John, Wilbur and Rod (Wilma's oldest son) to carry her back to her bed. Shortly after that she drifted into a coma. With an RN and her daughter, Tanya Bolger a student nurse, by her side, Wilma remained alive all night before Jim pronounced her dead for the fourth and final time, the next morning, July, 29, 2004, at 10:30 AM. Vicki said Jim told her he'd "never believed in miracles but we all witnessed them with your mother."

Part V

At The Heart Of It All

"For where there is love of man
there is also love of the art. For
some patients, though conscious
that their position is perilous,
recover their health simply through
their contentment with their physician"

---Hippocrates
The Father of Medicine
4th Century BC

Chapter 17: Jim Reed and the Art of Medicine

Over the past century, doctors have changed much, much more than patients. Patients today want the same two things from their doctors that they've always wanted. They want a doctor who can figure out exactly what's wrong with them, how to help them feel better. That's the 'science' part of the profession of medicine. The second thing patients have always wanted is to be treated by their doctors in a compassionate, empathetic way, with humility and devotion. That's the 'art' part of the profession of medicine. Patients have only one doctor but a doctor has thousands of patients. The onus for the relationship rests clearly with the doctor.

There are two kinds of doctors: those who interact with patients and those who don't. Here's an example of the kind who don't. When I was 62, a cardiologist whose name I can't recall because I saw him only once, correctly diagnosed me as needing bypass heart surgery. As soon as I got up off the heart cath lab table, the nurse handed me a list of four heart surgeons to choose from. I had no idea who any of them were, so I just picked one and called his office. After the specifics were dealt with, his nurse asked if I wanted to meet the doctor before the surgery. That upset me a lot. Wouldn't everyone want to meet ANY man who held their life in his hands? So we met and talked for all of ten minutes. The surgeon was highly skilled and may have well saved my life. That was ten years ago. When I recently asked my brother to guess something strange about my surgery experience, he didn't hesitate, and hit it right on the head. "You can't remember the surgeon's name." The name had vanished from my memory because there had never been a doctor-patient relationship.

Serious diseases like the one I had, and an encyclopedia of other debilitating medical problems, are treated by specialists in hospitals. They don't interact much with patients. But patients needing those types of services comprise only about 20% of the country's medical caseload. The other 80% are patients being seen in the offices of primary care doctors for problems like the four most common reasons patients see doctors: upper respiratory infections, back-related pains, headaches and digestive disorders. Of course, family doctors do a great deal more. They're the 'gatekeepers' to specialists. They need to recognize every possible symptom of every known problem in medicine. To do their job, they have no choice; they have to have a lot of interaction with their patients. To one degree or another, they practice the art of medicine.

The basic reason the art of medicine is so important is the effect of the mind on the body. That concept is neither new nor radical. As far back as the 16th century, a famous Swiss physician named Paracelus said, "you must be aware that the will is a powerful helper of medicine." The instincts of wise doctors in those early centuries of medicine were borne out later in highly regarded research studies. A 1904 study at the famed Mass. General Hospital found that 47% of the patients visiting their outpatient clinic had diseases caused by stress or psychological factors. Then, in 1964, a similar study at the same hospital revealed that the number had risen to an extraordinary 84%.

One of the most famous cases of the power of the mind on the body was reported in the 1996 book, "The Lost Art of Healing," by Nobel-prize winning cardiologist, Dr. Bernard Lown. When Lown was in training, the doctor in charge was taking a group of students on rounds. They happened to pass the room of a woman who had been a patient of the doctor's for thirty years and trusted him implicitly; she was hospitalized for a serious but not critical condition. The doctor was in a hurry that day and as he passed her room he hollered out to his students that she had a case of "T.S.". That's medical shorthand for tricuspid stenosis, a narrowing of the tricuspid valve. But the patient didn't know what T.S. meant, so she used her imagination. In her mind, she interpreted it to mean 'terminal situation.' Later that same evening, she died.

The early 1900's marked the turning point in American medicine. That's when the scientific method became pre-eminent in American medical schools. Rapid progress was made in the understanding and control of the great diseases. In 1900, the three leading killers were TB, influenza and pneumonia. They accounted for 383 deaths per 100,000 people. By 1950, their death toll was reduced to only 69 deaths per 100,000. Due to remarkable advances in science, research and public health, the American life expectancy rocketed from 49 in 1900 to 68 in 1950.

An unfortunate side effect of the great advances of science-based medicine was that the art of medicine became science's ugly stepsister. It was predictable and understandable: in the rush to embrace science, anything that smelled non-scientific tended to be discarded. While the science of the mind—which might be thought of as the father of the art of medicine—should have been integrated with the science of the body into medical education, it did not happen.

Reason, science and logic have always been the backbone in the education of doctors. But in his 1986 book, "Doctors, Patients and Placebos," Dr. Howard Spiro, then Director of the Yale University Program for the Humanities in Medicine, opined that "reason, science and logic are of no value—and in fact may be detrimental—to the physician's ability to practice the art of medicine." While at first glance Dr. Spiro's assertion seems far-fetched, consider other sources.

In the 1970's, Dr Stanley Riser, Director of the Program on Humanities and Technology in Health Care at the University of Texas, conducted a study in which "we videotaped first year medical students taking patient histories before they had gained any clinical knowledge. Then we taped third year students, who had gained clinical knowledge, taking histories. The first year students did a better job at taking the histories. The reason was that they weren't on a quest to find a disease."

At the dawn of the 20th century, the respect for physicians in the eyes of the American Public was surpassed only by that for the U.S. Supreme Court. By the middle of the century, that perception had changed dramatically. In a 1955 poll reported in the American Journal of Public Health, the chief complaint of 64% of the patients was that doctors lacked 'human warmth'. In another 1955 poll, conducted by the AMA, 43% of the patients thought doctors were 'arrogant'. Year after year brought great advances in the science of medicine: imaging inventions, new drug therapies, advanced surgical techniques, life-saving research—all rightly garnering news headlines. Meanwhile, the art of medicine continued in its downward spiral. The blending of art and science, critical to the oath keeping of all family care doctors, was very elusive indeed. But not for Jim Reed.

Mind you, Jim didn't learn the art of medicine at the famed McGill University School of Medicine in Montreal, Canada. No medical schools anywhere taught the art of medicine to any students. Where and how then did Jim Reed acquire the unique 'art of medicine' abilities that set him apart from other doctors? It's very tempting to attribute Jim's 'art of medicine' skills to some sort of mystical source because it brings an element of the supernatural into the human equation, and adds to Jim's persona of being somehow more than a mere human. While all of that is tempting, the truth, in my opinion, lies somewhere else.

I think the foundation of Jim's unusual doctor-patient relationships was day-to-day actions like his 24/7 availability, his laudable dedication, his clinical skill, his affordability and his genuine feeling for patients. The icing on the cake of Jim's development was the fact that he was a hometown boy; nothing had ever changed who he was—not the war, not the University of Illinois, not McGill University and not his internship in Knoxville, Tenn.

The key ingredient in the art of medicine is empathy. Empathy goes far beyond sympathy. In his book, "The Power of Empathy", Arthur Ciaramicoli, Ph.D., expressed this opinion:

> "In my work and life, I have discovered one absolute truth: empathy is the light that shines through the darkness of our pain and our fear to reveal what we have in common as human beings ….the most important element of empathy is not the words we speak but the underlying message we communicate….it's most enduring quality is that of focused attention….empathy requires objectivity to maintain it's balance and a certain emotional distance….empathy is always action oriented."

Dr. Ciaramicoli's description of the concept of empathy seems to have been written with Jim Reed in mind. He's always been action oriented. He's always been there for his patients, anytime, anywhere. He has a certain emotional distance in that by nature, he's not an extrovert. His patients know he understands them and know he places their welfare above his own. Finally, they know he has the trait Dr. William Osler, the 'Father of Modern Medicine' considered the most important one of all; equanimity, or the ability to remain calm and collected in the midst of turmoil, and life and death crises.

Another very important factor in the doctor-patient relationship is the psychological phenomenon known as the 'placebo effect.' Here's how it works. You go in to see your doctor with a symptom like a headache, a backache or a digestive disorder, and after talking with you and checking you over, he gives you some pills, tells you that they have helped other patients with the same symptoms. You leave his office, go home and start taking the pills. In a few days you're feeling much better…but the fact is you hadn't taken any medication at all. They were nothing more than sugar pills. The reason you got better was because your mind went to work on your body. You cured yourself.

By coincidence, the very day after I wrote the above words, a front-page story in our newspaper reported a survey indicating that 50% of doctors admitted sometimes giving their patients placebos. Nonetheless, a large portion of the medical profession refuses to admit to the power of placebos because it's not science based—in spite of the overwhelming evidence proving its existence and power. For example, all new medications are required to undergo 'blind' tests to prove their effectiveness. Such tests have to include a placebo test group. For various reasons, the true results of those tests are often very hard to come by. Such was the case for years with tests for antidepressant drugs. Finally, the July, 2002 issue of Prevention and Treatment, published an analysis of 47 placebo-controlled short term clinical trials involving the six most widely prescribed antidepressants from 1987-1999. The study, conducted by Dr. Irving Kirsch, PhD, of the University of Connecticut, found that the difference between placebo and drug was clinically insignificant.

But there's another way to look at the placebo effect, a broader, more philosophical way. Webster's dictionary defines placebo as 'something to soothe.' I'd suggest it's impossible for a good family doctor not to have a soothing effect on many of his patients. I think it's especially true in Jim Reed's case: he makes his patients feel better just from being with them and from the way he relates to them.

Of course, more often than not, the patients won't be consciously aware of what is going on between them and Jim; that's just the nature of the human mind. But there are exceptions. "I can go to Dr. Reed," Bonnie Danner told me, "and be assured that everything will be okay. He doesn't say that, but it's just the way he talks to me. His professional treatment of me makes me feel I'll get better and everything will be alright." While talking with Bonnie, I could see concern on her face, and hear it in her voice, about what she would do if Jim retired. What could anyone say that would reassure her?

The Rev. David Swain of Rapatee, Il. related a more specific example of this phenomenon. "I was in the hospital with a serious gastrointestinal problem and I suddenly started hemorrhaging. The nurses very quickly wheeled me into the intensive care unit. That's when I started to fear for my life, lying there in a cold bed, in a sterile room, being looked over by strangers. "Then," Pastor Swain went on, "all of a sudden the door to the room swung open and Jim walked in. I'll never forget the strong emotional feeling that immediately came over me that now I wasn't going to die."

This concept of the doctor himself as a sort of placebo is not new. In 1937, Dr. W. R. Houston gave a speech to the American College of Surgeons entitled, "The Doctor Himself as a Therapeutic Agent." Moreover, one of the profession's leaders in trying to keep the art of medicine from becoming extinct was Dr Howard Shapiro, and he said this in his 1986 book referenced earlier:

> "Not all patients are the same, some require more art and some more science. Science and intuition are not mutually exclusive, certainly not in the care of people...sometimes poetry may offer the patient more than physics...someday

I hope the placebo will prove unnecessary even as a symbol of the physician's willingness to help. Let the physician only realize that they are therapeutic, that by suggestion and persuasion by words and little deeds, they can influence and comfort many patients and the placebo will serve even less purpose."

I think it's accurate to say that many years ago, Jim Reed reached that high plateau of care that Dr. Shapiro so eloquently described. Sadly, the medical profession as a whole has lagged far behind. If one key unlocks the gateway to excellent doctor-patients relationships, it may be the element of trust. You could search from now until the Cubs win a World Series and you would not find a doctor who had gained as much trust as Jim Reed. The loyalty they felt may have been summed up best by one old timer—whose family has been seeing Jim for five generations. "Of course I've met the young doctors who've worked with Jim over the years, and they seem like nice young fellows, but why in the hell would I see them when I can see Jim."

In the midst of writing this book, I picked up our local paper on Nov. 29, 2008 and saw this tempting headline: "Personalized Medicine a Goal of President Elect Obama." I eagerly dove into the article because I'd come to think personalized medicine was at the heart of Jim's practice. I was shocked and disappointed in the article. Their new definition of "personalized" medicine was an individualized DNA genetics map! I have to admit, to most people that probably sounds pretty impressive. But not to Jim's patients. They much prefer his old-fashioned style of personalized medicine. Here's the way one of them, JoAnn Huffman Smith put it: "In these days, when most doctors are too busy to stay and talk with patients, Dr. Reed is rare. He once told my husband Paul that if a doctor would just talk with a patient for awhile, he would probably hear what his or her problem is."

Jim has proven himself to his patients over and over again. They know that he has always been there for them, whenever and wherever he was needed. They know he will leave no stone unturned in efforts to help them. They know he's always put their welfare above his own. The beauty of all this is that's it's not conjecture, or the rantings of an adoring kid brother. It's simply self-evident. All we have to do is what Jim told me to do the very first time we sat down to talk about the book: "Talk with my patients." I didn't know what he meant then. Now I do. I think you will too by the end of the book.

Chapter 18: Three Families: 150 Years

Jim Perelli

His was the only house in Farmington I didn't need an address to find—he's lived there about sixty years. My brother told me I would never see Jim Perelli without a hat on. He was wrong. As I pulled up in his driveway, Jim Perelli was standing out in his yard, hatless. After we'd visited for 30 minutes, I no longer noticed the large scabbed-over spot on his head, a souvenir of his cancer treatment.

I idolized Jim Perelli—or "Coach" as we called him then—when I was a boy. He was my first male teacher and first coach, but more than that, he was a kind, friendly, young man who made kids feel good. My feelings for him were so strong that 50 years later when I wrote a volume of poetry about my adolescence, I honored him with a poem. Now here we were, two old men, and when I told him I could still recall—and proceeded to name—the clothes he wore to every basketball practice, he screamed out to his wife Pat, who was busy in the next room, "Did you hear that Mother?"

I guess Jim was hatless because he felt so comfortable with me that he didn't need to cover up anything. Later during our visit, he said "I've always had a special spot in my heart for the Reed family." He knew all the Reeds. He was a classmate of Hubert and Barb. "Barb was a brilliant student. Wasn't Barb in the top 5 of our class with you Mother," he hollered out again to his wife. "I was number 11!" she screamed back. During our visit, Coach would yell out like that to Pat a couple of more times, and I enjoyed hearing it.

Coach told me that while he was stationed at the Harlingen Air Force Base in Waco, Texas, during WWII, he happened to run into our brother Cotton, four years his senior. Cotton had just married Violetta Davis, and invited Coach Jim to have dinner a couple of times with them. After the war and some college, Jim started teaching health and coaching at Farmington Junior High in 1947. Harp Reed was on his first basketball team, and I was on his teams from 1950-1952; also, he hired our brother Phil to referee those games. "I argued successfully with the school board," Coach said, "to get

Phil $5 a game instead of the $3 they wanted to pay him. I impressed upon them," he went on, "that Phil was a professional baseball umpire." And finally, Coach had the youngest Reed, Alicia Rose, in his health class.

Before I arrived for my visit, Coach's wife Pat had laid out a photo from a 1940 edition of the Chicago Tribune. A large 3 by 6 inch shot, it showed 18-year-old Jim Perelli standing in his basketball uniform. Oddly, in one outstretched hand he was holding a twirling baton, while in the other, he held a trumpet.

You see, during his high school years, Jim won two national twirling contests and two national music contests. But despite his own extraordinary youth, this day he was more interested in talking about his granddaughter. (A few years ago, she had the honor of performing in the Macy's Christmas Parade as a dancer.)

On this 1940 Homecoming Parade postcard, drum major Jim Perelli and his drum majorette sister Pat lead the high school band.

In addition to his other skills, Perelli had also been an outstanding all-around athlete in high school. It wasn't easy for him to refuse Coach Grebe's plea to play football. But he did because "I could make good money teaching baton to a lot of young kids, and I knew I would need the cash to help pay for college." He began at Knox College in nearby Galesburg in 1941 but it wasn't long before he was called to serve his country. Not in the usual way, however.

"Have you heard of Glenn Miller?" Jim asked. Silly question. Everyone in America around my age knows who Miller was. "It was his job to go around to all the Air Force bases to establish bands," Jim went on. "One day while I was stationed at Miami Beach, I was told to report to the headquarters office and there sat Glenn Miller, holding auditions. After I played trumpet for him, he told me it wasn't official yet because tryouts weren't over, but I would be in the band. So throughout the war, at different Air Force bases, I played with guys who had been in all the big bands—like the Dorseys,

Harry James and Fred Waring. After the war, I got a call one day and it was a guy who was leaving the Waring band. He offered me a job in New York City with his new band. I would have taken it but Pat didn't want to leave Farmington." The Big Apple's loss was Farmington's gain.

Jim and Pat Perelli settled into married life in their hometown and they've been there ever since. In short time, they had three daughters: Cynthia and twins LuAnn and SueAnn. When Mary B. Wright, a local who'd been principal of the junior high forever, finally retired, Coach took her place. He subsequently became assistant superintendent of the entire school district. But it wasn't until 1983, when Coach retired after 33 years in the school system, that his relationship with Jim Reed became closer.

Like most people, Coach experienced good health throughout his working years. From 1956 to 1983, his contacts with Jim Reed focused on the routine care of his three girls and the occasional bouts with flu and colds for himself and his wife. All of that changed abruptly in 1983 when, at age 60, Coach noticed a small lesion on his head. It was hard to miss because—like many of us—with each passing year, Coach had less and less hair to worry about. Anyway, when the lesion failed to heal and disappear, Coach didn't ignore it like many others do. Instead he went to see his doctor.

As soon as Jim Reed looked at the lesion, he was pretty certain he knew what was going on. He had never been one to dance around issues, and this directness was one of the qualities his patients admired in him. So Jim presented Coach with the single most feared word in the English language: cancer. Jim said he'd arrange for the next step—a biopsy to microscopically examine the tissue and provide the detailed information needed to proceed with treatment.

Like so many others who've gone through cancer scares, Coach said the two week wait for the biopsy procedure and the report of findings was the longest, most anxious wait he and his wife ever experienced. When the news came in, it was good and bad. The bad part was that his skin lesion was cancerous. The good news was that the type of cancer was determined to be basal cell carcinoma, the least deadly of all skin cancers. It's a very common cancer, striking 3 of every 10 American Caucasians. And while every form of cancer is dangerous because of its ability—when left untreated—to spread to other parts of the body, basal cell carcinoma responds very well to early detection and surgical removal, which is why Coach is still around 27 years later to talk about it.

All the while Coach was being questioned, poked, examined, treated and operated on by specialists and nurses he didn't know, he took great comfort in knowing that keeping a very close eye on everything was the family doctor he'd come to trust implicitly. Coach was fully confident that no error in diagnosis, testing, or treatment would ever happen under the watchful eye of Jim Reed. But errors or not, there were bound to be other emergencies.

"In 1995 I was experiencing some symptoms which concerned Dr. Reed," Coach said, "so he arranged for me to have a heart angiogram." Coach's daughter, Cynthia, returned home to provide family support. It's a good thing she did, because the night before the angiogram, Coach began experiencing classic heart attack symptoms. In the midst of the turmoil and crisis, Coach's wife reacted like a lot of us would: she fainted. Fortunately, Coach's daughter remained calm enough to phone Jim Reed. He told her to get her father in a car and to the hospital as fast as possible, and he'd call ahead and have staff waiting. (While Cynthia was speeding to the hospital she was forced to stop twice so her dad could throw up along side the road.)

In a matter of hours, Coach was undergoing successful quadruple bypass surgery. "I'll never forget my first day back home," he told me. "It was dusk and there was a knock at our door. It was Dr. Reed, there to check up on me. Of course, I knew that he had been through the same operation I had, so it meant more to me. He told me what I could expect with recovery and rehab." He paused, then added, "I wouldn't be here today if it weren't for Jim Reed." I asked Coach if he was sure of that. Without hesitating a second, he responded, "I'm positive of that."

I asked Coach how often he'd been to my brother over the years. "Probably about three times a year for thirty years," he replied, "for the cancer, the heart, prostate problems, diverticulitis and various other ailments." At this writing, Jim Perelli is eighty-five. He plays golf and goes to exercise rehab a couple of times a week. He doesn't twirl the baton anymore—but he still plays a mean trumpet.

I think Jim Perelli enjoyed visiting with me as much as I did with him. He was emotional and excited, warm and exuberant. But he became calmer and more contemplative as he related the story about his small-college ROTC unit, which had stayed together for combat in WWII. Nineteen of the twenty-two young men were killed or injured at the Battle of the Bulge. Within a few minutes of telling me that horrific ratio, Coach repeated it again, as though it were a re-occurring dream over which he had no control. Never forgetting the fallen, in honor of our Armed Services veterans, Coach has been playing the heart-rending "taps" at local funerals for many years.

In 2010, Jim Perelli celebrated the 100th anniversary of his paternal family's arrival in Farmington. His grandfather came here to mine the earth. His father was a fixture at Page's Clothing Store for forty years; hired, Coach said, "to lure all the Italians in by talking their language." In honor of his lifetime spent in Farmington, his career of service as an educator, his high respect in his hometown, and his more than 60 years in his present residence, the Farmington City Council in the Spring of 2010 honored Jim by naming the back alley directly east of his home, Jim Perelli Way.

Jim Perelli in the thoroughfare named in his honor by the City Council

The Dikemans

Ms. Nancy Dikeman and her family

Nancy Dikeman didn't know it, but she was my guinea pig. She was the first person I interviewed for the book. As it turned out, she was also the only patient I would interview who didn't know anyone in the large Reed clan before she met Jim Reed.

Even though 54 years have come and gone since Nancy first saw Jim, it's a day she's never forgotten. She wasn't ill at all on that gorgeous spring day in May, 1957. In fact, she was feeling downright giddy, and at the same time a little nervous—who wouldn't be, facing a life-changing event like hers. She was 23 then, decked out in her prettiest sundress, waiting to see Jim for a blood test before she could wed and change her name to Mrs. Robert Dikeman. The thing is, when she told me that happy story, she unintentionally led me into the first of many flashbacks I had while working on the book. I had no control over these of course, and in time I came to embrace them, view them as connectors, helping tie all of life around Jim and Farmington together into a whole.

When Nancy related that story to me of her first encounter with Jim, my mind meandered back to 1962 when a beautiful young gal from Decatur named Mary Barr went to see Jim for the same reason as Nancy. Mary wanted to change her name to Mrs. Rudy Reed. Since Mary was about to join forces with the Reeds, Jim thought he'd spring a little mischief on her. He'd brought a huge horse syringe from home and given it to his nurse, Babs Hedden, to hold onto. When Mary entered the exam room, Jim asked Babs to bring in a syringe. And when Babs walked in with the super-sized needle, Mary nearly jumped out of her skin. Since she's been recounting that story for 49 years, it's qualified for our family lore scrapbook. (Of course the syringe grows a little every year.) But Nancy Dikeman had gotten off prank free, probably because her intended was in the room with her and they were both strangers to Jim.

At that first meeting between Jim and Nancy, neither one had any idea they'd be seeing so much of each other during the ensuing seven years. Over that time, Nancy would be pregnant for 36 months. By her fourth delivery, she was such a relaxed babymaker that when she was on the delivery table, she joked to Jim that she was "getting too old for this stuff." Jim told her that it was too late to stop now.

All four of Nancy's pregnancies and deliveries were as smooth as her newborn's behinds. Jim said that 95% of childbirth happens naturally and his main job was just to be there in case something unexpected occurred. Nancy laughed as she recalled Jim almost missing her first delivery. "As my due date approached, suddenly I had a feeling something fast was happening, so my husband rushed me to the hospital. There was a quick exam and the nurses said I was right so they called Doc at home and he sped to the Graham Hospital just in the nick of time. After that, he watched my next three pregnancies like a hawk."

One recurrent theme expressed by Jim's patients was his willingness to always be available for them, and nowhere was that more evident than with his maternity patients. He never strayed more than a half hour away from home whenever a patient's due date neared, ever aware of the emotional need of young mothers-to-be to have their family doctor near at hand.

After her last delivery, Nancy's contacts with Jim centered on the development of her two girls and two boys. In 1969, the children endured several nasty bouts with tonsillitis, and a decision was made to be done with them for her 3, 7 and 9 year olds. Nancy rightly knew that doing them one at a time would be emotionally tough on the ones waiting their turn. So she came up with the idea of doing them all at the same time; while Jim was briefly taken aback by the idea, he decided to go along with her wishes. On the appointed day, Nancy showed up at Graham Hospital with the three young ones and her suitcase. She fully intended to spend the night with them—until she was advised that administrative policy would not allow it, in spite of her pleadings. Luckily, Nancy happened to have an aunt living very nearby; but after being there just a couple of hours, she got a frantic phone call from a hospital nurse telling Nancy that her three-year-old was terribly upset, and wouldn't settle down until they told her that her mother could come back to stay with her.

The tonsillectomies, performed by Jim, went off without a hitch—but Nancy almost threw a wrench into the recuperation process. A few days after the kids got home they were feeling fine so Nancy proceeded with their Sunday family tradition of popcorn. A few days later when she took them all in to be checked by Jim, he explained she'd been lucky because the popcorn could've easily interfered with the healing process in their tender throats.

Nancy's husband, Bob Dikeman, a lifelong farmer in the Maquon area, contracted rheumatic fever as a child, so he'd see Jim about once a year for a checkup. In 1976, when Bob was forty, Jim discovered a suspicious growth on a lung x-ray and referred Bob to a specialist in Peoria who confirmed Jim's fear of cancer. The specialist felt Bob's growth did not yet necessitate aggressive treatment and recommended what doctors refer to as watchful waiting. Three months later Jim thought the growth had enlarged. The specialist agreed and a thirty-day course of radiation was begun.

Three months after radiation treatment finished, Bob suffered a convulsion, and a brain scan revealed another cancerous growth. Cobalt therapy was begun but the doctors told Nancy they thought Bob only had six months to live. Nancy's first thought was sorrow over Bob not getting to see any of their four kids grow up into adults. At the time, they were 18, 16, 14 and 12.

The agony of an entire family living day to day with a death sentence inching ever closer is one of those experiences impossible to understand unless you've lived through it yourself; it takes a very strong, tough, special woman to endure what Nancy lived through without losing her mind. With that said, Nancy and her family received a huge gift when, a few months later, Bob's condition inexplicably stalled instead of worsening. It was one of those things doctors seldom experience and cannot translate. "Doc told me," said Nancy, "that if he ever came down with cancer, he wanted to come out and get some of Bob's blood."

Incredibly, Bob would go on to live another 25 years. They weren't all problem free years, however. He endured a quadruple heart bypass surgery as well as back surgery. Through it all, Nancy was able to maintain a strength of spirit that transferred to both Bob and her children. Jim also praised Nancy's general attitude and demeanor, and I've learned he isn't one to toss out meaningless compliments. Nancy is not an effusive woman, but she did say "I was always appreciative of Doc's being there whenever we have needed him for the past fifty years." He was there for their marriage blood test, and there for her four pregnancies. He was there for three tonsillectomies, and there for Bob's cancer, back operation and open-heart surgery. And he was there at the end for Bob in 2002, to help ease the trauma and grief of death.

In 1980, when she was only 47, Nancy suffered a mild heart attack. She was hospitalized for two weeks, but in the end didn't need surgery. She laughingly remembered having two cigarettes in the hospital while waiting for her cardiologist to show up. Those would be her last ones, on doctor's orders.

In December of 2002, Nancy was having breakfast in a Yates City restaurant with her closest friend, Pastor Mary Babcock of the Yates City Presbyterian Church. Pastor Mary asked Nancy if she was feeling okay, because she just looked a little off. Nancy said she felt fine, but while in line to pay the bill she suddenly fainted. While Nancy was taken to Methodist Hospital in Peoria, a guy in the restaurant (who was married to a woman working in Jim's office) called to notify Jim.

At the hospital, Nancy was examined and received an EKG. All the results were negative, and they were preparing to discharge her when her bedside phone rang. "It was Doc and he said that under no circumstance was I to leave the hospital until we found out what had happened to me." Upon further testing specifically ordered by Jim, Nancy was found to have significant heart artery blockage, requiring triple bypass surgery. Later, Jim explained his thinking to me. "The key was that I had treated her for 44 years and knew that her behavior and symptoms were not normal for her. And since you don't just faint for no reason, I wanted to know what that reason was."

Nancy Dikeman was 23 when Jim became her doctor. Now she's 74 and Jim is still her doctor. No one knows how long the relationship will go on.

The Bowhays

Danny and Marilyn Bowhay and their son Larry

My usual routine while interviewing patients for the book was to do it on Wednesdays, Jim's day off, so I could also visit with him. On this particular Wednesday, I was at Jim's and told him I was headed out to meet the Bowhays. They live and farm a few miles east of Elmwood. Jim said I'd never find the place.

Mr. Bowhay had given me pretty detailed directions, so I started to read them to Jim, slowly. As I was doing that, I could almost see his brain racing, his mind tracing the route. As I mentioned each turn—and there were many—he nodded his agreement. When I finished, he said, "those are good directions and you should actually be able to find their farm." I didn't grow up on a farm and I've been a 'big city boy' for some fifty years now, so I've enjoyed scouring the countryside around Farmington looking for Jim's scattered patients. They're all over the place; that's why Jim has been back and forth over every country road for miles around for the past fifty-three years. And that's why nobody knows these roads better than he.

After introductions—"Danny will do fine," Mr. Bowhay told me—Marilyn Bowhay said "you look just like your brother." Hearing that always makes me feel good. But her next comment made me break out laughing. "Are you younger or older than him?" "Good Lord," I roared, "he's eleven years older than me and looks every day of it!" Like many of Jim's patients, the Bowhays know a lot about the land. (The Bowhay family started farming in 1800 in Pennsylvania.) On the other hand, Marilyn's family was a latecomer, not having started until 1918.

The Bowhays were one of the very few families I interviewed for the book who hadn't had some type of personal connection with at least one other member of the Reed family. They thought Jim had about seven sibs and were surprised to learn that it was nearly double that. But while they didn't know any Reeds, they were one of the few families who knew the Myers family, one of whose members would eventually become Mrs. Jim Reed.

Marilyn and Dan Bowhay both grew up in the Elmwood area, and went to school with the four Myers children. They weren't close friends but in a small town, at least back in those days, there weren't any strangers. Dan is eighty now and Marilyn is seventy-five but they both look younger than that. Though they seem very fit, I was nevertheless surprised to learn that Dan still farms. Marilyn also works in the fields driving a tractor, but Danny jokingly assured me he doesn't overwork her.

Marilyn Weber married Dan Bowhay in 1951. Their two children, Linda, 56 and Larry, 57, were delivered by Dr. Clinton McKnight. When Dr. McKnight left the area in late 1956, the Bowhays chose young Dr. Reed as their new physician. And they've stayed with him for over 50 years. At the same time the young Bowhay family retained Jim, Marilyn Bowhay's mother, Etta Weber, did the same, when she was fifty-two. She was under Jim's care until she passed away in 2007, one month shy of her 102nd birthday. She is the oldest person Jim ever cared for. (Her husband, Lee, passed away in 1997, at age 94.) I'd take my chances on their daughter Marilyn making it to 100.

In the course of interviewing Jim's patients, one thing they all remember in detail is any type of serious ailment their young children experienced. The Bowhays were no exception. "One day when Larry was six (51 years ago)," Marilyn said, "he became dehydrated real fast, in about twelve hours. And he couldn't keep anything down. So we rushed him to Doc. Larry fell asleep in the examining room while we were waiting for Doc, and when Doc came in, he couldn't wake Larry up. He looked a little worried and that really concerned me. He said maybe Larry would respond to my voice, and asked me to talk to him. I did, and he did respond. But when Larry opened his eyes, he was convulsing."

"Jim had us immediately put Larry in our car (this was before there was any ambulance service), and drive him straight to the hospital where he'd have a specialist waiting on us. They ran a lot of tests and didn't find anything—but they gave him intravenous feedings for thirty-six hours, and then somehow he was okay. Until a month, later, when the same thing happened again. The treatment was repeated but another month later, it happened for the third time. That's when Doc said he thought Larry should have his tonsils out. He referred him to Dr. Mc Knight, who by that time, was an eye, ear, nose and throat specialist in Peoria. The tonsils came out and Larry was fine after that."

Unlike most of Jim's 50-year patients, both Danny and Marilyn experienced serious health problems while still in their twenties. Marilyn was suffering from bad headaches when she was only twenty-four. Now headaches are the leading reason patients see doctors, and they can be caused by and related to a huge number of other problems. In Marilyn's case, Jim could not find the cause, so he referred her to the famed Mayo Clinic for a complete workup. Much to Marilyn's surprise, Mayo's couldn't find the cause either. "They concluded that my headaches were caused by nerves, stress or some psychological problem but I had a strong feeling it was something else." At that point, Marilyn did what a lot of patients do; she sought out 'alternative' care. (A 1993 study revealed that of the roughly 800 million annual patient visits to medical providers in America, more than half were to providers of alternative therapies: acupuncture, chiropractic, hypnosis, message therapy, meditative therapy, etc.)

"About that time a friend suggested that I might benefit from seeing a chiropractor," Marilyn went on. That was something she'd never done before, but feeling at her rope's end, she thought why not. "So I did, without discussing it with Jim because I was a little afraid of what he might say." After x-rays, examining her and taking her history, in which the chiropractor learned she had taken a bad fall many years earlier, he concluded her headaches were referred pain from a misaligned back. "He began a series of treatments," Marilyn said, "and slowly, I began to feel better. After about three months, the headaches were gone. I was going in to see Jim for something else and Dan and I decided I should tell him what I had done, even though I was afraid of what his reaction would be. When I told him the headaches were all gone, his response was, 'I don't care if you took snake oil, if your headaches are gone, that's all that counts.' Boy, was I relieved!" She added that her headaches never returned with the intensity of those she experienced 50 years ago.

In 1957, the same year of Marilyn's terrible headaches, her young husband contracted a bad urinary tract infection; it was so serious that Jim admitted him to the hospital. During his immobilization there, he developed what Jim called a deep-vein thrombosis—a blood clot—always a serious condition because if it dislodges it can travel to the brain or heart with fatal consequences. As soon as the hospital staff feared a clot, they called Jim and he immediately ordered a Heparin IV drip, a medication that acts to dissolve the clot. Jim said it worked very well and Danny was able to return home in a few days. "We feel Doc saved Danny's life," Marilyn said. He's never had a reoccurrence.

"Doc can tell a lot just by looking at you," she continued. "Just a few weeks ago, I had a fainting spell." At that point Dan excitedly jumped into the conversation and took over the story. "We were just sitting here at this table on a Sunday morning when all of a sudden, her head dropped down on the table. I raised up her head up and all I could see was the whites of her eyes. I didn't call 911 because I was afraid to put her head down to go for the phone. Then she came out of it in about five minutes, so we didn't call Doc."

"But the next morning," Marilyn said, "I was standing here fixing breakfast and I started to feel faint. So we jumped in the car and headed for Doc's office. I was sitting on the exam table when Jim came into the room and the first thing he said was 'I've known you a long time and I don't like the way you look.' He checked me over and couldn't find anything. So he put one of those monitoring belts on me that records everything for twenty-four hours. It didn't show anything bad so he said we'll just watch it and that it might never happen again. Sure enough it hasn't."

The biggest medical scare the Bowhays have experienced happened to Marilyn in 1985. "I became real sick one night and laid on the floor all night long, throwing up." "We called Jim that morning," she went on, "and he immediately put me in the hospital and ordered some tests. They indicated I had a large, cancerous growth on my colon, and the biopsy showed it was malignant. Dr. Gibbs operated on it; he said we were lucky, that they thought they got it early and they thought they got it all out." She added, laughing, that "for years after that, when I'd see Dr. Gibbs, he'd say I wasn't supposed to be here."

In 1985, Marilyn began to notice that she was tiring more easily. Of course, that's a symptom in multitudes of illnesses, but what she began experiencing next isn't. "My legs began feeling weaker," she told me, "and they got harder, almost like wood. At the same time, I was having more trouble walking. So I went to Jim and after talking with him and being examined, he said he suspected a problem called Collagens Disease. He sent me to the hospital where testing confirmed it."

Collagen's Disease is an inflammatory autoimmune vascular disease related to arthritis and strikes only about 1,000 Americans a year. Treatment consisted of administering prednisone, a steroidal medication, and rest. The rest part was easy because Marilyn felt exhausted most of the time. "I was sleeping 15-20 hours a day," she said. Recovery was slow but steady.After a few months she was back to normal and has not experienced any symptoms since then. The rarity of Collagens made Marilyn wonder just how Jim knew what it was. So later, I asked him. He said Collagens wasn't easy to diagnose and that 30 years of clinical experience probably made the difference.

A couple of years ago, Danny paid the price a lot of farmers pay at some point in their deceptively dangerous occupation. "One day," Danny said, "I was changing the oil in the combine. After all the old oil was in my bucket, I started to climb down and the next thing I knew the oil bucket tipped over and the oil spilled all over me and the concrete floor. Everything happened so fast. I don't recall even moving, but the next thing I knew, my feet went out from under me and I hit the floor very hard on my rear. I heard something pop and then the pain hit me. The pain was bad but I managed to crawl to the barn door, then to my feet and out the door. My son was there and got me to the house. We cleaned up and then he drove me to the hospital. The x-rays showed I had broken my pelvis in two places. We rented a hospital bed and I had to lay flat on my back for six weeks. My wife and son had to do all the harvesting that year. The pain I had during those six weeks in bed was the worst I've ever had." He feels most fortunate to have made a full recovery with the ability to return to all his former farm duties.

"We have the greatest respect in the world for Doc Reed," said Marilyn and Danny. "Just the other day I was in his office," Danny said, "and he asked me if I was still farming. When I told him I was, he wondered when I was going to retire. So I just asked him right back when he was going to retire. When he replied, 'when I die,' I said it was the same for me. He's always been there for us and he still is."

As I drove away from the Bowhay farm home, I found myself nostalgic and sentimental, the same immediate reaction I had after leaving my visits with most of Jim's patients. I noticed the silence out here in the country, an appealing silence I've never really known. I wondered if I could live out here, if I could make the change. Then I wondered if folks like the Bowhays could move to the city. I think it'd be easier for me than them. It seems to me they might have more to lose than I.

Later that evening, listening to my tape of the Bowhay visit, I was having some trouble making out the conversation. Then it dawned on me why: There was almost always a lot of laughing going on whenever one of us was talking. I thought of my other interviews and I remembered the same thing happening. Why all the laughter? It was because they so much enjoyed reminiscing about years and years of their experiences with Jim Reed. For many of them, he's been an important part of their entire adult, married lives. And they're remembering my brother with deep gratitude and affection.

Alone in my study that night, for the first time the magnitude of what I was involved in really sank in. I was now seeing and experiencing something that had been going on in Farmington for decades, and I never knew it existed, even though my own brother was the one who made it all happen. As much as I didn't want to admit it, I knew it couldn't go on much longer, no matter how hard everyone wished for it. And I knew it was a huge piece of small town America that would never be seen again. I felt very sad. Sad for my brother, sad for his patients, sad for small towns and sad for the medical profession. And sad for myself. Tears came. But that was okay. It would keep me going and determined. I felt much closer to my brother, and maybe even more importantly, closer to the folks he'd taken care of for more than half a century.

Chapter 19: Uncensored Patients

The best way to get to know a doctor is to be his patient. Unfortunately for me, I never could do that with my brother since I've lived 100 miles from him for the past 54 years. You could of course learn a lot about a doctor by following him around for days at a time, but that's not feasible since patients don't really want anyone else there when they're being seen and examined by their physician. One option open to me was to spend hours visiting with Jim, listening to his unbelievable tales and bombarding him with tons of questions.

The last—and best—way for me to get to know my brother as a doctor was to talk with his patients. After all, they were the end product of all his time and efforts, the reason why he's been doing what he does for more than 54 years. In fact, the only piece of advice Jim ever gave me about the writing of this book was to talk to his patients. There were way too many for me to see, so I put an ad in the paper asking them to write to me and share their experiences with Jim. And they did.

There is no reason to think the scores of patients who wrote and/or spoke to me weren't representative of all of Jim's patients. The responses I received are dispersed in the various chapters throughout the book because that's where each seemed to best fit, but since it was impossible to include all the responses in those chapters, we devoted two chapters to nothing except letters from patients. Most were written after Jan., 2008, when I started the book, but some came to Jim in 1997 when a surprise community-wide open house was held to honor him on his 70th birthday.

There are several common threads running throughout all these letters. Most touching—and most revealing—are the deep, personal feelings that Jim's patients felt free to express. Those strong feelings often resulted from a doctor-patient relationship forged over the span of several decades. And the one comment heard most often is Jim's willingness to be available 24 hours a day, seven days a week. Now let's see what the patients have to say.

"I was a young kid in need of a shot. I was throwing a fit on Dr. Reed's table. The next thing I knew, I was coming to with Dr. Reed smacking my cheeks, saying, "Diane, wake up." I had fallen off the table, hit my head on something and knocked myself out. Dr. Reed carried me down the stairs to our car."

--Diane Burgess

"I truly believe Dr. Reed did all he could and more for my husband Paul all those years and I'll always be grateful. I know I could have lost my husband in 1986 and several other times because he had other close calls. Thankfully, because of Dr. Reed, he lived through many problems. Dr. Reed has given his life for our communities and many people like Paul. The Smith and Huffman families know that for sure."

- Jo Ann Huffman Smith

"You took care of me when I was growing up, and my mother, Barbara Hefley Howard and my grandparents, aunts and uncles. You are part of our family, as any stories I have heard about my family being ill, or injured have always had your name mentioned."

-- Kristen Weldon Middleton

"You have gone out of your way to help me over the years and you won't know how much I appreciate it. Your wife was a great help when I called you at home. I will be at a complete loss when you retire."

-- Peter Yancik

"Thank you for being there for our whole family all these years, for my mother and father and all six kids. I remember when my Dad's fishing buddy, Gilbert Dikeman, passed out down by the lake and you were there in a flash. Thanks for all the special things you did over the years."

-- Berniece and R.L.Porch

"After several physicians gave us crackpot ideas and proved their lack of diagnostic skills, my wife came to you and received your correct diagnosis of an allergy to pesticides. We followed your advice to move to a place near the ocean, and it worked. I think you may have saved her life."

-- Steve Hawkins

"May I say that there aren't any more doctors that I've found that truly cared for their patients as has Dr. Reed. He opened his office one Saturday morning just to see my husband. When I had some surgery, he was the first doctor to see me the next day."

-- Mrs. Ramona Johnson

"You have been a significant person in many peoples lives, not the least of whom are my parents—who hold you in the very highest regard, as do many, many others, both near and far."

-- Janet Agnoletti Tylshe

"My Dad was Dr. David Bennett, who practiced medicine at the Coleman Clinic in Canton from 1934 to 1964. I remember Dad always spoke so highly of "young Dr. Reed.""

-- Carolyn Bennett Armstrong

"Dr. Reed told me I had high cholesterol and needed to lose weight. As he was leaving the room, I asked him how I was to do that. He turned around and just said, "stop eating." It was a simple answer to a complex question."

-- Mrs. Ramona Johnson

"I want to thank you for caring for my family all these years. The excellent care we receive must be the reason my sister and I have lived as long as we have. I also want to thank you for helping me get through those terrible migraines for such a long time. You were always there to help me."

--Lois Sandberg

"When my daughter, Susan White, had a broken leg, the hospital had it set in a cast that didn't appear right to her. She went to see Dr. Reed. He agreed with her, so he broke the cast and fixed it for her. She thinks he is one step below God, maybe even one step above."

-- May Jean White

"My little girl fell off a merry-go-round at a Little League ball game and her head was bleeding bad. I held her while my mother drove us to Dr. Reed's house in Trivoli. I was crying, as I thought she might be dying. When we got there Dr. Reed said everything would be ok, that head wounds bleed a lot. He stitched it up and I was so happy. He didn't mind us coming to his house."

-- Mrs. Joyce Bennett Pero

"In essence, Dr. Reed works seven days a week, 24 hours a day. He makes himself available whenever he is needed. His medical knowledge is overwhelming. There is no medical problem that he ever walks away from. He has the needs of his patients at heart. Between his concern for his patients and his medical knowledge, when a patient leaves his office, they have one thought in mind--" Dr. Reed has saved my life again."

-- John and Lena Gagliardo

"We are so pleased you are being recognized for all your hard work as a beloved physician of Farmington. God blessed you with the high energy it takes to be the best of the best for many years. Know that a lot of people all over Fulton County love and respect you."

-- Lois Parsons
--Charlotte Moffitt

"We have always felt comfortable knowing we could depend on such a great doctor. My uncles Freddy and Richard were horse buddies of his and liked to go to his stables. Our granddaughter is best friends with his granddaughter, Kristen. He has come to our home to help and we have gone to his house. What dedication!"

-- Joe and Judith Tusek

"When my youngest granddaughter was about two, she had a cold and so I took her to Dr. Reed. He sat her up on a table and asked if she was taking any medication. Kaylee blurted out, "amoxicillin." Dr. Reed started laughing and said, "anyone her age who can say that word doesn't have to have a shot." Kaylee was very happy and smiled."--- Mrs. Bonnie Danner

"Following surgery for kidney stones, I had to get a urine sample at home to take into Jim. I got a small sample for the girls, (Jim's nurses) but for Jim I got a one-gallon glass jar and filled it with water and just the right amount of yellow food coloring to make it look exactly like urine. The girls put it on Jim's desk while he was out and when he returned he shouted out, "What's this!" When they told him it was my sample, I think the joke made his day."

-- Tom Anderson, (Jim's childhood friend
and famous "hearse ambulance" driver.)

"Dr. Reed has been our family doctor for 35 years. He has always been caring, curing and reachable. House calls have not been unusual. Over the years, at one time or another, he has quietly saved all of our lives, from my 92-year-old dad to my two months old premature daughter. The following incident has not been the exception, but the rule. Some years ago, on a miserably cold, icy Christmas night, my adult daughter was bitten by a dog. When I called his house for advice about treating the bite, he simply said, "meet me at the office." Dr. Reed is what doctoring is all about. We love him."

-- Jan Churchill

"Dr. Reed is the most caring, thorough, unconceited doctor I have ever dealt with. A Dr. Welby type in reality, he would at times call us to ask about someone's health problem and then come to the house because he was concerned about what was happening. He came when our elderly parents couldn't or wouldn't go to him when they needed to. He diagnosed my husband's brain aneurysm over the phone and rushed him to the hospital for surgery. And we're convinced he helped save the lives of our two precious grandchildren with his very keen attention, care and experience. He figuratively and actually has wrapped his arms, his brain and his heart around our family and community. We have never deserved him but we will always love and appreciate him."

--Mrs. Bethea Harding

"Dr. Reed, you have done a lot of things for me in my life. You delivered my son Eddie and saved his life in the process. His head was turned in my womb so they thought I would need a C-section to relieve the pressure on his brain. You turned him so I could have him naturally without any complications. Later in life, I was diagnosed with Crohn's Disease. I had reached an all time low in weight of under 100 pounds. I was under an extreme amount of stress and severely overworked. You talked my husband Arnold into leaving the farm and me into closing my restaurant in Yates City to get my disease under control. You sure don't find doctors anymore who care about their patients and the whole family. You always had time to listen and care for your patients. If I was sick, you'd see me right away and I wouldn't have to wait two or three weeks like I do here in Florida. Dr. Reed, you're the best."

--Mary Hahn

"Dr. Reed, at our office, Karen, Debbie and Betsy all think they have seniority over me, but you and I know who is really your longest tenured employee. I remember when I was just a little kid counting pills for you with your son Brent in your back office. We had a lot of fun getting paid for it while we drank Pepsi. You've known me ever since you delivered me in 1963. On a more serious note, you have always held my deepest respect. I count it a privilege to know you, work for you and be a friend of you and your family."

--Lynn Wagler Stewart

"Shortly after our parents, Maurice and Goldie Negley, moved from Trivoli to Farmington in 1956, you hired our mom to work in your office. She enjoyed and worked with you and your wonderful staff until 1977, when a serious illness would not allow her to work anymore. We personally experienced your caring and compassion when Dad died suddenly in 1960. We experienced it again when Mom's health worsened. We wanted to care for her at home and you and your dedicated staff gave us that privilege by guiding and helping us immensely during those months until her death in 1978. Thanks Dr. Reed from a grateful Negley family—not only for our family's association and care for over 20 years, but for what you have done for so many, many others as a truly dedicated family doctor."

--Donna Negley Vroman and brothers Jim, Dick and Jack Negley

"I'm writing to you Dr. Reed to thank you for spending time to talk with me and allowing me to spend a day monitoring your patient contacts with you. I came away quite inspired by your commitment to the medical profession, to the importance of the family physician, and above all, to the patients who rely on you. I will try from here on in my career to do justice to the enormous privilege I have received in being able to observe you and absorb a small amount of your enthusiasm for our calling. I find myself challenged to provide more comprehensive care, be more available to my patients, and take myself more seriously as a family physician after my encounter with you. The past month has been more enjoyable and fulfilling for me professionally than any time previously. Thank you again for this great gift. If you would be willing to bear with me visiting you again in your practice, I would be very glad for the opportunity on my next visit to Illinois.

Best wishes and again, thanks, Kris Percy

(Ed. Note. Dr. Kris Percy, nee Potter, is a former resident of Farmington and a family physician with a practice in California.)

Chapter 20: More Q. and A. With the Doc

RR—Let's get back to fat. Obesity in America is growing to epidemic proportions. While I know your focus has always been on treating individuals, I think you also came to view the "community" as your patient. What impact do you think you've had on obesity in Farmington over the past thirty years?

DOC—I don't think I've had much impact on the problem. My experience over the past half-century of dealing with the problem has been that people are going to eat whatever they want, whenever they want, as much as they want, no matter what I or anyone else says. Overeating is a habit every bit as hard to break as addiction to drugs.

RR—I have friends whose loved ones have had serious, "mystery" ailments. They mistakes were made because their family doctors didn't want to refer them to a specialist. What do you think of that?

DOC—I think those patients should find a new doctor.

RR—So when my family doctor tells me something and then says "why don't you ask your brother what he thinks," that means I have a good doctor?

DOC—Not necessarily, because there are a lot of factors that go into being a good doctor, but if he welcomes input and opinions from colleagues, that's a sign he may be a good doctor.

RR—You told me you're opposed to the type of "assisted suicide" medical practices made famous by Dr. Jack Kevorkian because they're illegal. But what if they were made legal tomorrow?

DOC—I'd still be opposed to it. First of all, it would be a violation of the Hippocratic Oath. And I also think the practice would probably be abused by too many doctors and hospitals. Finally—and maybe most importantly—how would you feel if you performed an assisted suicide and the next day a cure was found for the problem.

RR—Do a very large percentage of gravely ill patients really want to die?
DOC—I don't know about that but I'll tell you one thing. The closer patients come to dying, the more they seem to want to live.

RR—Since you started practicing medicine in 1954, what do you think has been the single most important advance in the field?
DOC—Cardiac catherization labs, in about 1963. Heart-related problems were, and are, our number one health problem. Since the onset of cath labs, there has been a marked reduction of cardiac deaths. With their great diagnostic tools and use of heart stents, cardiologists have greatly reduced the need for dangerous open-heart surgery.

RR—My wife and I were in one of those specialty herb stores. I was waiting on her while she browsed through two or three hundred herbs, so I picked up one of those natural health food magazines, and these were some of the headlines of their stories:
"Natural peptide clathration therapy can help your autistic child."
"Broccoli protects women from diabetes."
"Dried prunes please your bones."
"Soy isoflavones may help prevent prostate cancer recurrence."
Stories like that can make average readers like me feel like we're missing out on a lot of important stuff. I was wondering how doctors respond to stories like that?
DOC—The practice of good medicine is science based. None of the so-called treatments mentioned above has been proven to be beneficial.

RR—I saw something amazing and unbelievable the other night (Jan., 2009) on "60 Minutes." Researchers have developed a brain scan that can literally "read your thoughts." While it's in its infancy stage, the researchers felt confident it would be highly developed in ten years. The implications feel very scary to me. While we all recognize the human body is the most complex machine known to man, do you ever think to yourself that maybe we're starting to go a little too far with things like cloning and the computerized reading of our thoughts?
DOC—I think human beings are already being cloned. They're already doing it with animals, so there's no reason to think human cloning isn't happening.

RR—Can you tell me a couple of funny incidents that have happened recently with your patients?

DOC—Just recently a middle-aged man presented at the front desk and asked to make an appointment for an appendectomy. The girls explained to him that he would first have to be experiencing some rather severe symptoms. "Well," the man responded, "I'm not having any problems now, but I just wanted to be sure I didn't have any more children." It was all the girls could do to keep from cracking up right in front of the gentleman.

RR—That was a good one. Do you have another?

DOC—A lady came in recently suffering from hemorrhoids. We gave her a few suppositories and asked her to come back in a week for a check-up. When she returned, she was upset and yelled at me, "how in the hell did you expect me to get better by putting something wrapped in foil up my rectum?"

RR—For all us weekend gardeners, how dangerous can mowing the yard be?

DOC—I had a patient, a little girl about three or four. She was standing in the doorway to her backyard where her dad was mowing. The mower threw a rock and hit her right in the eye. It was an amazing thing. It removed her eyeball as cleanly as if a surgeon had done it. Then I had a neighbor out here whose mower threw a nail into his knee. Soon after that his son was mowing and it threw a nail through his abdominal wall. If they had had to drive to my office in Farmington instead of just coming across the street to my house, he would have bled to death.

RR—Right up to the time I had open heart bypass surgery when I was 62, I had exercised religiously, running 3-5 miles every day for 20 years. I wasn't overweight, I never smoked and my wife watched my diet like a hawk. What did all that good stuff mean with regard to still having heart problems?

DOC—It didn't mean crap. About half of all people with heart disease never had a symptom.

RR—When Dr. Dimmitt set up practice in Farmington in the early 1900's, the life expectancy of a woman was about 50. When you came to town in 1956, it had risen to about 70. Now it's about 80. Do you think it's reasonable to think that by the year 2050, it might be 100?

DOC—I sure do.

RR—We hear an awfully lot about the need for elderly folks to take extra care not to fall. Statistics say that up to 20% who do fall die within a year. Why is that? Exactly is it about falling that kills people?

DOC—First of all, you need to keep in mind that a certain percentage of those 20% who die would have died even if they hadn't fallen. But most importantly, accidents involving falls don't usually kill people. What happens is that a fall can make it harder for an older person to cope with the problems they were already having. And it can precipitate other problems related to their serious medical conditions. For example, falling can be related to the formation of blood clots in senior citizens. And patients might become less active from fear of falling again, and that inactivity becomes problematic.

RR—The airwaves, newspapers and magazines are filled with information about the importance of leading a healthy lifestyle. My wife had an uncle who smoked all his life, ate anything he wanted and lived to be 90. And I had a 65-year-old friend who never exercised. He took a stress test that showed his heart to be perfect. His mother was 90 as were her two sisters and brother. Here's my question. If you had to choose one or the other, which would it be: an unhealthy lifestyle with good family genes or a healthy lifestyle with bad genes?

DOC—You can't beat genes.

RR—An opthamologist told me everyone would be better off if they'd wear sunglasses all the time. We've had two brothers die from skin cancer. Yet, in all my life, I've never seen you wearing sunglasses or using sunscreen. What do you have to say for yourself?

DOC—There have never been any controlled studies on the effectiveness of either of those products.

RR—I think about 17 states have passed laws legalizing medical marijuana. Do you feel you need to add pot to your arsenal of treatment options.

DOC—Absolutely not. There are ample medications available now for nearly all types of pain and suffering. I wouldn't be opposed to a patient trying it in response to a rare, intractable pain, but only under strict medical supervision.

RR—I have a friend who's a philosopher by training, vocation and avocation. His wife told me that whatever he's doing—be it taking a shower or eating a sandwich—in the back of his head, he's always got a philosophical thought going on. Is that the way it's been with you and medicine?

DOC—No, not at all. Medicine is a profession that's action oriented, dealing with harsh realities. When I'm with a patient, all my thoughts and energies are focused on that patient. But when I'm not with a patient, I try to relax. I've never considered myself a workaholic. I simply answer the call for help whenever I can.

RR—Being a man, here's something I've wondered about for years, and now that you're near the end of your practice—and too old to be embarrassed about anything—I feel more free to ask the question. So here we go. Over the years, how difficult was it for your female patients to talk with you about the more intimate details of their personal lives?

DOC—(chuckling at my question) It was never difficult. As a matter of fact, it was just the opposite. They always seemed to feel free to discuss everything. In fact, they seemed eager. I didn't have to do anything to encourage them either. I was always careful about expressing myself in a manner that encouraged their frankness. Sometimes I wish they hadn't revealed so much to me. I guess they trusted me to keep everything they told me in strict confidence.

RR—Of all the popular TV medical shows over the past five decades, like Marcus Welby, Ben Casey, Dr. Kildare, ER, Chicago Hope and House, which one did you like the best?

DOC—I never watched any of them enough times to comment on that. I'd only seen them maybe once a year. But I had a friend who'd been a surgeon in a MASH unit in the Korean War, so I watched that show more than the others and I thought it was pretty realistic, based on what my friend told me.

RR—The diet supplement industry has grown to a staggering behemoth of 26.7 billion dollars in 2009, with 54,000 different products produced by 1,500 manufacturers. Yet, in the June 28, 2010 edition of Newsweek, Dr. Marc Garnich of the Harvard Medical School said, "I tell all my patients to throw away essentially every supplement they swear by...if people eat a healthy diet, they really don't need supplements." What's your opinion?

DOC---I agree with Dr. Garnich completely.

RR—The other day I saw a letter to you from the McGill school of Medicine and it was addressed to James M. Reed, M.D., C. M. That's the first time I've ever seen a "C.M."after a doctor's name. What does that mean?

DOC—It's the initials for the Latin phrase 'magister chirurgiae' meaning Master of Surgery. I think at the time I was in school only McGill and one school in Europe were awarding that degree. I stopped using the initials after my name because I got tired of people asking me what it meant.

RR—I retired when I was only 53 because I was burned out after 31 years of child welfare social work. Why didn't you retire after you had your near-fatal heart attack and quintuple heart bypass surgery in 1986 when you were sixty-one?

DOC—I still enjoyed my medical practice a great deal and couldn't think of anything else I'd rather do.

RR—I know that you know that there are some people who think that you're too old (82) to still be practicing medicine.

DOC—(laughing) Yes, I know there are. I'll know when it's time for me to go. It'll be when my mind begins to slip. I'll know when that is. It hasn't happened yet. At a recent national accreditation education seminar in Kentucky, we were given a test in which a New York hospital fed us symptom information via computer on 20 patients and we had to diagnose their problem. I got all 20 correct.

RR—I'm serious now so be honest with me. I've read and heard that some patients think of you like they do God. How do you keep from getting the big head?

DOC—My patients really appreciate my help. I try hard to give them the best I've got. I try to keep up with the latest developments in the field. And I try to be sympathetic. I think I'm just doing the job I was trained to do.

RR—I'm glad I'm retired. If I wasn't, this book wouldn't exist. One last question:why don't doctors make house calls anymore?

DOC—Good question.

Part VI

The Doctor Is Out

Chapter 21: From Doctor to Patient

Common sense tells us that a skilled family doctor like Jim Reed would constantly monitor his own health. And furthermore that he would always seek care and treatment whenever experiencing a potential problem. But common sense in this instance would be wrong.

From 1956 to 1986, Jim Reed was an unstoppable workhorse. He labored—albeit a labor of love—long, tough hours, sacrificing himself for his patients. Night and day, every day of the week, he treated patients anywhere at anytime. He performed what people around Farmington considered heroic deeds of medical daring: in farm fields, in strip mines, on rooftops, wherever needed. He had, in the eyes of a great many people, taken on a larger-than-life persona. He seemed indestructible and invincible.

During those years, the only problem to befall Jim was one of the most common—a bad back. While on a family hunting expedition in 1971 Jim's teenage son, Bryan, bagged a huge black bear. Wanting desperately to take the creature home as a trophy, Bryan, the guide and Jim dragged the heavy monster back to their truck. There were no immediate aftereffects, but two weeks later Jim experienced severe back pains in the area at the base of the spinal column. He was hospitalized, and received the standard treatment at the time—confinement to bed with 40 lbs. of traction (legs wrapped and tied to a system of pulleys) to immobilize him from the waist down, taking as much pressure as possible off his back. There was also some physical therapy involved. After enduring four weeks of confinement, there appeared to be no improvement at all in Jim's level of pain. Therefore, he consented to having surgery. The night before surgery, feeling he had nothing to lose, Jim decided to free himself from his traction contraption to allow him to change his body position for the first time. Magically, as soon as he did that, the pain disappeared. The surgery was cancelled. After that, his back bothered him from time-to-time, but taking it easy for a couple of days usually resulted in improvement. Other than those occasional back problems, Jim remained in good health for the next decade plus. But that came to a screeching halt on October 28, 1986.

Before that day, Jim had never experienced one symptom—but he knew that was true for about 25% of all heart attack victims. "I felt some tightness in my chest," Jim said, "and right away I thought to myself that it might be coronary insufficiency. I was just out the door at my home on the way to the hospital to see a patient so I asked my wife Jan to drive me, without telling her what I suspected was going on. On the way to the hospital, I knew I was having a myocardial infarction." (During my interviews with Jim, I quickly learned that after using medical terminology for 54 years, it was difficult for him to speak in layman's terms. What he'd just told me was that he was actually having a heart attack.) "That's when I broke the news to Jan. She remained calm, understood what was going on and handled it very well."

"I immediately called the hospital," Jim went on, "and asked them to have a cardiologist meet me when we got there. We arrived in a few minutes and I was met by Dr. Rahman, who quickly administered an EKG. As soon as we looked at it, we knew I had in fact just experienced an acute myocardial infarction. We made a quick decision to transfer me to Peoria Methodist Hospital because of their advanced heart catheterization lab. Dr. Rahman was kind enough to ride with me in the ambulance with a heart defibrillator, in the event I might have a cardiac arrest on the way." A cardiac arrest means your heart stops beating entirely; the defibrillator's purpose, of course, is to shock the heart into restarting. Fortunately, that did not happen to Jim on the way to Methodist.

As soon as the ambulance arrived, Jim was met by his close friend and colleague, cardiologist Dr. Thanad Shay, who immediately administered a heart angiogram, the procedure allowing the doctor to view the amount and location of the blockages in the arteries. "It showed I had a severe, advanced five vessel occlusion," Jim related. "My left main artery was too occluded to catheterize," he continued, "leaving me in a very vulnerable position." Layman's version? There was nothing that could be done about the left main artery, and Jim's chances of survival at that point weren't good. I asked for some particulars about his heart surgery. (Remember, this is a man with a burnished steel trap for a brain, thousands of detailed case histories inside his head.)

"It sounds crazy," he replied, "but I don't know the date. I didn't make a note of it. Things like that don't interest me. I never even looked at the angiogram. I just said to Dr. Shay, 'you have to do it, okay fine.' You have to have faith. I didn't even ask them afterwards what veins they used for the bypass, because it was done."

On October 30, 1986, Dr. James Munn performed a successful five-vessel open-heart bypass surgery, though there may have been one slight mishap during the procedure. A catheter is always placed down the patient's trachea to assist with breathing; Jim thinks some of his vocal chord tissues may have been damaged during that procedure. Then, he thinks his vocal chords took a second hit, a couple of days later, when the nurse removed the catheter. As she was right in the middle of that process, the patient in the next room suffered a heart attack. So Jim's nurse left him to rush to the rescue of that patient. "There I laid," Jim said, "with the catheter half in and half out. I began to have trouble breathing and knew that I had to do something, so I decided to remove the catheter myself. I think in doing that, I may have damaged my vocal chords some more." He laughed when I asked if he billed the hospital for providing service to himself. Twenty two years later, he says, "It seems to affect my voice as I begin to tire at the end of the day."

Jim had to remain in the hospital for nine days after surgery, twice as long as the typical bypass patient. "Everyone always wants to know how a doctor feels when he becomes a patient," Jim continued. "The impression it made on me was to give me a greater appreciation for all the little things the medical staff can do to make the patient and his family more comfortable."

Even when Jim was ill, he was never far from his patients. "Dr. Reed and my husband Paul both had heart problems at the same time," JoAnn Huffman Smith told me, "and their cardiologist, Dr. Shay wanted them both to get some physical rehabilitation. So Dr. Reed's wife asked Paul if he'd mind driving her husband to rehab, so he did. They'd talk about horses because Paul's folks had Tennessee walkers. I believe these two men found several bonds in their doctor-patient relationship that went deep. The morning that Paul died in January, 2007, Dr. Reed was there and was as sad as all of us."

After being back home for about two weeks, Jim developed post-operative blood clots in his jugular vein. This was obviously another dangerous situation for Jim, requiring another two-week hospitalization to successfully dissolve the clots. Jim emphasized how helpful it was, emotionally, to receive special TLC from the staff at Peoria Methodist Hospital. "But," he went on, "most helpful of all was that Jan spent almost 24 hours a day at my bedside." Jim's positive memories about his hospital stay, however, do not jibe completely with everyone who helped care for him. Reverend Larry Kirk is a retired hospital Chaplin who had many dealings with Jim over the years. "He wasn't a good patient," Rev. Kirk told me. "He was impatient and restless, so I gave him a book on philosophy that I thought might help calm him down. He still has my book," he added, laughing.

Upon his second return home, Jim had to undergo four long, difficult weeks of rehab and recuperation. After that he successfully tore back into his life's work—for a time. "I got along okay for about two years," Jim said, "until one day while I was making a house call, I was pretty sure I was developing an abnormally slow heart beat. I decided to go home and see if resting would help. It didn't. So I called my office and my associate, Dr. Mark Baylor came right out to the house. We decided I should get to the hospital quickly and see Dr. Shay." After testing and consultation, Dr. Shay recommended Jim receive a surgically implanted cardiac pacemaker to assure the heart doesn't beat at a dangerous rate.

While the pacemakers were a wonderful medical advance for heart patients, one drawback is that they're battery operated, and therefore need regular checkups. That's where the problem came in for Jim. "I must admit I wasn't as diligent as I should have been," Jim said. All the patient has to do is call the hospital regularly to activate a computer analysis of his pacemaker. Not doing so resulted in Jim's having to make a couple of emergency trips to the hospital. After that, Dr. Shay's staff was kind enough to take the initiative in contacting Jim instead of waiting on him to call. During the past 20 years, he's had five different pacemaker implants.

Jim Reed knows better than anyone that his heart attack probably could have been prevented. You see, Jim had three brothers (Phil, Red and Hubert) who'd experienced serious heart problems, and Jim knew full well that the most serious risk factor for heart disease is a strong family history with the problem.

The other thing Jim well knows is that if he'd had a treadmill heart stress test at an earlier age, he likely would've had pre-emptive bypass surgery before he suffered his severe heart attack. But he didn't. And the reason he didn't was that his entire waking life was so deeply committed to his patients that he neglected his own health.

Typical of Jim, the first thing he did after his heart surgery was call his brothers and sisters, urging them to undergo the aforementioned treadmill test. I for one took his advice to heart (so to speak) and ended up being very glad I did. I had several stress tests over the next fourteen years, and they were all normal in their findings. But the one I had in 2000 wasn't normal. It led to an angiogram, which in turn led me into triple bypass surgery. The point is my problem was caught before I had a heart attack, and before I had more than one badly blocked artery. In fact, Jim described my surgery as "preventive."

Jim knows that he dodged a deadly bullet in 1986. And he knows he has been fortunate to live for more than 24 years after his heart attack and subsequent surgery. Off the top of his head, he can spit out survival rates for every known medical condition; he knows the odds were stacked against him. But he licked them.

After his 1986 heart attack and bypass, and his pacemaker troubles in 1988, another two years passed before Jim's next medical crisis. Once a patient survives a serious heart condition, a major ongoing priority becomes avoiding infections of any kind. (To emphasize that, after my own bypass, Jim advised me to take a dose of antibiotics before I went to my dentist for something as simple as regular cleanings.)

At age 63, in 1990, Jim developed a sudden and severe case of chills and fever. "I felt something serious was going on," he said, "so I was admitted to Peoria Methodist Hospital, and once again to the care of Dr. Shay. After extensive blood work, Dr. Shay's diagnosis, which I agreed with, was that I had an extremely serious condition called bacterial endocarditis. That's a condition in which colonies of germs form on the heart walls and heart valves. If not halted, it can lead to congestive heart failure."

Of course, this was a doubly dangerous situation for Jim, given the already weakened condition of his heart. Once again, Jim was staring death in the face. He knew it. Dr Shay knew it. His wife, Jan, and his children knew it. But no one else did. None of his brothers and sisters knew, and none of his thousands of patients. That's the way Jim wished it to be.

Treatment for Jim's latest crisis consisted primarily of closely supervised intravenous doses of multiple antibiotics. So serious was the situation, he had to remain hospitalized for a very long eight weeks. Once again, it was made bearable principally due to the constant presence and support of his wife, Jan. That Jim was seldom alone did much to ward off the severe depression that can understandably overcome patients facing life-threatening illnesses. Of course, he also received special care from hospital staff whose respect he'd earned over many years. "And all the cards and well wishes," Jim said, "from my patients, friends and my family helped a great deal to keep up my spirits. During all this time, I never felt like I would be forced to give up my medical practice, but I was very worried that I might not be able to carry the workload I had before."

The eight-week treatment of Jim's bacterial endocarditis was successful but he'd become very weak and developed a case of anemia. This is always a major concern to doctors because it can be symptomatic of more serious ailments, including the most feared one of all, cancer. This was a psychological setback for Jim since he had been about ready to leave the hospital. While he disliked the idea of a longer hospital stay, he knew what he had to do.

He underwent a colonoscopy, the gold standard procedure for colon cancer detection. Performed by Dr. Paul Paulsen, a Peoria general surgeon, the procedure involved the removing all suspicious looking polyps, and performing a biopsy of them to determine whether they were benign or malignant. The bad news was that Jim's was malignant. But the very good news was that it was in an all-important early stage of growth. Agreeing with the recommendation of his surgeon, Jim had part of his colon removed. (And he is pleased to report in the ensuing 18 years, his regular follow-up colonoscopies have not revealed any further malignant growths.) After what seemed like an interminable two-month stay at the hospital, home never looked so good to Jim.

It was 1990, Jim was now 63 years old, and he'd just survived his second life-threatening crisis in four years. Many friends, patients and loved ones thought that he had made his last house call. They thought he'd just lay back and enjoy his retirement—but they didn't know Jim as well as they thought they did. His deep love and commitment to doctoring was something he simply couldn't walk away from. He'd received too much personal satisfaction from it to walk away. And he was too much in demand to walk away. Thousands of patients breathed a sigh of relief when Jim returned to doctoring.

Jim's third and fourth personal medical crises involved mishaps at his horse farm. No one who's been to the races can doubt the pure beauty, grace and power of a majestic thoroughbred speeding around the track. On the other hand, few of us give any thought to all the grunt work done every day to produce the final gorgeous product; Jim Reed knows because he's done it.

"Horses are so strong," he told me, "and so dumb, you have to be very careful around them. They may behave well 95% of the time," he went on, "but the other 5% can be very dangerous." And he has the scars to prove it.

"One day in February of 2006," Jim said, "I was working at the farm with my son Bryan and our part-time farmhand, Mike Park. I was moving a young stallion from the barn to the paddock. When we got to the big steel gate, he bolted and knocked me down. Then he knocked the gate right down on top of me and ran right over the gate with me under it." It was the worst pain Jim had ever experienced in his life. Bryan summoned the Hanna City Rescue Squad which arrived within a few minutes. Jim was rushed to Methodist Hospital where testing indicated he'd broken his sacroiliac joint and pelvis in four places. He also incurred a pelvic hematoma, involving blood loss—an especially dangerous condition for Jim because, being on two anti-coagulants, he could have bled out. His injuries necessitated a two-week hospital stay, plus three more weeks of home recovery. There were painful rehabilitation sessions two or three times a week, "the toughest thing, physically that I'd ever been through," he told me. "It was so bad I thought I might not ever walk normally again." When he was in fact able to walk, he did so in the privacy of his basement. He didn't want anyone outdoors to see him in his weakened condition.

Jim's fourth medical crisis happened on July 8, 2008, also at his farm. Earlier that year, he'd taken two spills there, and fortunately, come out unscathed. I witnessed his second accident and can attest how easy it is to fall, because the area around the barns is riddled with uneven, dried, dirt ruts. Jim was not so lucky with his third fall because he slammed his head on hard ground. The ambulance was immediately summoned and he was rushed to Peoria Methodist Hospital where a brain scan confirmed Jim's fear of a concussion. (On top of that, he also re-injured his previous pelvic fracture.) But the immediate danger was the concussion, because there was blood seeping into the brain. Fortunately for Jim, the amount of blood making its way into the brain was minimal, because he said there is really no specific treatment for that condition except complete rest and constant observation. The after effects of the concussion were minimal. But he still had to undergo a difficult six weeks recovery at home.

I visited Jim six days after his hospital release, (early on Friday, July 18, 2008) and was shocked at how bad he looked. In a bed set up in his living room, Jim was flat on his back. He seemed worn out, his face very drawn. He shifted and squirmed, searching for any position in bed that might lessen his discomfort. He could barely leave bed to do anything.

I had multiple interviews scheduled with Jim's patients later that day and knew I'd be asked how soon Jim would be back in the office. So I asked him and he said two weeks; Jan was standing where he couldn't see her and rolled her eyes. So I said maybe I should tell them three weeks. Jan immediately chimed in, "No, no, tell them whatever he says."

Jan and their daughter, Cindy, were upset that particular morning because Jim needed to be measured for a back brace and the medical supply people refused to come to the house. They wanted him brought to their offices even though Jim could barely move. Ironic, huh? Here was a doctor who'd been making house calls for 50 years and now when he needed the simplest in-home service, he couldn't get it. Cindy told me she'd made attempts to contact the company and they didn't even return her last couple of calls. Finally, she went on the internet, found what they needed and it was in their home the next day.

After my interviews, I returned to Jim's home later that same afternoon and was taken aback to see two strange cars in the driveway. Then an unrecognizable younger couple came out of the house. This was particularly surprising because Jan had put a sign on the door saying Jim wasn't able to see any visitors. After the couple drove away I asked Cindy what was going on. She said Jim was seeing a patient. I thought she was kidding, but of course, she wasn't."He's an old friend and it's pretty bad," she said.

I was dumbfounded. At 9 that morning, Jim was barely able to move, in misery, looking terrible. And then, at 4:00 P.M., he had a patient, a man, sitting at the bottom of his bed while Jim was propped up at the top of the bed. And just when I thought I'd seen everything, there was more. Three days later, I called Cindy to double check what I'd seen.

"The same day you were here," Cindy told me, "the phone rang at midnight. It was Debbie." Debbie is Debbie Bozsoki, Jim's former daughter-in-law, who has worked for him for over thirty years. Debbie called because she feared her daughter (Jim's granddaughter), 20-year-old Kristen, was having a gall bladder attack and she wanted Jim's advice about whether she needed to be hospitalized. Jim told her to immediately bring Kristen out to the house for him to examine. Debbie proceeded to do this because she was unaware of the kind of shape Jim was in. She found out when she got to his house, but of course, by that time there was no way that Jim was not going to examine his own granddaughter.

So, with Jan, Cindy and Debbie looking on, Kristen laid down on the bed next to Jim and he examined her. His verdict was that she was indeed having a gall bladder attack but didn't need to be taken to the hospital on an emergency basis, not at one in the morning. Jim told Debbie to take Kristen to his office and give her a couple of shots. Later, when I interviewed Debbie about this strange saga, she told me how sorry she was that she'd called Jim and would never had done it if she'd known the shape he was in. But she wasn't at all surprised that he did it, and of course his help did keep Kristen from the emergency room. She did eventually have her gall bladder removed, but it was done by schedule, not on a terrifying, emergency, middle-of-the night basis. The most amazing part of this whole saga happened a couple weeks later when Jim was feeling much better, and I asked him about the incident. "You saw Kristen just because she was your own flesh and blood, right?"Without hesitating, he replied, "No, I would have seen anyone who showed up needing help." Less than two years later, Jim himself would be the one needing help again

Jim has lived in his large, comfortable, wood-sided (genetically incapable of retaining paint) two-story home in Trivoli for 53 years. He could easily find his way around the house blindfolded. The uncarpeted stairway leading from his front hallway up to the second story has 15 steps. Assuming Jim's gone up and down those stairs four times a day, then he's made the trip 137,000 times. In all that time on the stairs, he'd never fallen. On March 9, 2010, fall #1 happened. Because of Jim's age (82) and his physical condition, it was a potentially life-threatening tumble.

"I was at the top of the stairs." Jim said. "I was barefoot and just as I was about to take the first step down, I somehow stubbed my toe. I instinctively reached down to check it out and that's when I lost my balance. Before I could grab the banister, I started tumbling down. I rolled head over heels all the way down, hitting and banging every part of my body."

When you fall down a few steps, it happens so fast that you don't have time to think of anything. But with 15, you have time. Jim didn't mince words. "I thought I was going to die." At the least, the chances of his NOT being seriously hurt were very, very slim. As you can imagine, over the years, Jim's seen many fall victims with broken necks, backs, arms, legs, etc.

When Jim fell, Cindy was two rooms away. When she heard the noise, Cindy knew what had happened, and she immediately called 911. Meanwhile, when Jim finally reached the bottom of the stairs, he knew enough to lie there quietly. After a minute, he was pretty confident he hadn't broken anything. He looked around for blood but thankfully didn't see any. The Rescue Squad arrived very quickly and rushed Jim to Methodist Hospital in Peoria. Cindy told me that on the way, Jim was giving orders to the medics! (I'm surprised that this surprises me.) Hospital testing revealed the only damage done to my 83-year-old brother was a broken toe.

Folks around Farmington aren't much different from folks anywhere else. A 2008 poll by the Southern Methodist University Institute for Religious Studies revealed that 55% of all people believed in the existence of guardian angels. It's safe to assume that most of Jim's patients think he's had one for years, and after surviving his brutal fall, he just might agree with them.

Chapter 22: After Hours

Our brother Sonny died too young. In 1982 when he was only forty-nine, he lost his battle with malignant melanoma, the deadliest form of skin cancer. Five years older than me, Sonny could run like the wind, and I watched awestruck as he sped around the base paths. He played a mean game of billiards too, and I watched him shoot pool at Ernie's Pool Hall. And he was smart. Russell Troxel, our high school principal who knew all thirteen Reeds, told our brother Red that he thought "Clayton"—the only people in town who ever called him that were teachers—"was the smartest of all the Reeds." He was nice, too; I can't recall his ever doing or saying anything to hurt my feelings. He wasn't a complainer, either: from an early age, he was blind in one eye. You never heard him gripe about it, though.

A few weeks after Sonny's death, I was visiting his wife, Donna, when she happened to mention how much he'd loved dixieland music. I vividly recall my surprise when she told me. Later, I figured out why I'd reacted that way. It'd upset me that I didn't know Sonny's taste in music; but more than that, it dawned on me that there'd been a lot about him I hadn't known. Well, time passed and I forgot about my guilt feelings. But then when I started on this book, those feelings returned. I realized I didn't want to make the same mistake with Jim that I'd made with Sonny. I wanted to really know Jim. That's the main reason for this chapter, but there's one more.

I was surprised to learn that some folks around Farmington (I know how ridiculous this might seem) really thought Jim wasn't a mere mortal. Of course, sometimes a special 'aura' builds up around people of unusual accomplishment. Admirers of such people often prefer not to know much about the personal lives of their heroes because the more they know, the less mysterious and exciting their hero becomes. Admirers would prefer to have their fantasy remain untouched, untarnished.

While the scenario above is appealing, it's not a desirable one, because it doesn't reflect reality. It implies that great things can only be accomplished by people who are somehow superhuman. But better we should learn that great things can be accomplished by mere mortals. So, in this chapter, I present Jim Reed, mere mortal.

Throughout his life Jim's demonstrated one of the keys for people who handle stress well: a highly developed sense of humor. That part of Jim was evident in his youth, (as described in earlier chapters) and he's never lost it. His long-time nurse, Debbie Bozoski, told me she'd never forget the day the phone rang at the office and when she answered it, a patient, John Behrends, told her he had a headache and wanted to know what he should do. "He was so upset," Deb told me, "that even though Doctor was with a patient, I went in and asked him what I should do. Without hesitating, he said I should tell John to go stand on his head in a corner for half an hour and if that didn't work he should call back. I was surprised by Doctor's answer so I asked him if he was sure that's what I should tell John. With a straight face he said yes. So I left the room and then I heard this loud laugh from Doctor and he yelled out that he was just joking and that I should tell John that he would call him back in a few minutes." I think most folks around Farmington who knew the eight Reed brothers very well would tell you that one thing they shared in common was a sense of humor.

The eight Reed brothers shared a few characteristics in common. For example, all of us ended up being about average in size.I say 'ended up' because, while most teens reach their full growth by age 18, the Reeds grew more from the ages of 18-21 than they did from 14-18.I was surprised to see one family photo in which Phil, who was two years younger than Jim, was a couple of inches taller.I know it wasn't a nutritional problem because while we were a poor family, food was always plentiful and fattening. While we all tended to be small in stature, we all had the big head—literally. When Jim went to Montreal, one of his first stops was a department store to find a warm hat; the average winter temperature there was roughly 20 below zero. Well, the saleslady brought out the largest hat they had and on Jim's head it looked like a yellow delicious apple perched atop Johnny Appleseed's noggin. He finally settled for one of those wool pullover, one-size-fits all caps.

As far as appearances, there'll always be a difference of opinion among family members, but I have to admit I always felt Jim was the best-looking Reed brother.He was the only one with black hair.He resembled a mixture of two actors: one was a character actor named Dane Clark and the other the more well-known Ben Gazarra.Brothers Harp and Cotton were blonds. Cotton always reminded me of Roy Rogers and Danny Kaye.

In terms of personality types, you often hear people labeled as either extroverts or introverts. I think four of the Reeds—Cotton, Hubert, Red and Phil—were extroverts and Harp, Sonny, Jim and I were more introverted. Red liked to strike up conversations on the street with complete strangers.

Cotton was a super salesman. Phil was a college teacher and politician. Hubert's favorite hangout in his Chicago neighborhood was the corner pub. Those are all extrovert activities. Harp was a minister, alone a lot with his thoughts. Same with me as an amateur poet. Jim would rather be at his farm than anywhere. Those are obvious introvert activities.

In contrast to his unpredictable, remarkable, complex life as a doctor, Jim's personal tastes and habits were always basic and simple. He never had the least interest in following styles or trends. He never sported a beard or moustache, and never changed the way he combed his hair. It was as though everything unrelated to his passions of medicine, farm, or family was wholly unimportant to him. For example, he was never concerned about his wardrobe; he always wanted to look clean and neat, but he didn't care how old his suits or shoes were, as long as they were serviceable. On the other hand, our older brother, Red, was just the opposite. A few years back, Red was so upset over a pair of old shoes that Jim was wearing that without even telling him, he ordered an expensive new pair, and Jim wore them—but he told me the only reason was to please Red.

Jim couldn't be more old-school about his professional appearance.He would never be seen at his office in anything but a white shirt and tie. That habit was instilled in him at medical school, where it was required attire of all students. He expressed his disgust to me about an incident in the 1970's when he arrived at the hospital for a meeting and two young doctors drove up on motorcycles, wearing leather jackets and sporting long ponytails.What disturbed him even more than their attire and grooming: a couple of years later, Jim learned that (despite their relatively unsuccessful family practice) the ponytails were on the faculty of a medical school! While it's common now to see doctors wearing sneakers, the chances of ever seeing Jim in a pair are less than the Cubs winning another World Series.

Jim's preferences in food and cooking parallel his tastes in grooming and wardrobe; namely, basic and simple. His disinterest in cooking stems from all the teenage time working food preparation at the Betty Anne Bakery, and even more so in his 12-month stint as a cook in the Navy. (My wife Mary's homemade chicken noodles have been a hit at our family reunions for 50 years. My mother taught her how to do it. Mary noticed that Jim never ate them so she finally worked up the courage to ask him why. He told her our mom fixed them every Sunday while he was growing up and he simply tired of them.)

When it comes to food, Jim's tastes haven't changed much since he was a kid. Our mom always saw to it that we ate well, but nothing fancy: meatloaf and pot roast, scalloped corn and creamed asparagus on toast.

Ham is Jim's preferred meat and he occasionally enjoys franks and beans. Like most folks in central Illinois, Jim can't wait for fresh summer sweet corn and tomatoes.

When it comes to desserts, Jim's favorite is chocolate pie. Now, my wife happens to be a very good cook and in the summer of 2009 she decided to make one such pie for Jim. What she also did—that Jim said he seldom sees anymore—was to make a meringue topping five inches high. He was crazy about it!

As for entertainment, Jim was never one to laze around in the evening and watch 5 or 6 hours of TV. He had neither the time nor the inclination. My hunch is that if he did sit down in front of the boob tube, he'd probably be asleep in five minutes.I say that because when our mom was still alive, he'd stop by our home for lunch every day and after he ate, he'd flop down in the comfy chair and be asleep almost instantly. Jim has never seen any of the popular TV doctor shows like ER, Chicago Hope or House.Recently he asked me to explain the popularity of Oprah Winfrey to him because he had never seen her show. (I told him I was sorry, I couldn't, because I'd never seen it either.)

Jim never took the time for movies, so after my seeing the great horseracing picture, Seabiscuit, I made a point of telling him how wonderful it was. He finally went and loved it of course.He said it was the first movie he'd seen in five years.Music, though, is the one art form Jim has enjoyed over the years. That's probably because you can listen to it while you're involved in other activities like driving. Over the years, I didn't get many small talk phone calls from Jim or his family. When the phone did ring, it was usually about family medical news or a question about child abuse, my area of social work. So I was really surprised one night when Jim's wife Janet called and asked if I could find a particular music CD for Jim. I told her I'd be glad to… and was floored when she said he wanted an operatic piece by a female diva. His other musical preference is classical, but he also enjoys Irish/Scottish folksongs and occasionally, old-fashioned mountain music, as a reminder of his Tennessee days.

Puttering around the house, doing odd repair jobs was never Jim's specialty—never much time for that. His wife was smart enough to never have a 'honeydo' list for him. However, Jim's closest friend in the Farmington area is Dick Westerby, and the two of them cut a deal 50 years ago: Dick would do Jim's repair jobs in return for free medical care. As for other domestic tasks, one might assume he'd been involved with the ritual of changing diapers, since he fathered four children. But no. The well-guarded family secret was that he'd never raised a finger to change a diaper on any of his babies!

One of Jim's few returns to his alma mater for the 1983 Ohio State-Illinois football game. Red Reed stands in front of—from left to right—Scott Reed (Red's son), the author, Jim and his wife, Jan.

Like every good doctor, Jim maintains a calm, cool demeanor during medical crises.But that doesn't mean he doesn't have a temper. The angriest I've ever seen Jim was during the public furor a few years ago surrounding Chief Illiniwek, the famous athletic symbol of the University of Illinois. Those who aren't UI alums or rabid UI fans can't understand the deep feelings those folks felt for the Chief.The NCAA, in all its stupidity, ruled the Chief to be a racist symbol and ordered the UI to discontinue the Chief.When I picked up my phone one night in 2007, Jim unleashed a torrent of outrage: he beseeched me, thought there must be something I personally could do to save the Chief—mostly because I'd had a series of poems published in a UI sports newsletter. I suppressed a bitter laugh. When I explained there was nothing I or anyone could do, Jim thought we should just tell the NCAA to 'go to hell'.

Earlier in the book, I presented evidence that Jim Reed really is human: he knowingly and officially lied to the federal government to join the Navy during WWII.Now here's more evidence of a different sort. It seems that when Jim was a young man, he indulged in the dangerous, unattractive, expensive, vile, smelly habit called smoking. (To be fair, smoking was much more acceptable back in the forties and fifties.)Of the eight Reed brothers, at one time or another seven were smokers (You can probably guess which one wasn't.)Red told me he started during WWII in Europe just to help him keep warm. As for Jim, he started while in the Navy and quit a few years later, thank heaven.

(Pre-paragraph disclaimer: I am a liberal democrat. Always have been, always will be.) I recently learned that when Jim returned to Farmington in 1956, he allowed himself to become involved in a questionable activity. I think it happened because he hadn't yet built up a very large medical practice and so he had too much free time on his hands. You see, for years, there was a huge metal sign hanging in his garage proclaiming "Republican Headquarters," and I'd always assumed this sign was just an antique, a quaint artifact. In fact, when Jim came to town in 1956, he and some other misguided youths established a Young Republicans Club. He recalled that their big triumph was to go into a local precinct that had voted the most heavily democratic in the previous election and win it for the Republicans. Fortunately, Jim's political activism lasted only a few years, until his practice mushroomed, and time demands precluded politics.

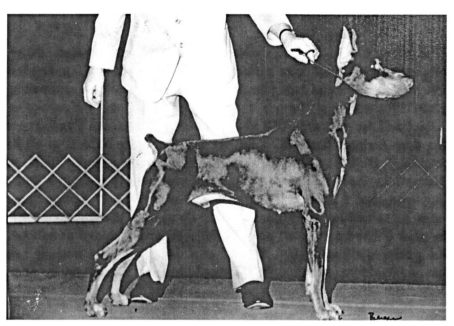

One of Jim's champion Doberman show dogs

But enough about elephants and donkeys; let's talk dogs. When Jim began his internship in Knoxville, TN in 1954, his wife was pregnant with their first child. Jim knew Jan would be spending long hours alone due to his hectic work schedule. Thus, it was primarily for security reasons that they decided to bring a dog into their family.Since small dogs don't scare people much, they decided on a Doberman Pinscher. Security or not, it wasn't long before Jim and Jan fell in love with Dobermans. Soon, Jim's competitive nature came to the fore and he became involved in show dog competitions.

But there was a problem. Showing dogs is a time-consuming hobby and when Jim's medical practice took off, he simply didn't have the available hours. Of course, Jim was too competitive to just stop, so instead he hired professional trainers and handlers. All the while, Jim and Jan always had a dobie in their home as a house pet.No one can recall just how many dogs they owned, but in 1990, Jim acquired a dobie with the AKC registered name of Wingate's Miss Monte Penny. She had champion blood lines all over her family tree, and while she quickly became a champion, her true fame would not come until after her own show days were over. That's when she became a virtual breeding machine—before her mothering days ended, she became the all-time second leading producer of Doberman champion show dogs in America.

Before televiewing professional sports became a religion for every red-blooded American boy, it wasn't uncommon for small town kids to hold a special fondness for the outdoors; and so it was for Jim and several of his closest friends. He had to put hunting and fishing on hold for eleven years after high school, but after Jim returned to Farmington in 1956, he quickly returned to his first love. He and his buddies also enjoyed golf outings, but that didn't really satisfy Jim's desire for the outdoor life. Pigeons, however, would help.

As boys, Jim and his buddies caught pigeons on local farms under the cover of darkness.Now, twenty years later, every time Jim drove to the hospital in Canton—an almost daily occurrence—he went right past 'Spot' Gale's homing pigeon farm, on the north side outskirts of Canton. After doing that for a few years, Jim finally gave in to temptation; he converted his large backyard dog kennel into a homing pigeon haven. For decades, Jim would occasionally race his birds but it was a time-chewing diversion. It involved caging your birds, then driving 50 miles or more for a meeting with other hobbyists. They were then released and timed to see which ones returned the fastest to their roosts. (the birds, not the hobbyists) To this day, Jim still has some birds, but he no longer races them. Jim's dogs, birds, hunting trips and golfing couldn't fully slake his thirst for the outdoors… but horses would.

Among the doctors Jim met when he began his practice was Canton physician Dr. Mark Nelson, a devoted enthusiast of harness racing. He

Jim's mother with Miss Pam   **Jim hold's Pam's 1960 State Championship trophy**

not only owned race horses, but even had a farm with his own half mile racetrack. Through their friendship, it wasn't long before Jim was hooked as well, and bought his first horse in 1957.Unsure how his wife would respond to the news, Jim handled it by simply not telling Jan.

Jim's first horse wasn't a winner, but in 1958, he purchased a filly named Miss Pamela from Farmington furniture owner, Clyde Turl. Jim hired crusty old Trivoli horseman Glenn Johns to train and drive Miss Pamela. Before long, Jim and Glen realized they might have something special. Harness horses begin racing as two-year-olds at county fairs, in preparation for the state championship races at the Illinois State Fair every August in Springfield. Pam proved to be a consistent winner at the 1960 small county fairs and hopes for a good showing at Springfield began to build. Well, she wouldn't disappoint. With a large contingent of Reed family members cheering like crazy in the packed grandstand, Pam won going away and was crowned the Illinois two-year old filly State Champion.

After that, Pam raced from one coast to the other.One day when she won a race at the famous race track in Santa Monica, California, a movie film company was there shooting a scene for the blockbuster movie, "The Days of Wine and Roses," starring Jack Lemmon. Jim was told the race scene would be in the movie, but unfortunately, at the last minute, they cut it from the film. In the decades that followed, Jim would own many winners, (including the 1963 Ill. State champion, Gaytime's Best) but none remembered as fondly by all the Reed family as Miss Pamela. Of the scores of horses Jim would own, Pam was the only one so gentle he let our mother to go nose-to-nose with her.

After several years racing horses, Jim decided to focus instead on the breeding and selling aspects of the business. It wasn't uncommon for him to have as many as forty horses on his farm at one time. Coming up with enough monikers was a pleasant problem.He began naming colts and fillies after his family, and therein lies one of the great coincidence stories of all time.

Idlewhile's Hubert was named after Jim's older brother who lived his adult life in the Chicago area. Hubert and his lovely wife, Leona, had two daughters, Vicki and Karen. (while having race horses named after us was exciting, business was business, and Jim sold most of his horses—including Idlewhile's Hubert.) Hubert's daughter Karen was a hospital executive in Baltimore. Once when she was in Los Angeles for a conference, she was at a party and struck up a conversation with a stranger. When he learned she was from Chicago, he told her he'd recently been there on his way to buy a race horse. Karen then mentioned that her uncle had a horse farm, near Peoria. The man said that was where he'd bought his horse. When Karen told him the name of the farm, he said that was the place! Then the story really got strange: when Karen asked the name of the horse, he said it was Idlewhile's Hubert, the horse named for Karen's father!

At first, Jim leased a piece of land just north of Trivoli to house his growing horse stable.Then in 1968 he purchased 80 acres just south of Trivoli and built his own half- mile race track. He incorporated as a business and named his farm Idlewhile Stables. (As of this writing, it is the oldest continuous family owned horse racing stable in Illinois.)In 1994 Jim decided to fulfill a dream and took the plunge into thoroughbred racing. He got lucky that year while visiting the Pinecrest horse farms near Lexington, Ky. The 1990 Kentucky Derby Champion, Unbridled, had just sired a foal with a serious leg problem, making racing impossible. Usually, the big time horse farms would have a foal like that put down, but Jim examined the injury and was fairly sure the colt could be saved. So he bought the colt cheaply, had him successfully operated on, named him Unbridled Success and made him the centerpiece of his new thoroughbred breeding operation.

The Reed brothers and sisters at the Annual Reed Reunion in 2004. Top row, L to R : Barbara Reed Osborn, Warner Reed, Willard Reed and Alicia Reed Aden. Bottom row, L to R : Marcia Reed Little, Rudy Reed, Greta Reed Kumlander and Jim Reed

Anyone's who's lived has been beset with at least a couple of personal regrets, and Jim is no exception. One thing he's always regretted was that he didn't spend more time with his family: his brothers and sisters, his wife and his children. Jim treasures the time he did have with his four children... but as he aged, he appreciated perhaps even more the outings spent with his grandchildren. Evidence of that is preserved in the precious letters presented here, on the occasion of Jim's 70th birthday, in 1997.

"I think my favorite events to remember with Grandpa is when we went under the little bridge when you are going to the farm. We went under it and threw a soda can in the water. Then we got the 22 shotgun and tried to shoot the can. Usually it was me and Kevin and Grandpa. Another thing I always liked to do with Grandpa was gather up some pigeons at night then we would get up a little earlier than we usually do and take them out in the country somewhere since grandpa knows just about every back road in Illinois, then we would dump them off and if they found their way home they were good ones, and if they didn't they were stupid and would go live in a barn somewhere. Well those are some of the great events I had with Grandpa and I hope we will have many more of them."

Matt Reed (age 10)

Happy 70th b-day Grandpa. I hope you enjoy it. I want you to know how much I love you. And that I know every one loves you. We've been to and through a lot of things together. I enjoy going to the farm with you and practicing with hunting arms. I know you have been through a lot of hard and happy times as a doctor and being in the NAVY. I think more and more about taking the job you have. I know it will be tough though. I try to visit you a lot but your not home usually. I have not much to say except you are a wonderful Grandpa and dad and I love you very much."

Kevin Reed (age 12)

"This is about my Grandpa and I want to tell you how special he is. He is nice, kind, loving sweet. He buyes me cookies. One time he bought me a marshmelo cooky. He got me flowers yesterday. I love him very much. Well I have to go. Bye."

Love, Kristen Reed (age 9)

"I think the best time I ever had with my grandpa was when he, Cindy, and me went hunting for graveyards. We went about 35 miles from London Mills and then saw a sign that said it was a cemetery, so we decided to take a look. We went down an old driveway to the cemetery and came upon a couple of bushes that were in the way. It took about a half hour to clear. When we were done we proceeded to the cemetery. They had been there before and wanted to dig a couple spots to see if there were any graves that had fallen over or were buried. I was stuck with the hard part, I had to dig up at least three places and we found nothing. Then on the fourth spot we hit the jack-pot. We not only found a grave but it was an ancestor of ours. It had to take two hours to get all the pieces out and five hours in all. We recovered all the pieces and decided to go home. I thought I was done but they asked me to help clean the pieces. What could I say? I said yes and helped clean the head stone. Finally when we were done it was someone whose name was Mason. It was good to know I helped. I hope grandpa got a good kick at what I looked like after that. I also hope grandpa had fun. Happy Birthday Grandpa!"

Love always,
Your grandson, Jason, (age 16)

While personal dilemmas like those of fathers regretting the lack of time invested with their children always seem real, quite often the emotional guilt being carried is disproportionate to the perceived injury. Dr. John Rosemond, a nationally renowned psychologist, has made a career explaining why modern parents worry way too much about their children, and in fact, would be well advised to practice more "benign neglect," much like their grandparents did. If Rosemond's theory catches on—and I for one hope it does—it will change child rearing in America.

The other personal dilemma Jim has been doing internal battle with for decades is the mystery of the soul and death. While most physicians—and for that matter most humans—are constantly faced with these issues, Jim has wrestled with them more often and more deeply because he's had unusually close relationships with thousands of his patients. And thoughts of death have never left him for long periods of time. I don't think it's farfetched to suggest a connection between Jim's interest in visiting cemeteries and his service to the dying.

Jim has never belonged to any church or attended church services. His lack of affiliation resulted, I think, from several things. We weren't reared in a very religious environment. I can't recall our father ever attending church. Our mother was more outwardly religious than Dad, but she never talked of religion around the house, and one had the feeling that religion was not a major factor in her day-to-day routine. For example, she left the Baptist church in favor of the Methodist simply because the Baptists didn't have an organ and the Methodist did. As kids, we weren't cajoled into attending Sunday School or summer Bible School.

Another factor playing into Jim's reluctance in fully accepting religious doctrines is the fact that his adult life has been dominated by scientific thinking. The philosophical underpinnings of science tend to fly in the face of religion, which is to say that a scientist is disinclined to accept anything strictly on the basis of faith.

The third factor influencing Jim's relationship with the unknown is a little more subtle. There tends to be a personality trait among many older, accomplished men—men from Tom Brokaw's Greatest Generation—who take a certain amount of pride in being self-reliant, of not needing to be dependent on anyone for anything.

Jim's ongoing internal philosophical entanglement with death, the soul and afterlife took on a much deeper meaning for him in the fall of 2008 when he lost his beloved wife, Jan, after 54 years of the closest relationship. Two things—and two only—kept him going. One was family and the other was his patients. Still, during his grieving process he was consumed with sadness. He desperately needed someone upon whom he could unburden himself. He'd never talked with anyone except dying patients about religious matters. Now he was drawn to a man named Dave Swain.

David Swain is the pastor of the Union Church in tiny Rapatee, a few miles west of Farmington. A patient of Jim's for about 30 years, Pastor Dave is not a typical minister. He didn't enter the preaching profession until 1990, when he retired from Caterpillar, where he'd been a machine operator. In my one visit with Pastor Dave, I found him to be a friendly, unpretentious, warm person. Most importantly, he was a good listener. It was easy to understand why Jim would've been drawn to Pastor Dave for counsel. If that wasn't enough, there was another important factor the men shared in common: they both loved the outdoors and had since childhood. Pastor Dave is so skilled, in fact, that he's led numerous hunting expeditions in Canada.

Jim always wants to know what Pastor Dave has been up to in the great outdoors. "I can see it in his eyes and hear it in his voice," Pastor Dave said, "that Jim almost lives those times vicariously through me. I know we both feel that being out in the woods alone is the most soothing thing in the world."

Pastor Dave spoke slowly and warmly of his great admiration for Jim. Then, after a long pause, he said"one of the most touching things I've ever encountered in my life happened a while back when I was driving by the deserted Trivoli cemetery on a dark, gloomy day. I happened to glance to my side and there at a distance, silhouetted against the foreboding sky stood Jim, standing all alone over Jan's grave."

There've been many amazing aspects to the life saga of Jim Reed, maybe none of them more mystifying than the way he's coped with intense, constant levels of stress. Jim has fortunately had the many hobbies and interests we've talked about in this chapter. They surely helped him to unwind, relax and enjoy what little private time he's had over the past half century. At the end of the day though, my gut feeling is that interests and hobbies haven't been the true key to his coping. I think it probably boils down to one thing: people.

Chapter 23: Comfort Zone

The rate of suicides among doctors is higher than any other profession. Not surprisingly, researchers think the main cause is depression. While the degree to which stress is a factor is debatable, its presence is not. Stress was the cover story in the Feb., 23, 2009 issue of NEWSWEEK magazine. In that article, UCLA psychologist, Shelly Taylor said , "Being surrounded by loved ones plays a major role in stress response." It's hard to imagine anyone who's been surrounded by more affection and respect than Jim Reed, and it's been going on for more than fifty years.

When Jim returned to his hometown in 1956, he had one thing on his mind, one thing he'd trained six tough years to do: practice high quality, effective medicine. He hadn't learned anything else, like managing an office, providing a gentle bedside manner, or handling stress—but he did have a huge advantage right from the start. It was what in sports parlance is called 'the home field advantage,' and it would be the rock solid foundation of his comfort zone.

Four different kinds of relationships meshed to form Jim's stress safety net. Two of them—family and close friends—were already in place when Jim hung his shingle. The other two—colleagues and patients—would be added very quickly. When those four powerful forces melded together, the resulting emotional support system for Jim was nearly impenetrable by stress or any other problems.

From the very beginning, Jim was pleasantly engulfed by familiarity. On his first day, he treated a young woman who'd been a first grade classmate. His ambulance driver was a childhood friend. He began caring for several elderly women who'd been his elementary school teachers. Earlier, we heard of the great affection Jean Fidler, his first aide, held for him even after 50 years. Fellow doctors immediately recognized his abilities and dedication. Last but far from least, within a few years, a strong bond forged between Jim and his patients.

Fifty-three years and about 20,000 patients after he began his hometown practice, only three people shared each of the following life experiences with Jim:

- All became close friends in their youth.
- They all remained in the Farmington area into adulthood, thus allowing their friendships to grow and deepen. They all married and their families became close. Two of the wives were even hired to work for Jim. Jim was the family doctor for these friends, as well as their families, even delivering some of those children.
- All three close friends of Jim became gravely ill as they aged and all were cared for until their passing by Jim with devotion, emotion and compassion.

The three people who've been the only ones in Jim's life to share all of those experiences were Virgil Hedden, Art Pille and Bill Thomas. One of the most difficult tasks Jim ever had to perform was to sign the official death certificates for his dear friends. Perhaps the most difficult of all was Bill Thomas, the very first friend Jim made when he arrived in Farmington in 1933 as a six-year-old boy. Jim has never had the luxury of time, time to properly grieve over the loss of loved ones. There have always been patients waiting on him for help. But who really knows, maybe that was the best medicine for Jim.

Apart from his family, there is no one Jim feels more comfortable being around than his two closest living friends, Dick Westerby and Bud Toft. I wanted to spend some time with them and hear what they had to say about their old life-long friend. I'd known both Bud and Dick since I was a kid because our house seemed to be the gathering spot for Jim and his friends. After a lapse of forty years, I saw them briefly in 2004 at the city-wide celebration for Jim's 50th year as a doctor. As they approached me through the crowd, I thought of their card games of hearts and pinochle at our home fifty years ago, and how they were always smiling and happy. After exchanging pleasantries, they disappeared back into the crowd. Now, as I pulled into Dick's driveway, it was four years later.

I barely recognized Dick when he answered the door; he'd changed that much in the just four years. As he led me into his dining room, I nearly tripped over the long plastic tubing running from his nose to an oxygen tank.

As soon as we were seated, Dick said he just got home from three days at the hospital. "I was having a lot of trouble breathing last Sunday and so I called Jim. He told me to call 911 and get to the hospital. I did and Jim almost beat the ambulance there." According to Jim, "Dick could have died but made a nice recovery." This day, Dick seemed to have no trouble breathing and clearly had a good time reminiscing about his old friend and doctor for the past fifty-two years.

Dick suffers from asbestiosis, a serious impairment in the functioning of the lungs, caused by repeated exposure to the chemical asbestos when he was younger and worked in the construction business. Dick said his health was so good until about age seventy that he seldom had a need to see Jim.

"I've been a patient at the hospital several times over the years," Dick said, "and whenever I tell the staff that Jim is my doctor, I notice a slight change in the way they react and treat me." (Dick meant that in a positive way.) He enjoyed repeating an incident when Jim was hospitalized for several weeks. By orders of Jim's doctors, visitors were restricted to family members. In spite of that, Dick went to the hospital, only to be told by the nursing staff that he couldn't see Jim. He pleaded with them but to no avail. So he asked them to please tell Jim that he was there. They begrudgingly agreed to do that. After being gone a minute, the nurse returned and told Dick, "Dr. Reed says you should come right in."

I'd been wondering about something for quite awhile, and I thought Dick could answer it better than anyone. I asked him if, following the deaths of their other two closest friends, Art Pille and Virgil Hedden, when Jim went into his office, his patients would be able to tell that he was mourning. Dick didn't hesitate with his response. "No they wouldn't. He always has the same demeanor, calm and cool. Only someone close to him like me might have noticed a little difference." I decided to pose another nagging question to Dick. "Do you think Jim gives any special treatment to his close friends?" Without blinking, he gave a definite "no." "He has always treated everyone the same," he added. He was also highly complimentary toward Jim's office staff. "Jim's tough and demanding. They all know what he wants and that patient care is his priority. His attitude and habits have rubbed off on them. They all work together very well."

Then, right in the middle of this serious talk, Dick asked if I'd ever ridden much with Jim. I told him I hadn't. "Good, because he's the world's worst driver," Dick said. While I was laughing, Dick went on. "He wants to look at you when he's talking to you, so he's weaving all over the road. Then, when he's on his phone, he's not paying attention to the road." As I got my giggling under control, Dick told an even better story.

"We were on the golf course at Galesburg once and Jim drove the golf cart right into a mud swamp. Virgil Hedden had to take off his belt and use it as a rope to pull it out." "Then the next time we were there," Dick went on, "the head lady took our money for the cart and handed us a rope saying she thought we might need it." Not surprisingly, Jim's take on these tales differed from Dick's version. While Jim admitted that when behind the wheel he often turned to look directly at Dick, he claimed he had to because Dick was hard of hearing. Now, with regard to the golf course mud swamp incident, Jim said that Virgil Hedden, like a lot of folks (including me) had a fear of bodies of water. So, being the prankster he was, Jim liked to frighten Virg by driving the cart as close to the water hazards as he could.

At a golf outing in Galesburg in 2000, from L to R, Leno "Twitter" Agnoletti, Bud Toft, Jim and Dick Westerby

Speaking of golf and Jim's driving skills, a number of years ago Dick built a putting green on Jim's farm, about thirty or forty feet on the north side of a pond, at the top of a slight incline. One day he and Jim rode out there in Jim's big sedan to practice putt; they parked on the incline and exited. Sadly, Jim neglected to put the car in "park" gear. After a minute of gravity, the sedan began rolling toward the pond. Dick was closest to the car, so Jim hollered "grab the damn car!" Now, this wasn't some VW bug. "I knew," Dick said, "there was no way in hell I could stop that big car by myself, so I just watched it roll toward the pond. The front end rolled into the pond but it must have gone right into some mud because it stopped before the whole car went in." With the help of Jim's son, Bryan, the three of them tried to extricate the car from the pond with a tractor. When that failed, they got the large Caterpillar bulldozer used on their racetrack and completed the rescue mission. When word of the runaway car spread around town, Jim's pond began being referred to as the Trivoli Car Wash.

Dick talked about Jim's ability to get away from it all and relax. "He has an ability to leave his job behind," Dick said. "When we're out on the golf course, you'd never know that he was a doctor, or that he had a care in the world, and Jim never loses his cool out on the golf course." Then Dick verified the report of others: on their way home after golfing, "it wouldn't be uncommon," Dick said, "for Jim to all of a sudden pull off a side road and stop at a patient's house."

Dick has experienced two unusual medical situations with Jim. One Sunday about a year ago, Dick developed a redness and rash on his arm. He decided he should have Jim take a look at it, so he drove down to his home. Jim was perplexed by Dick's symptoms, so the two of them drove to his office and ran a couple of tests. It turned out Dick had contracted a rare skin condition, probably from some vegetation in his large backyard. Jim said a strange coincidence was that a treatment for that very skin condition, (called micrococcus species) was just developed one week before Dick had contracted it. "The case was written up on the internet," Dick said.

Dick talked about his five daughters. He and his lovely wife of over sixty years, Helen, had had a son, Jimmy, but Dick said he was killed in an accident when he was only twelve, about forty-five years ago. I expressed my sympathy, but left it at that, and we moved on. Dick hadn't become upset when he related that sad news to me. So I didn't think any more about it until a couple of weeks later when I was talking with Jim about my visit with Dick.

One of my early impressions during my visits with Jim was that while he clearly had a good sense of humor, when discussing a patient, he was always unemotional and calm, regardless of how complex and serious the situation was. I was so struck by this that I was beginning to wonder if he had been practicing for so many years and had seen so much raw life that nothing phased him, emotionally, anymore. But, as we were ending our visit about Dick, I learned that I was dead wrong. And it would be the most touching, human moment I would have with Jim while working on the book.

It was not an easy revelation for Jim to make, but just as I was about to leave that day, he mentioned that dealing with the death of Dick's son was the hardest thing he had ever done. The boy, Jimmy, was twelve years old in 1963, and a big go-cart enthusiast. One day, his mother was hosting a party and some of her friends had brought their kids along. Jimmy was demonstrating his driving skills when suddenly his cart went out of control at a high speed and crashed into a parked car in the driveway.

Jim was called immediately, as was the ambulance. A team of surgeons was assembled at the hospital; Jim and the Westerbys arrived shortly thereafter. The surgeons tried valiantly to save Jimmy's life but he was too severely injured. The boy lay very near death, and it fell upon Jim to break the unbearable news to Dick and Helen. "Dick immediately began begging me," Jim said, "to have the surgeons try once more." In spite of Jim's assurance that everything that could be done had been done, Dick continued to implore Jim. Finally, Jim relented to his close friend's pleas. "Then I had to go back to the team of surgeons," Jim went on, "and beg them for a special favor." Though they all knew further efforts would be futile, they finally agreed to do it, just for Jim.

After the surgeons' last efforts, Jim returned to the surgery unit where young Jimmy lay barely conscious on a cold steel table. Jim was the only other person in the room. As Jim stood over Jimmy, the boy looked directly up at him and asked him, "Am I going to die?" At that point in the gut-wrenching story Jim began to chock up. "It was the most difficult emotional thing I've ever faced in my medical career," he said. "I couldn't bring myself to tell the boy he was dying," Jim continued, "so I told him no." Jim had never told this story to anyone, including Dick and Helen Westerby.

In one of our earlier sessions, Jim had emphasized the importance of a doctor always remaining calm and collected and thoughtful. But he hastened to add that everything changes in emergency, life and death situations. Instinct takes over, with no time for thought. When Jim stood over Dick Westerby's dying son, instinct told him to tell a lie in order to spare the young boy further anguish.

I happen to have a wise old friend, a professional philosopher, so I sought him out for his view of Jim's ethical dilemma. His considered opinion was that any caring doctor would have been terribly distressed regardless of whether or not he had told the boy the hard, cold truth or the white lie. In sparing the boy the agony, Jim made the agony his own. My friend felt there was no way that Jim could be faulted for reacting the way he did. By the way, when Jim told me this story, my gut response was that I thought he hadn't done anything wrong. Jim had burdened himself by keeping this story to himself, buried for the past forty-five years. He can be assured of one most important thing: Dick and Helen Westerby have never forgotten the way Jim and the team of surgeons cared for their young son.

Seventy-five years ago, when Jim Reed started the second grade at Chapman School, he got to know a first grader named John Toft. For the rest of his life, to his friends, John would be called "Bud." Now one of Jim's two closest living friends, Bud should actually never have attended

Chapman School. Living in what was known in Farmington as the "West End," Bud would have gone to Harris School in normal times. But the Great Depression did away with normal times for several years; as a result, the Harris School closed down. And Bud and Jim met.

A month after visiting with Dick Westerby, I returned to his home, where Bud had agreed to meet me. He'd driven down from his home of the past 50 years, a small town named Woodhull about forty miles northwest of Farmington. (Bud's always returned to Jim if he's had a serious medical concern.) He said he'd recently seen his heart specialist, Peoria cardiologist Dr. Thanad Shay. Then he nonchalantly threw out the comment that "Dr. Shay told me that Jim had the sharpest eye he had ever seen in a doctor."

While I was stunned by that remark, I was equally taken aback by the fact that both Dick and Bud didn't seem either particularly surprised or impressed. My first reaction was that Bud probably misinterpreted what Dr. Shay had said, and so I felt I needed to verify it. Later, I did just that by sending the quote to Dr. Shay (Jim had told me he'd be impossible to talk to since he was so busy.) Sure enough, Dr Shay wrote me back and verified Bud had quoted him correctly. Bud ended that story by paying Jim a great compliment which I would hear more than once while working on the book. "Jim's patients have the idea that he isn't human. I just know that I'd stake my life on him."

In appearance, Bud's changed less over a span of several decades than anyone I've ever known. (Though Bud's apparent robustness didn't necessarily reflect how healthy he was on the inside.) It's a little hard to figure what he and Jim shared in common. Jim had ten years of post-high school education and training. Bud had none. It didn't matter; the rather unusual nature of Jim's intellect seems to have never been a factor in any of his friendships, probably because Jim always looked upon his intellectual abilities as a "gift," rather than a hard-won skill. And as such, in his mind, it was just the luck of the draw, and therefore nothing to be especially proud of. At an unspoken level, his humility and lack of pretense has always been recognized and appreciated by his friends.

Jim enjoyed over 55 years of marriage to a wonderful lady. Bud never married. Jim had four children. Bud had none. What the friendship boils down to, for Bud as well as Jim's other close friends, is shared childhoods, teen years and young adult years. They all came out of those times with such a strong, secure bond that nothing could break it. That Jim became the doctor for his friends and all their loved ones further strengthened those bonds.

Those bonds could be seen when Jim set up his practice in 1956. Sometimes Bud would drive Jim around to his house calls if Jim's wife needed to use their only family car. The bonds were seen when Bud's mother became terribly sick, and Jim stopped at her home every day to see her. They were there when Virginia Thomas moved her gravely ill husband (Jim's first friend in Farmington) back from Nebraska back to Farmington to be cared for by Jim. They were there whenever Tom Anderson got out of bed in the middle of the night to drive his ambulance/hearse for Jim. The bonds were there when Jim's college roommate, Art Pille, was dying of cancer. "Jim," according to Art's widow, Marilyn, " stopped out three or four times a week" And I saw the bonds when, after burying our mother, we all returned to Jim's to visit and have a bite to eat, and there was Virgil Hedden standing at the sink, washing dishes. And the bonds were seen in 1980 when Jim signed his contract to work for Peoria Methodist Hospital—and had it stipulated that his close friends would continue not to be charged for office visits. The only two close friends left, Dick and Bud, said they had a hundred stories. Here are a few.

There were a couple of memorable fishing trips to the northlands of Minnesota involving Jim, Dick, Bud, Art Pille, Peelie Swartwood and Russ Risdon. Russ, one of Jim's best college friends, was the only one who wasn't a Farmington area native. A lifelong resident of Chicago, Russ didn't know anything about fishing. After settling in at their camp, they arose about 5:00, while the other campers were still asleep. As they readied their small boat, Russ figured he could just get into the boat off the pier like he was walking concrete steps. Of course, as soon as he put one foot into the boat, it moved forward while his other leg was still on the pier, and so he did the splits, but fast. As Russ flopped into the lake, his buddies broke out in uncontrollable laughter. All of them, that is, except Art Pille, who screamed so loud it woke the whole camp.

Their other fishing trip involved Peelie Swartwood. Peelie was one of the most nervous guys you'd ever run into. "He'd always been that way," Jim said. "His mother was the same way." Peelie could also be pretty argumentative at times. All of his buddies knew that and just put up with it...most of the time. In the confined quarters of a car, on a long trip to Minnesota, it was pretty easy for Peelie to get under your skin. He and Jim got into a big argument over something no one can remember. So they stopped the car and just kicked Peelie out, right in the middle of nowhere. "After we drove on for about twenty miles," Jim said, "we started feeling guilty, so we turned around and went back to get him."

"My favorite story about Peelie," Dick said, "was when he and

Bud and Jim were driving around and ended up out at one of the 'slope' mines." (a slope mine is a deep shaft mine but instead of going straight down, via elevator, you reached it on a gradually sloped track in a small car.) Dick went on: "Jim and Bud grabbed Peelie, threw him into one of the small cars and gave it a shove. But they didn't know that it would get going pretty fast. Before long, Peelie was screaming, going crazy, fearing for his life." Luckily the car gradually slowed down of its own accord, then came to a stop after a couple minutes.

As the years passed, Peelie, (never the most stable block in the pyramid) moved around from town to town in various sales jobs. He would come back to Farmington from time-to-time, and more often than not, would ask Jim for a 'loan.' Jim always obliged, knowing full well that he'd never see his loan again. At one point, Jim heard that Peelie had married a woman whose father was involved in some sort of 'mob' activity, perhaps in Florida. Jim didn't have details and didn't want them. Well, before long, Peelie's marriage fell on hard times. It was rumored that he may have gotten physical with his wife. And when word of that got back to her father, Peelie feared for his safety. That's when he showed up at Jim's home one day and said he wanted to get out of the country fast. But he didn't have any money. "So I opened my billfold," Jim said, "and gave Peelie everything I had, about $200. And I never saw him again after that." Jim went on, "For years I never told that story to any of the guys because I was afraid of putting them in jeopardy." After that tale of woe and suspense, Jim closed by saying, "Peelie was the only person who rode with me on the bus from Farmington to Peoria when I went off to the Navy." That's the sort of thing about friends that tends to linger forever in your memory and in your heart—at least for a man like Jim.

Part VII

Along The Way

"You owe it to us all
to get on with
what you are good at."

--W. H. Auden
Anglo-American poet
1907-1973

Chapter 24: The Outsider

Throughout the course of his medical schooling and training, Jim's focus had been on the treatment of individuals. So when he began his hometown medical practice in 1956, his only concern was being of service to people who sought out his help. However, as he gained both experience and age, a subtle, gradual change took place in his outlook toward professional responsibilities. While his great passion—and number one priority—would always remain providing high quality medical care on a personal, one-on-one basis, he began to view the city of Farmington itself as a sort of patient, worthy of the same care and attention as any individual. One of the things that meant was in addition to promoting healthy lifestyles inside Farmington, Jim would be vigilant in deflecting unhealthy, outside influences from entering the area. This chapter chronicles one of his best and most bizarre efforts.

Jim's never been an easy man to rile. In fact, his equanimity has always been a key ingredient of his success as a physician. On the other hand, Jim would never sit idly by if anyone tried to place a roadblock between him and the high quality medical service his patients deserved.

On a simmering summer day in 1986, a personable young man I'll call J. T. Madix (a fictional name for this chapter) strolled into Jim's office and introduced himself at the front desk. There was no way for Jim to foresee the havoc about to be wrought upon him and his family by this stranger in town; but there was also no way for the stranger to know that this time he'd picked the wrong man to try and bedazzle. Madix, who presented himself as a doctor, wondered if he "might have a few minutes of Dr. Reed's time." Jim granted his request, as he would with any professional colleague. Madix presented to Jim a medical-business proposition that he asserted would be an improvement in medical services for the residents of the local nursing home, where Jim served as Medical Director.

Madix said he had a mobile medical van that would provide X-ray and lab work services right there at the nursing home, thereby making a trip to a distant hospital unnecessary for the Home's elderly, physically-limited patients. Jim listened intently to the young doctor's convincing presentation and concluded the idea had merit. "So I asked him to meet with the Home's Director of Nursing as well as the Home's Board of Directors," Jim said. Madix proceeded to do just that, and he impressed the administrators just as he had impressed Jim. So a deal was signed and the plan was put into motion.

It wasn't long before the first case came up with a need for the new service. A lady at the nursing home had fallen and an X-ray in the new mobile van service was taken immediately to help determine the damage done to her hip. Jim was told that the X-ray film would be evaluated by a physician in nearby Macomb, who would advise Jim of the findings.

When the report came into Jim, it indicated that the patient had suffered a fractured hip, so Jim had her admitted to the hospital for treatment. "At that point," Jim said, "I had developed a kind of funny feeling about Madix." The term "funny feeling" was Jim's way of saying that based upon his many years of practice, with thousands of people, on an intimate basis, he'd developed a pretty sophisticated sixth sense about people. He could get a good read on their sincerity, motivations, attitudes, etc.

"Because of my funny feeling," Jim went on, "I decided to have the hospital do their own X-ray. They did, and it showed that the patient had, in fact, NOT suffered any hip fracture. So I talked with the Home's Director of Nursing about what had happened. Unfortunately, by this time Madix had ingratiated himself not only with her but with several key Board members. So, she asked me to give him another chance. I did so, with some reluctance." (It was Jim's responsibility and duty, of course, to oversee all medical services at the Home.)

"The next time the mobile unit took an X-ray," Jim continued, "I decided to examine it myself. I was surprised at the inferior quality and knew something was wrong. So, I checked into Madix's credentials and found out he wasn't a physician at all, as he had presented himself when I first met him. He had practiced hypnotism and acupuncture. I immediately contacted the Director of Nursing at the Home," Jim went on, "and told her we could no longer use Madix's services. She became so upset with me that she contacted the President of the Board of Directors of the Home, who had also decided to side with Madix. The President then called me at my home. He was upset and got out of line with me professionally. About that time, I lost my temper with him and told him he didn't know what he was talking about. I also told him I wouldn't change my mind."

(When Jim first related this story to me, he omitted an interesting piece of information I became aware of later. It seems that a few years prior to this run in with the Board President, Jim had been summoned to his home, where the President had been working on his roof when he suffered a major heart attack. Jim arrived on the scene in short order, just like he always did in emergencies. Knowing every second was important, Jim didn't hesitate in scaling the ladder up to the second story roof to administer life-saving care to the Board President.)

Just 24 hours after his confrontation with the Board President, Jim got a phone call from Farmington Mayor Jim Hurst warning him that he might be contacted within the hour by the Illinois Bureau of Investigations. Hurst said that two of Madix's vehicles had just caught fire and that Madix had publicly implied that Jim was an arsonist. The Mayor furthermore said that his own son had been listed as a suspect by Madix, because a vehicle similar to Hurst's son had been spotted leaving the scene of the crime (the younger Hurst was cleared by the authorities in short order). Sure enough, an investigator did arrive at Jim's office. "He just asked me a few questions," Jim said, "and I told him how I viewed the situation and that was about it." (Meanwhile, in an about face, the Nursing Home Board of Directors took steps toward terminating their business arrangement with Madix.)

The following morning, when Jim arrived at his office, he found that the building's handicapped entrance ramp had been ripped apart. The State Bureau Investigator was called to the scene, examined the situation and told Jim that it looked like the damage had been done "with a truck or some kind of machine." Incredibly, just as the Investigator and Jim were examining the damage, Madix happened to drive by in his truck. Jim said it looked like the truck had been damaged.

By this time, the unfortunate affair had become newsworthy. The Peoria Journal Star newspaper assigned a reporter to investigate the controversy and submit his story. Unfortunately, one huge misstep in his efforts was his failure to talk to one of the two principles: Jim Reed. Not surprisingly then, his article painted Madix as the innocent victim of wrongdoing. He reported Madix as saying that he'd seen a big, young, white-haired man leaving the scene of his burning vehicle. That description happened to fit Bruce Reed, Jim's son, to a tee. Bruce thinks that largely because of that article, the FBI requested an interview with him.

Tiring of being on the defensive, Jim took the initiative in hiring a professional lie detector service to administer tests to his sons, Brent, Bryan and Bruce, all of whom lived in the immediate vicinity. (Of course, they all passed the lie detector test.) In the meantime, Peoria County detectives interviewed Bryan and Brent. After those first interviews, none of the three brothers was ever contacted again by police authorities. At about that same time, another incident occurred that came too close to involving Jim's wife. One evening after Jim and Jan had retired, they heard a loud bang downstairs. When Jim investigated, he found a smudged handprint on one of their family room windows. Police were called to the scene but nothing came of it.

"It was about at that point," Jim said, "I decided I'd had enough. I contacted a doctor in nearby Lewistown who had had some dealings with Madix and he agreed to come with me to Springfield [the Illinois state capitol] and talk with our State Representative, Mr. Tom Honer." After hearing all that had transpired, Representative Honer assured the two doctors he would take immediate action to rescind Madix's license to provide medical services, and he did just that, proceeding to convince the State Licensing Committee. The very next day, Madix was officially notified by the State Committee that he was out of business in Illinois. But unfortunately, that wasn't the end of the tale.

"One morning a few days later," Jim recounted, "as I was leaving home at about 6:00AM, I heard the fire alarm whistle, so I stopped by the scene, in case medical help might be needed." A fire was raging at the farm of one of the Nursing Home Board members, where Madix had been parking his vehicles. As Jim pulled in the driveway, he spotted Madix. Yet another of the Madix vehicles was on fire. "He was ranting and raving," Jim said. "His behavior was out of control. The firemen were there and heard Madix make verbal threats to kill me and members of my family."

About that time the State Police arrived. Seeing that Madix was completely irrational, they determined he was interfering with both the firemen and their own need to investigate, so they handcuffed him and put him on the ground. At that point, Jim decided it was time for him to vacate the premises. "That was the last time I ever saw the man," he said. So, in the end, the question of who had torched Madix's vehicles was never officially answered.

Whatever he was, Madix was not an idiot. He was smart enough to see the handwriting on the wall, so before he dug himself into a deeper hole in Farmington, in November, 1986, he quickly and quietly pulled up stakes and moved to another state where he'd previously lived and where, as it turned out, he'd been convicted of theft in 1980. (He served three years probation for that crime. Several years later, he was pardoned of that crime after making a sizable contribution to the governor's campaign.) After leaving Farmington, Madix became involved in the purchase and operation of nursing homes. In late 2007, a verdict was entered against Madix and three other defendants in the amount of 3 million dollars for nursing home negligence. The plaintiff had alleged that Madix negligently understaffed the nursing homes he operated. (Madix was determined to be 50% at fault.)

A reporter from a large metropolitan newspaper contacted Jim a couple of years after Madix left Farmington and said he was doing a feature on Madix. He wanted Jim's version of his dealings with the man. Jim's response was that he didn't want to bother unless the reporter guaranteed him the matter would be fully aired in his paper. The reporter agreed, so Jim told him the story—but in spite of the assurance, the article never appeared in the paper, as far as Jim knew.

Jim never felt personally threatened by anything which Madix may have done. Part of that was just his nature and part of it stemmed from his 24-7 work ethic, which made any distractions seem relatively unimportant. That being said, there's no question he became distraught when his immediate family was thrust into the fray. So it was that in the middle of this mess that Jim suffered his near fatal heart attack, on October 28, 1986. While Jim denies that there was any connection between the two, his family is not so certain.

(I'll never forget the time I was eleven and being bullied badly—including a pencil stabbing in my leg—by a kid named Herbie, who had moved into town a few months earlier. One day, our teacher announced that Herbie's family had left town. That was easily the happiest day of my childhood. When I related that story to Jim's daughter Cynthia, she said that was exactly the way her mother felt about Madix's departure.)

In retrospect, Jim lamented that he was "disappointed with a number of my patients who asked me if I had really set fire to Madix's vehicles." But I'd suggest there's another way to look at those comments. First of all, the mere fact that they felt free to ask Jim the question indicates their relationship with him was close enough and open enough that they could approach him so directly. And secondly, everyone likes reassurance. You can be pretty sure that once Jim answered the question put to him with a firm "No," that was all his patients needed to hear. At the end of this bizarre story, Jim added that most of the people who'd offended him during the strange episode apologized to him later and returned to him as patients, and while many of Jim's strong supporters would've personally preferred that he refuse to treat the doubters, they also knew that was not his style.

Chapter 25: Uncensored Again

"I love Dr. Reed. I admire him for his kindness and compassion for his patients. There hasn't been a finer doctor in my long life and he's always been there when I needed him."
  --Vi Branden, 94

"Dr. Reed has been our doctor since 1957. He delivered our four children. Three of them were preemies weighing 3 lb.10oz. 3 lb.7oz. and 2 lbs.11oz. Our fourth child weighed 5 lbs.13oz. Needless to say, we called on Dr. for more help than I can recall. He was always there for us. If we couldn't get to the office he'd make house calls. He really cared about his patients. He was there for us from birth of preemies through mumps, measles, colds, flu, diabetes, stitching cuts, and caring for our parents as they aged. He's been a good and caring doctor, man and friend. Farmington was lucky he came back here to practice. There isn't any way we could thank him enough for all the time and energy spent on us. Thanks to Dr's wife, Jan, for graciously sharing him with Farmington."
  --Frank and Phyllis Sprague

"It's not very often you can say one doctor has treated six generations in one family, but Dr. Reed has with the Kimbrells. I know at times I've been one of those patients that makes him want to tear his hair out. I know everybody hates to go the hospital, but I wait and wait until he usually has to put me in as an emergency patient. When my son was graduating from eighth grade and my daughter from college the same weekend, he told me I couldn't wait any longer, I had to go for surgery. I said I couldn't miss the graduations, and he said to have my family take lots of pictures, so I reluctantly went to the hospital. Another time when my first grandchild was going to be born I had to go for another surgery. I said I couldn't go and he told me I didn't have a choice, but I did get out in time to see my grandchild born. Last year he made a house call (that's unheard of nowadays) but he came once for me and once for my husband. We can't go to Methodist Hospital because of our insurance, so Dr. will call or have his nurse call to see how we're doing. He's such a kind, compassionate and caring doctor about his patients. There will never be another Dr. Reed, and I feel so blessed he has taken such good care of me and my family all these years. He's the best there is and nobody can replace him."

    --Cindy Kimbrell Meeks

"My husband's had a lot of broken bones and surgeries. He had a heart attack in Dec., 1983 and in Feb., 1984 they did triple heart bypass. On July 30, 1995, we came home from church and my husband had real bad pain and I called Dr. Reed. He said 'you bring him right up to my office and I'll be waiting.' We live in Canton so it took us 15 minutes to get there and Dr. Reed was waiting with his nurse and also had an ambulance come, and Doctor got him stabilized and they put him in the ambulance and I'm sure it saved his life, He is 77 now and has 13 stents in his heart and had 14 angiograms and he keeps busy every day.On Feb., 12, 1986, my granddaughter was 6 months old and was really sick.We called Dr. Reed and told him the symptoms and he said get her right up here.He checked the soft spot on her head and it was swelled.He rushed her to the hospital. They did a spinal tap right away, couldn't even wait til her dad got there. She had spinal meningitis, but with Dr. Reed's fast action he saved her.You would never know now she had it other than just a little slow on thinking. We think a lot of Dr. Reed and I wish we had more doctors like him to take his place when he retires."

    --Ivy and Lyle Hebb

"One of the things that stands out most in my mind about Dr. Reed is that he takes his time and doesn't jump to conclusions."

    --Pastor Mary Babcock, Yates City Presbyterian Church

"I was a lineman for CILCO (Central Illinois Light Company). This was back in 1971. Me and three other linemen were out in the middle of the night in a terrible storm.We were out on route 116 by Cramer Corner when we came upon a bad accident.There had been a collision between a truck and a car. The car, driven by one of the Korth brothers, had ended up in a field about 150 feet from the highway. We could see Mr. Korth was in bad shape.It was like he'd been scalped.About that time Doc Reed pulled up. As soon as he saw where the car was, he hollered out that his back was killing him and he'd need someone to carry him out to Mr. Korth.So me and another lineman—I can't remember who it was, either Joe Evans, Chubb

Carson, or Don Bridgestock--went over to Doc, crossed our arms, clasped our hands and placed them under Doc's rear to lift and carry him.I'll never forget helping Doc like that as long as I live."
    --Wilbur Pettett

"Forty years or more or less is a long time to depend on someone. That is what I have done. Dr. Reed was always there when I needed him. He was a friend as well as a doctor.A pat on the back meant more than a dose of medicine."
    --Genevieve Sheets

"For nearly 70 years, our family has known Jim Reed as a student, athlete, physician, valued friend and trusted advisor.He has always been there for us whenever we needed him, and he has truly been our special friend.He will always have our love and affection, for he has enriched our lives."
    --Pauline and Mike Grebe and Sally Grebe Seaman (ed. note: Walter Grebe, legendary coach at Farmington High School from 1937-1969, was the husband of Pauline and father of Mike and Sally. He died in Sept, 1995. Pauline died in Aug., 2007. Mike was General Counsel to the Republican National Committee from 1996-2000.)

"I've been proud to work with Dr. Reed for the past 30 years. A quiet, gentle man with soft, knowing hands and gentle voice, he's never pretentious nor boastful, yet he's confident.He's not afraid to tell the truth nor back his opinions with the wisdom of years of experience.No matter the time nor the day, he's never too busy nor too tired to see a patient in need, a dedication and caring not often seen these days.By bringing about and helping with new ideas and changes, he had made his mark on hospitals, Rescue Squads, nursing homes and this community.I wish to thank Dr. Reed for all the years of friendship and caring he has shown to me and my family and for his patience and wisdom during the difficult and wonderful times of our lives."
    --Mrs. Karen Peterson

"While I was in grade school, back in the early 1930's, a family moved into town from London Mills.We became acquainted with several of these youngsters.Our family lived south of the M and St. L railroad on South Cone Street, an area known as Steenberg Addition. We passed the Reed residence every day on the way uptown.My father, Bill Cline, was a barber and had also come to Farmington from London Mills, where he knew Mrs. Reed's family. When my oldest son, Bill, was 5, we lived upstairs in the Leeper home.Mrs. Reed climbed our stairs seeking to enroll Bill in her kindergarten program and I was sorry I couldn't afford it.I think my son still feels sorry about her climbing those stairs and not being able to attend her school. In Feb., 1960, as I like to tell my friends, Dr. Reed "took me in off the streets." He hired me and told me he'd teach me everything I needed to know.I guess I must have learned it as he let me stay until I retired in 1989. By then he'd helped me make college a reality for my three sons.As he watched them grow to men, so I helped keep an eye on his four youngsters when the need was there.We made a lot of changes in 29 years. My hat's off to Dr, Reed, the best boss, teacher, friend and family physician in anyone's book."

    --Mary McMaster

"The New World Dictionary of American English does not have enough words from the front to the back cover to say what a young man can accomplish with a dream.A young man who grew up in Farmington to become a doctor—and came back to serve his friends, raise his family, and everyone knew him.Dr. Reed has been my neighbor and friend for all these years and there has not been anytime that I or anyone else in the community could not call upon him for medical help.That is what a dream did for Dr. Jim Reed."

    --Kay Gibbs

"Dr. Reed, you've been a friend and doctor to our family for five generations.You've cared and doctored the grandparents, parents, Don and I, our children, and now the grandchildren. I should say you've put up with us for a long time. You knew just how to handle my mother. She always told the story about the time you made a house call. You left the room and went to the front door. Then you came back and said, 'Gladys, did you know there is a dead dog in the dining room.She replied,'No, not quite.' (By the way, the dog lived another month.)She always said you didn't quite approve of her dogs. She said that was okay, but she never said anything bad about your horses.Speaking of horses, there were many years of horses for our family, from Dr. Nelson's barn to the track in Trivoli.Don was in his glory working with horses on your farm with Buck. You always knew how to handle Don too. I think Don respects you more than anyone he has ever known. We all thank you for being there for us for so many years."

    --Mary Ridenour

"My younger brother, Lloyd Smith, and Jim were classmates and friends from the first grade through junior high. Jim was always little and short for his age. I remember Lloyd asking Mom if Jim would ever grow up to be tall—which he did—not only in stature but stands "tall" in his hometown as well. My father-in-law to be, Don Lercher, was Jim's coach in junior high. He said Jim wasn't a star on the court but he was always was in the classroom. Jim and my father-in-law remained good friends. When he needed to see Jim at his office, his visit would often end with a discussion of their mutual interest: the Civil War. I think at times that was better than a dose of medicine. My cousin, Fern Taylor, told me her visits to Jim usually ended up with a discussion of their Kentucky connections."
    --Amber Smith Lercher

"Having worked for several pharmacies in the St. Louis area before coming to Farmington in 1969, I was immediately impressed with Dr. Reed's medical knowledge and practice. In St. Louis, I was used to having physicians who would see 10 or 15 patients a day during regular hours (and think they were busy). I compared that with Dr. Reed who was seeing 100 or more patients a day and then be called at all hours of the night by patients. It was amazing to me to see him in the office the next day after being awakened five or more times during the night. A more dedicated physician would be impossible to find. Whereas most doctors in St. Louis were specialists and would see the same symptoms over and over in their patients, Dr. Reed took care of patients with all kinds of problems.During the last 27 years, I have had the opportunity to talk to many of Doctor's patients, of which the overwhelming majority have had nothing but praise for Dr. Reed. Another testament to admiration by his patients is the great number who drive 30, 40 or more miles to come and see him. I have had a multitude of his patients who've told me they value his opinion more than any others. Dr. Reed has always been available to my family when we needed medical help, from chicken pox to Mary's broken leg. I had called him from the hospital after Mary had broken her leg to ask his advice and the next thing I knew he was at the hospital to see her. I can't think of anyone who makes that kind of effort. Of all the doctors I have worked with over the past 30 years, there are none that come close to Dr. Reed's dedication or expertise."
    --Bill Rogers

"I'll never forget the first time I met Dr. Reed, many years ago. We were living about two miles north of the Trivoli Grade School. One day our 5 1/2 -year-old son, Jay, was walking home from school, and when he was crossing route 116, he was hit by a passing motorist. Someone called me. Of course I was in shock, but I grabbed my two little kids and drove down there as fast as I could. Well, we'd gotten very lucky because moments after the accident, Dr. Reed happened to pass by on his way home (just south of the school), and he was already helping Jay when I arrived. Jay suffered several cracked ribs and a bad cut in his leg. Dr. Reed took care of Jay just like he was one of his own patients, even though at the time we were going to another doctor. Dr. Reed was so helpful and cautious that from then on we were converts to his care."

--Jo Ann Huffman Smith

Chapter 26: A Work Day at 82

There are three ways of finding out what a family doctor does. One way is by actually watching him at work with his patients, but that's usually impossible since most folks don't want a stranger in the exam room with them. The second way is to talk with patients about what goes on between them and their doctor. We did a lot of that—and it was perhaps the most important part of this book. The third way is to have the doctor talk about what he does.

In what follows, Jim Reed talks about each of the patients he saw in one day. "There really is no such thing as an 'average' day for us," Jim emphasized, "but this comes about as close as we get to one." This then is a summary of one day of his patient visits, not a verbatim account of everything that was said or done. Individual identifying characteristics of patients, such as gender and age, were altered in order to protect confidentiality. This day at the office took place in the late winter of 2009. "It was a terribly foggy day," Jim said, "so several patients cancelled their appointments, which was probably a smart thing to do."

Jim Reed is 82 now, and no longer has the remarkable physical stamina and energy that he was well known for when he was younger. He no longer sees 100 or more patients per day as he did for 25 years. "I spend more time with each patient now," he explained, "because my patients are a lot older than they used to be and require more time." Here is how he spent one day:

"At 8:15, I saw my first patient, a young girl. Her parents brought her in today to receive the results of the biopsy we had done on her a week ago for recurring skin lesions. The results were negative and of course the parents were very relieved. One of the worst things patients go through is the anxiety and worry of waiting for test results.

Next I saw a husband and wife who were both experiencing the same symptoms of sore throats and coughing. Upper respiratory ailments like theirs have always been the most common reason for patient contacts. (The second most common complaint has always been back-related pain.) Even though most upper respiratory problems turn out to be viral infections, my practice has always been to assume that they would develop into bacterial infections. So, I've always treated them aggressively with antibiotics, which is what I did for this couple. I also talked with them about limiting their activities. I didn't think they required lab work or X-rays. I advised them that they should feel marked improvement in 48 hours and if they didn't, they should call me or one of the girls or come in. I delivered this gentleman into the world about fifty years ago. I've also cared for his father for fifty years.

The next patient was a retiree who was returning for ongoing treatment for an extensive recurring skin infection on his arm. He wants to leave the country soon on a planned excursion. I'm concerned that the rather remote area where he plans to go might not have the medical care he'd need for his infection, so he's agreed to delay his trip until we can help his condition improve. At this point he doesn't need any additional workup. We'll have him return in three days for more treatment.

Next I saw a middle-aged lady who spends the winter months in warmer climes. When she returns, she usually comes in with a host of complaints, often on the unusual side. Today, her complaint was of diffuse muscle pain with weakness and tenderness. She thought she might have a neurological problem. Because of her state of anxiety we spend more time with her. We gave her a simple blood test to rule out an inflammatory muscle problem. My girls told me they recently saw her walking in the grocery store and she moving quickly and normally, but when she came to the office she was walking differently. This lady has a relative in the health care field who gives her advice which probably does her more harm than good. She's been with me for about thirty years and I've had several consultations with the Mayo Clinic about her.

My sixth patient is a farmer who was kicked by a cow last fall and as a result suffered a severe laceration with emaciated tissue damage all the way down to his gastroneius (calf) muscle. The wound was six inches wide and three inches deep. We did a culture of the necrotic (dead) tissue and it revealed the wound had become infected. Complicating the treatment was the fact that the gentleman was allergic to various antibiotics. So we may have to go to intravenous antibiotic enderling drip pic lines. If we're not successful in eradicating the necrotic tissue and infectious material, he might lose his leg, below the knee.

My next patient is a lovely lady in her early seventies. I've followed her for fifty-two years and I'm amazed at how well she manages, living alone and completely responsible for her own care. She's usually in good spirits but a week ago she came in complaining of back pain. So we started her on a workup for possible arthritis. We did some blood work but before we do X-rays or scans, we usually give an injection of Toradol or Depomedrol. Then we watch them for a week to see how they respond. So today was her follow-up appointment and she seemed like a different person. She was free of pain and happy. This was a rather remarkable recovery for a person of her age. She agrees to the line of treatment we provided and will return for more on an as-needed basis.

Our eighth patient is a lady over ninety who lives alone and cares for herself. She had come in a week ago to request blood profile because it had been a year since her last one. Today, she returned to get the results. The results were good and she was very happy. About three months ago when I was at home with my terminally ill wife, this very lovely lady came to our home with homemade soup. And it wasn't the first time she had done this. She absolutely denies having any problems except worrying about her health and not being able to care for herself at home.

My next patient was a young lady with a history of hypertension which has been well-controlled with medication. She had called in asking for a refill but since it had been about a year since we had seen her, we wanted to have her in before we gave her a new prescription. Today, she felt good and looked good. Her vital signs were fine. We did blood work to make sure no other pathology was developing. I agreed to give her a prescription for two weeks to carry her over until we get her lab results back.

Our tenth patient was an elderly lady who has a history of peripheral arterial occlusion disease. She's had her left femoral popliteal (back of the knee artery) bypassed three times, once at the University of Iowa and twice locally. Now she's getting to the point where there is less blood getting through the stents and grafts. We're starting her study of course with a Doppler but she'll need an arteriogram and a referral back to the University of Iowa for consideration of removing the grafts that they have in now and offering her something to deliver more blood to the lower limb. Unfortunately, this is all complicated by the fact that she has a chronic lymphoma that needs to be watched. She's beginning to show her age from the lymphoma and of course that's going to play an important part in her ability to respond to surgery.

My next patients were a married couple who I've cared for over the past fifty years. They seldom come in so we pay more attention to their complaints. The wife has recurring pan sinusitis with significant rhinitis requiring antibiotic therapy and oral decongestants. She has responded well to this course of treatment in the past. I met the husband fifty years ago when I was called out to his farm. He was semi-conscious and complaining of headaches. This was before the days of CAT scans and MRI's. I suspected a ruptured cerebral aneurysm and referred him to a Peoria neurosurgeon who confirmed my suspicion and operated immediately, basically saving the man's life. Since that time he's had no neurological problems. He came in today because he's been having tremors of his hand, a rather typical symptom of the beginnings of Parkinson's disease. He wasn't ready to go through a complete workup and neurological consultation because they had a trip planned. We started him on our standard medication for Parkinson's and agreed he'd come in for the workup after their trip. Both these patients were happy with our evaluation.

Our thirteenth patient was an 85-year-old lady brought in by her son. She has some cognitive disorders but is able to live at home alone with help from her family. She's a reclusive very pleasant lady bothered by cellulitis (strep infection of the skin) in her left leg below her knee. It started with a simple abrasion of skin but then became contaminated. I saw her two days ago and started her on antibiotics. This was a follow-up visit and her condition was significantly improved.

Our next patient was the 92-year-old brother of the patient just described. They live next door to each other. He was brought in today by his daughter. He was also suffering from cellulitis but worse than his sister's. Just a few years ago, he was having cardiac problems which required three trips in the middle of the night to the cardiac cath lab. The next day after he left the lab, I drove by his house and saw him cutting timber. Something he loves to do. These folks are very strong determined folks.

My fifteenth patient was a mother of three small children. She has to work at a physically taxing job to help support her family. She came in today suffering from a strained right biceps muscle. The muscle was quite obviously swollen and tender. Our standard treatment for a problem like this is an injection of Toradol and /or Depomedrol, and advice about minimizing stress on the muscle. I asked her to return in a week. If she's not better, then we'll have to go into a deeper evaluation. I think she'll be much better in a week if she babies the muscle for awhile.

Our next patient was a lady I've been providing care to for fifty years. A week ago she came with recurring bronchitis, and the chest X-ray we did concerned me a little so we proceeded with a CT scan. She came in today to receive the results. Her scan was fine and she was very happy to hear that. People are always afraid of what the test results will be and they're always greatly relieved that things are not that bad. Her condition had improved. There was no shortness of breath or coughing.

My seventeenth patient was a forty-five year old gentleman that we see on a regular six months basis because he has multiple dark flat pigmented skin lesions. He likes to say that I should know his skin by now since I delivered him forty-five years ago. We take the time to evaluate these lesions on a regular basis to be sure that if one of them should become cancerous we'd catch it in an early stage, making it much less dangerous.

Our next patient was a lady I had only seen once before. She has suffered four painful bouts with a right-sided perirectal abscess. I had drained the abscess a few days ago and that did bring her relief. But in view of her history, I suggested she undergo surgery to remove the fistula as a way of possibly averting future abscesses. She agreed with my recommendation.

Our nineteenth patient came in with a cough and sore throat, simple symptoms of an upper respiratory infection. We'll treat him with antibiotics. He said he is also developing symptoms of arthritis so we'll schedule him for a workup to determine that.

My last patient today was a middle-aged lady who had come in a few days earlier with an infected blister on her heel. It looked suspicious to me so we had lab work done and she was here today to receive the results. The lab work showed an early lymphoma so we'll refer her for an oncology consultation. Otherwise, she seems in good health."

Of course, Jim has many other professional responsibilities besides seeing patients. "There's an awfully lot of paperwork to do with insurance companies and governmental agencies," he said. "and we get a great many phone calls every day. And it's not uncommon to have several drug reps stop in every day. I ended this day with preparing to give a legal deposition tomorrow in a law suit involving a three year old case of a lady I'd once seen and who had subsequently died while undergoing surgery by a colleague of mine. I don't get worked up over things like this because I know there is no way any attorney can understand the detailed medical information usually involved in these matters."

Unfortuately, Jim's account of his 'typical' day didn't include much about the myriad management tasks doctors are saddled with. I felt this chapter would be incomplete without this kind of information, but knew I couldn't go back to Jim after the fact and expect him to detail the procedural chores of that particular day. I was pretty much stuck, so I just put this chapter aside for a few months. Then one day I got lucky. My computer-savvy daughter was always on the lookout for internet medical articles. On this particular day, she sent me a summarized report, authored by Dr. Richard D. Baron, which had just appeared (in full) in the April, 2010 edition of the prestigious New England Journal of Medicine. The project tracked all office activities of five Philadelphia family doctors every day for twelve months. So now all I had to do was ask Jim if the numbers in this report were reflective of his own practice.

Sitting around his kitchen table with Jim and his daughter, Cindy, (who was usually present for our visits to act as interpreter because I have a hearing loss and Jim tends to speak softly) I read him the results of Baron's study. The five doctors in the report had "averaged seeing 18 patients a day. In addition, each one made 24 phone calls, wrote 12 prescriptions, read 20 lab reports, examined 14 consultation reports, reviewed 11 x-rays and other imagery reports and sent 17 e-mails or letters to specialists, labs, etc."

As I finished reading the report aloud, Cindy broke out laughing. Having seen no humor in the report, I asked her what was so funny. She said the numbers I read "weren't even close" to Jim's. Whereas those doctors had seen 18 patients a day, Jim said until just recently, he'd been seeing 50 patients a day. He thought that increasing the other numbers of reports, phone calls, etc by 150% would reflect his daily workload. He recalled coming into the office after missing one day for illness and there were 200 letters, reports, etc. piled up on his desk. "I always tried to get to those things immediately," Jim said, "because I never knew when one of them might have an immediate, important impact on a patient's treatment needs."

In the NEJM report quoted above, there was also a response from Dr. David Blumenthal, President Obama's national coordinator for health information technology, who felt that there was "a pathway toward escaping at least some of those 'invisible' burdens: the electronic health record combined with changes in workflow and payment." Jim's attitude is simpler and more direct: he's never found governmental bodies at any level to be of much help to him, he's never used computers, and he thinks there would be far fewer problems if more doctors would just be willing to work harder.

Chapter 27: Change

When Jim Reed began his medical practice in 1956, his focus was on one thing and one thing only: caring for patients. That's all he was trained to do. He wasn't trained to administer an office. He wasn't trained in the art of medicine. And he wasn't trained in community health. What happened was that with each passing year, Jim developed a deeper feeling of responsibility for the overall health of the community. In fact, in the end, he took more personal pride in that area of his career than in the individual life-saving actions that brought him most publicity. There's little question his feelings were influenced by the fact that this was his hometown.

Seniors have always been the most in need of Jim's services. Of course, that's just the nature of health care anywhere. Older people need more help. Not many years passed after Jim's arrival back home before he realized Farmington was in need of a nursing home. Other small towns in the area had them; in fact, Jim was serving patients in 14 such area homes. Not having one in his own hometown was a burden on his patients, on their families and on Jim, who was forced to spend a lot of time on the road. So, in 1976 he decided to take action.

The nursing home in Farmington

Jim called together five local men he felt might be willing to invest in a sound business proposition. After explaining his thinking, Jim almost guaranteed them that a nursing home would be filled quickly. They were convinced, and with their seed money, they secured a bank loan to start construction on the south side of Farmington. The facility was completed in 1978, and just as Jim had predicted, the 92-bed facility was quickly filled to capacity. While the nursing home constituted a huge upgrade in the continuum of care in Farmington, it obviously had the added benefit of cutting back on the time Jim had to spend on the road traveling to those 14 other facilities.

"There was one unexpected downside to the nursing home," Jim said with a laugh. "Every time I went out there, I was swarmed over by all the residents." As the nursing home industry continued to expand all over the country, small individual homes were purchased by big conglomerates. Jim advised the local investors to sell. They took his advice and were pleased with the return on their initial investments. Jim felt that the high quality of services did not suffer when the change in management occurred in 1983.

From 1956 to 1962, the only available transportation for getting seriously ill patients to the hospital was a hearse, courtesy (free) of Jim's old classmate, Tom Anderson of the Anderson Funeral Home. However, in the early 1960's, the State Department of Public Health decreed that funeral homes could no longer be involved with the living. Of course, the state bureaucracy, in all its wisdom, didn't say what communities were supposed to do if they had no other service.

As it turned out, the new state regulation may have been a blessing for Jim, considering the many close calls he and Tom Anderson had had. The consensus opinion in Farmington was that both of them tended to be a little on the reckless side in their motoring habits. Of course, Jim always claimed that whatever he did he had to do for his patients. For Tom, on the other hand, some folks thought he simply got a thrill from high-speed trips. Either way, time was frequently of the essence.

Jim got a phone call late one night at home that there'd been a bad mine accident involving the electrocution of a man. When Jim arrived on the scene, he learned the victim was Wes Settles, Jr., who'd been a couple years ahead of Jim in school. (I'd learned by now that because of Jim's deep connections to our hometown, he always had personal anecdotes to accompany his medical stories. His Settles sidebar was that when Jim was in the Navy and in San Francisco for a couple of days—waiting to ship out to the Philippines—he ran into Wes at a

Naval base show starring the Marx Brothers. In fact, that was the last time he'd seen Settles until that fateful night.)

Wes was in critical condition. He'd fallen over a massive, downed collection of live electrical wires. He was very badly burned and otherwise injured, in extreme pain, thrashing, incoherent. Jim and Tom Anderson managed to get Wes into the hearse and they took off for the hospital, with Jim following Tom at speeds near 100. Jim saw that Wes was out of control in the hearse; unfortunately, at just that moment, Jim ran over something that punctured a tire. Showing no concern for his own safety, Jim just kept driving 100 mph on his flat until he caught Tom. They tied Wes down with Jim's belt and sped off, but despite their efforts Wes tragically died just as they reached the hospital.

Tom and Jim were doing all they could, but Jim knew it wasn't enough. Jim heard about a doctor in nearby rural Tremont who'd recently helped the local fire department develop an ambulance service and rescue unit. So Jim gave him a call, picked his brain, then approached the all-volunteer Farmington fire department to discuss the possibilities. Jim promised he would go out with them on every emergency call and provide all the training and help they would need. He sold them. The five community-spirited men who donated hundreds of hours were John Higgs, Don Bridgestock, Ken Holmes, Hike Johnson and Joe Evans.

John Higgs served as a volunteer fireman in his hometown for 43 years.

The 100th anniversary of the Farmington Fire Dept., in 1995

Chief John Higgs said that what most impressed him about Jim was "his willingness to go back to the firehouse after every call and take the time to talk with all of us about the call; what we had done right and how we might improve." Higgs said somehow Jim was aware of old—but still functional—WWII field hospital equipment being stored in Canton and Jim arranged to have it donated to the Rescue Unit. Higgs also said that Jim and local druggist Bill Rodgers provided free medications and supplies to the unit.

After a few years, around 1970, the State Department of Public Health assumed all legal authority for Rescue Unit operations. Each volunteer received 250-300 hours of medical training at St. Francis Hospital in Peoria. Soon after, the volunteers spearheaded local efforts in raising $22,000 for the building of a rescue unit vehicle. The firemen themselves designed the unit, and it was so well received they were asked to take it around the state to show as a model to other departments. Higgs said he and his cohorts would've preferred to be supervised by Jim instead of the State District Office in Peoria. It just made sense to them (and Jim) because most of the rescue calls were on Jim's patients. Instead, the Unit had to call the Peoria office before they called Jim. Whenever there was a dispute over service, Chief Higgs said Jim always went to bat for them and he and his colleagues greatly appreciated it. To tangibly show their gratitude, at the 2004 citywide celebration honoring Jim's 50th anniversary as a doctor, the Rescue Unit presented him with a beautiful plaque. And six years later, in December, 2010, they surprised Jim at their annual dinner by making him a lifetime Honorary Fireman. They presented him with a fireman's pager, a fireman's badge and one of those small, round flashing warning lights for the top of his car. Jim said the last item would have been very helpful in the old days when he and Tom Anderson often exceeded speeds of 100 mph.

People don't like change. We especially don't like to see things that we're happy with change. We get mad when our grocery store changes around the location of items we buy on a regular basis. I get mad when my wife—a very good cook—changes the recipe of a dish I love. Sometimes though, change is best embraced. By the mid-seventies, Jim had developed serious concerns about the wisdom of continuing his relationship with Graham Hospital in Canton. He knew—and they certainly knew—that his huge patient load was responsible for at least half of all the business at the hospital. In view of that, plus the fact that he was held in high esteem by his colleagues, Jim felt that his recommendations for changes and updating of hospital policies and facilities warranted more attention than they received.

While Jim was understandably hesitant to detail specific personnel conflicts, he did say his greatest concern was the hospital's refusal to establish a heart catheterization unit. This advance in medicine—which Jim considers the most significant since he began practicing—was in widespread use in Peoria hospitals by the late 1960s. So by July, 1980, Jim was seriously pondering his options, and just as he was, there was a bolt from the blue.

Jim got a phone call from a Peoria Methodist Hospital administrator asking to meet. At the get together, the hospital representatives told Jim they were planning to open their very first satellite medical clinic, and they'd selected Hanna City (half way between Farmington and Peoria) as their site. They simply wanted to pay Jim the professional courtesy of making him aware of their plans. Jim thanked them, but just as they were leaving, Jim blurted, "Do you think you might be interested in buying a very large practice?" After Jim provided some detailed information, the Methodist staff indicated they certainly would be interested. Jim retained Peoria attorney David Higgs, a Farmington native (brother of Fire Chief John Higgs) and a childhood patient of Jim's. Jim said the meeting went very smoothly. So much so in fact that after about a half hour, the hospital CEO dismissed himself with the parting comment to his attorney to "give him anything he wants." In short order the deal was sealed.

Peoria Methodist Hospital

One early morning not long thereafter, Jim's wife stepped outdoors to retrieve the newspaper. Once back inside she opened the paper and let out a scream. There, splashed across the entire width of the Peoria Journal Star with a large headline was a long article about the purchase of Jim's practice by the hospital. Until that article, Jim's wife was the only person who knew there were negotiations going on. Now, suddenly, everyone knew. The news sent shockwaves through Farmington, Canton and all the surrounding area. His patients were understandably upset and worried. Since they were more than happy with the way things had been working, they weren't receptive to the idea of a major change. "I think the immediate reaction of most people," said Jim's close friend, Dick Westerby, "was that the term 'selling his practice' meant that Jim was retiring."

Since the heart of his practice was the strong doctor-patient relationships he'd established during twenty-four years of service, the phrase did sort of imply that he was "selling his patients" to Peoria Methodist. Of course, that was not close to being the case. A more accurate characterization would be that Jim and Peoria Methodist had formed a "merger." A fair, successful merger means both parties benefit. And that's what happened. Jim was able to free himself of the growing administrative tasks he'd never enjoyed. He also received what he considered to be fair compensation. Lastly, and most importantly, he received sincere assurances that Peoria Methodist would not attempt in any way to influence the type of medicine Jim chose to practice with his patients.

From the perspective of Peoria Methodist, they realized they'd be receiving a massive influx of in-patient service referrals from Jim. What most of his patients didn't realize at the time was that Jim was very confident the new changes would actually result in an improved level of care and service for them. First of all, he knew his being freed of office administrative concerns would leave more time for his patients. And secondly, the growing array of high quality medical specialty services in Peoria would now be more available to his patients. As an example, Jim proceeded to form a close working relationship with a cardiologist he considered to be highly skilled, Dr. Thanad Shay—and that relationship benefited all of Jim's heart patients.

While it's commonplace now for hospitals in larger cities like Peoria, Champaign and Springfield to own and operate out-patient clinic offices in smaller towns, that was not the case in 1980. In fact, when Peoria Methodist Medical Center purchased Jim's practice in 1980, it was first time they'd done such a thing. Now, 30 years later, they own and operate 27 such clinics. That, together with their on-campus expansions, has made them into the 3rd largest employer in the city, with a staff of over 3,000.

Jim was very pleased with all the conditions of his contract. In addition to the nearly one million dollars the hospital paid Jim for his practice and medical office building, Jim was very satisfied with his yearly salary—which was not and never has been based on how many patients he sees each day. In addition, Jim retained a high degree of autonomy, never having a supervisor in the sense that most employees do. For example, he's never received a formal job performance evaluation.

Jim's staff pose at an office open house celebrating his 70th birthday party in 1997. Left to right : Tina Holmes, Jim, Ruth Ann Doubet, Betsy Kimbrell, Lynn Stewart, Deb Bozsoki, Margaret Morey and Karen Peterson

In the fall of 1980, when the merger became official, all of the staff in Jim's office suddenly became employees of the Peoria Methodist Hospital. And it's fair to say that their initial reaction was about the same as that of Jim's patients: namely, they weren't too crazy about it. As one of them put it bluntly, "On the day Peoria Methodist Hospital took over we went from being a purely medical service to becoming a business." To illustrate her point, she added that, "Just a few years earlier the patient office call fee was $7.00. In 1980, it shot up to $34." Another staffer: "Before 1980, it was more like a family atmosphere around here. Dr. Reed used to take the whole staff out for a long lunch whenever someone had a birthday. We'd even invite Uncle Phil (Jim's brother). But all of that changed after 1980." Their fears about change and the future of profit-driven (if not profit-obsessed) health care systems were well founded.

In his 1996 book, "The Lost Art of Healing," Dr. Bernard Lown, a renowned cardiologist and Professor at the Harvard School of Public Health, described the typical bureaucratic health care system:

> "The focus of the system, as it has become an industrial behemoth, has shifted from attending the sick to guarding the economic bottom line, putting itself on a collision course with professional doctoring......The foremost objective of the system is cost containment, and to accomplish this, hospitals create vast bureaucracies of economic managers, accountants and lawyers, now grown more numerous than the health care providers. Efficiency now becomes the byword dictating homogenization in dealing with any and all patient problems.... standard clinical guidelines and computer-driven algorithms define automatic courses of action for specified diagnostic categories....In this environment, doctors increasingly become technicians leashed to assembly lines, the aim of which is to maximize patient throughput.... The medical care system will not be cured until the patient once again becomes central to the doctor's agenda."

In spite of that accurate portrayal of the health care delivery systems over the past twenty years—and while not denying the sincere concerns of his staff in 1980—Jim Reed's focus after 1980 remained the same as the day he graduated from med school: providing quality care to everyone who sought his help. And Peoria Methodist knew better than to mess with a good thing. Said Jim in 2008, "No one on the staff of the Methodist Medical Center has ever interfered in any way with my practice of medicine. Not once in twenty-eight years."

Of course, in big bureaucracies there is, almost without fail, a tendency for leadership to lose touch with what's happening on the front lines of their operations. When that occurs, bad planning and poor decision-making results. Unfortunately, after 30 years that's what happened in the relationship between Jim Reed and Peoria Methodist Hospital. What the hospital upper level managers apparently never really understood was the deep loyalty and admiration that thousands of patients felt toward Jim Reed, many for as long as half a century. Methodist's eventual mistake was understandable, though, given that they'd never seen or experienced anything close to that phenomenon. But first a bit more background.

In September, 2004, an emotional city-wide Farmington celebration in the Dr. James M. Reed City Park was planned by the hospital for the dual purpose of recognizing Jim's 50th year in medicine, and also re-naming the clinic building in his honor. To those people who didn't know Jim well—and unfortunately that included the administrators of Methodist Hospital—the assumption was that Jim Reed would soon be retiring. (After all, he was 77 and not in great health.) But those who knew Jim well knew better, and when he stepped up to the microphone to make his comments, he made it quite clear that he was not retiring. That was six years ago.

So, at the beginning of a new decade, in February of 2010, Methodist management made what, frankly, must be termed a major public relations blunder. On February 17, 2010, they placed a press release—in the form of a letter to patients from their CEO—in the Farmington Shopper, the local weekly paper. In it, they stated that as of March 1, 2010, they would "begin the transition of Dr. Reed from full time to part time…in anticipation of his full retirement from the Methodist Medical Group in September, 2010."

Their massive mistake was that they'd failed to discuss any of the content of their press release with Jim before they issued it. Seriously. So not only was Jim shocked and dismayed when the press release appeared, but so were his patients. His office phone lines were swamped with distraught callers, and staff were bombarded with questions by patients wherever they went in town. To calm the devoted patients, Jim felt he had no choice except to issue an immediate rebuttal. So, in the next edition of the same paper, one week later, he issued his own press release, headlined "Dr. Reed is Not Retiring."

Following Jim's action, Peoria Methodist called an emergency staff meeting to confer about their PR disaster. They met quickly with Jim and apologized for what had happened. Gentleman as usual, Jim accepted their apology and left the meeting on cordial terms.

Jim's considered response to all the hullabaloo was that when his partnership with Methodist concluded in September, 2010, he'd return to a part-time solo practice in the offices connected to his home. Why would Jim keep working in his eighties? That's a question I asked myself repeatedly when I began this project. Over and over, in visiting with his 50-year patients, I'd ask them what changes they'd noticed in Jim over the decades. Invariably, their answers always seemed to be two words: "not much." "He's slowed down a little," they'd add, "but we've all done that."

Granted, his physical condition is a long way from that of decades ago when he never thought twice about throwing himself in harm's way: lifting heavy patients, driving dangerously, scaling huge mine shovels and leaping farm fences. Age put a halt to those headstrong actions. But, there are two key qualities that age has not yet stolen from Jim. One is his ability to think clearly, diagnosing accurately and prescribing appropriate treatment. And the other trait he still has inside him—one unfortunately missing in far too many younger physicians—is the fire in his belly. The unusual depth of his concern and commitment to his patients has remained unchanged. I offer this one example as evidence.

Jim saw his last patient in his Farmington practice in September, 2010. From then until early 2011, when he opened his small, part-time practice in Trivoli, he had no ethical or legal responsibility for any patients. In June, 2011, Jim's daughter Cynthia ran into Marilyn Bowhay in the grocery store in Farmington. (You'll recall we met the Bowhays earlier in the book. They had doctored with Jim for over 50 years, but, like most of his patients, as of October, 2010, they had a new family physician). Anyway, at the store Marilyn told Cindy she'd recently undergone surgery. It wasn't major or life-threatening ... but it was still surgery. When Cindy returned home, she told Jim of her encounter. He misunderstood, thinking Cindy had said Marilyn was contemplating surgery. So Jim immediately picked up the phone and called Marilyn to impress upon her medication regimen could react negatively with the surgery. This was at least twelve months since he had last seen her and nine months since she was officially his patient. In relating this story to me, Marilyn's reaction says it all: "That's just like Doc isn't it?"

Part VIII

Six Generations, Six Times

"We all belong to the same big family and have the same smell."

--Carl Sandberg
1878-1967
Three-time Pulitzer Prize winner for Literature

Chapter 28: Harding

Jim Reed has accomplished some hard-to-believe feats during his long career (for starters, eight years after seeing his first patient in 1956, he had a caseload of 16,000). Stories of his heroic actions—like amputating a farmer's arm using only a borrowed pocket knife, or saving a trapped miner's life—are locally legendary. His 24-7 availability and total dedication to his patients are well known. Too, his roughly one million patient visits are likely unequalled. But incredible as those accomplishments seem, for me they pale in comparison to one other: there are six families living in the Farmington area who've had the mind-boggling total of six generations in their families cared for by Jim Reed!

This nearly impossible situation becomes understandable only when you begin to think about it in detail, with as many specifics as possible. There are five conditions necessary for this six-generation phenomenon to happen:

- A doctor has to settle into his practice at the beginning of his career.
- Once arrived, the doctor has to stay for a very, very long time
- The first person treated in the first generation—or sixth, looking back—has to have been old when the young doctor started his practice.
- At least one member in each of the six generations had to remain in the area.
- Six generations had to decide to retain their doctor's services.

If just one of those five conditions ever went unmet, the six-generation link was broken. Very few doctors have ever had the privilege of caring for one extended family for six generations. Jim Reed has done it six times. There is nothing he's ever done in his illustrious career that's given him more professional and personal satisfaction than this. That's reason enough to talk with some members of this very exclusive "six generation club." When they describe their experiences with, and feelings about Jim Reed, the phrase 'doctor-patient relationship' comes alive and takes on a whole new meaning.

**Betty Harding, a classmate of Jim's,
poses for her 1945 yearbook photo.**

Betty Harding Tolf is 82 now. If all of Jim Reed's patients were sturdy like Betty, he would've spent a lot more time lazing at horse barns during the last half century. The medical genes that have grown and ripened on the Harding family tree for over a hundred years are as good as any Jim Reed has ever seen. When Betty's grandfather, A. J. Harding was born in 1864, the life expectancy was 40. If A.J. had been average, he would have died in 1904. But he wasn't average—not by a long shot. He lived to be 97, 142% longer than average. When A.J.'s son, Elwyn, was born in 1905, his life expectancy was 50. If he'd cooperated with the statistics, his body would've conked out in 1955. But it didn't. He also lived to be 97, nearly 100% above average. Point is, don't bet the farm against Betty Harding Tolf living to be a hundred. (In fact, maybe it was farming that kept them going.)

**Four generations of Hardings in 1957. Left to right:
Theodore, A.J., Bradley and Elwyn**

Some of the best farmland in the world is found around the Trivoli area. The Harding family bought a lot of it, a long time ago. "We got it for $25.00 an acre," 93-year-old A.J. Harding told Jim Reed back in 1957. "No one else wanted it because it didn't have trees or streams on it." Mr. Harding was born while the Civil War was still raging, in 1864, in an Illinois log cabin in an area called Texas, about two miles northeast of Trivoli. A.J.'s son, Elwyn, was born in Trivoli in 1905, and went into farming with his father. "Both my father and grandfather were married to farming," said Betty, the family historian. She sat at the kitchen table at her Trivoli home, just a couple of blocks south of Jim Reed's house. She stared out her kitchen window toward the west at a plain home 75 yards across an open field. "I was born in that home 81 years ago," said Betty. "It's been added on to, but I liked it better the way it was before. I remember the day when I was eight," she continued. "I was just standing out in that field when suddenly young Dr. Plummer—his father was also Dr. Plumer—crashed is airplane right in front of my eyes. He died instantly."

Betty Harding first met Jim Reed when they both entered Farmington High School in 1941. Since she was a farm girl, that was her first year in the Farmington school system. "I never got to know Jim very well in school," said Betty. "I remember thinking that maybe he didn't like girls very much." Having just interviewed a couple of Jim's childhood friends, I assured Betty that adolescent Jim had a normal amount of interest in girls. "I knew that he was working at the bakery," she added, "and probably didn't have much free time. I still have a clear memory of one situation," Betty went on. "Jim and I were in the same history class our senior year. Of course by then, everyone in the school knew Jim was the smartest kid in our class. I was such a flighty thing but I thought, 'By golly, I'm going to get as good as grade as Jim.' By sheer nose to the grindstone, I did get the same grade. I was so glad the class was not chemistry or physics. Life isn't fair to give more brains to some people. Of course, as my doctor, I'm glad he's got 'em." (Betty was selected to speak at the 2006 ceremonies naming the Farmington Methodist Medical office building in Jim's honor.)

I was taken aback when Jim told me neither A.J. Harding or his son, Elwyn, had ever suffered from any serious illnesses—between them they'd lived for nearly two centuries, after all. Jim added that Betty was following in their indestructible footsteps. In fact, looking at each of the half dozen families Jim had doctored for six generations, this family seems to have been the healthiest of all.

There are a thousand and one things that can go wrong with the human body. Most of them are the common garden-variety illnesses; things like colds, the flu, headaches, arthritis and backaches. A.J. Harding and his son, Elwyn didn't have time for problems like that. They led hard lives, farming before the age of all the machinery. If they didn't do the work— every day—it didn't get done. They didn't have time to be sick.

In many ways, Jim Reed is sort of 'old school.' His general approach is to leave them alone if they're doing well. That seems to suit his patients just fine, especially his senior patients. He doesn't believe in wasting their time, or his. Most of all, he doesn't like them incurring any unnecessary medical costs.

Betty has never felt the need to avail herself of the latest trends in the ever-changing world of modern medicine. She isn't much interested in the newest diagnostic testing machines, and she has little interest in learning about her own DNA genetic map. She thinks that if she did need any of those services, her doctor would tell her so. She's right. He would. The fact is, Jim Reed agrees with Betty.

Nationally, the medical profession generally recommends a yearly physical exam for senior citizens. Jim doesn't believe in that. "There are really only three reasons for a patient to see me," he explained. "One is if they are experiencing a current problem. Another is if they have a serious ongoing problem like heart disease that needs to be checked. And the third one is if they have a family history of a serious disease."

Betty and Bob Tolf had a daughter, Terrie, born in 1953. At that time, the family was doctoring with Clinton McKnight because Betty said, "he just lived two blocks away, in the house where Jim now lives." When Dr. McKnight decided in late 1956 to return to his roots in southern Illinois, the Tolf's began seeing Jim, who moved into Dr. McKnight's former home in January, 1957.

Terrie has continued the Harding tradition of good health, never having much reason to see Jim. The fourth generation of the family to be treated by Jim, Terrie grew up and married Jerry Loeuprecht. They had a daughter, Jenny, who's now thirty-one. Of course, she became the fifth generation to be cared for by Jim. Years later, after Jenny married Jerry Wheeler, their two girls, Kloey and Faith, became the sixth and final generation with Jim.

Those two little girls have a long history of healthy relatives. With all the advances sure to come in the future, they should have no problem living to be one hundred. Faith's one-hundredth birthday will be in the year 2105. It's also entirely possible that at that time, centenarian Faith will have some great, great grandchildren. So, in 2105, she can tell them that the span of time between the birth of the first Harding treated by Jim Reed and Faith's own 100th birthday, was 241 years! Furthermore, she can say to them, "Dr. Reed treated your great, great, great, great, great, great, great grandfather!"

When I dropped that story onto Jim, it was the only time during our work on this book that he was struck speechless.

Chapter 29: Murphy

LaVonne Murphy Welker, 18 and her husband, Harold "Pud" Welker, 20 in 1945

LaVonne Welker, 80, holds her twin great grandchildren, Avery, on the left, and Mylee

I'd never met Mrs. Lavonne Murphy Welker before today. The only thing I knew about her was that she was one of the six generations in her family treated by Jim. As I pulled into the driveway of her home, just a few houses west of the Alexander Lumber Yard in Farmington, it looked like she'd probably led a tougher life than the other folks I'd talked with. The outside of her tiny home was badly in need of repairs and looked like a strong wind might topple it.

There was a hand-lettered sign on the dilapidated front door telling visitors to come around to the side door. That door led directly into her kitchen, where I was greeted warmly by Mrs. Welker and invited to sit at her kitchen table. Mrs. Welker shocked and surprised me with the most humorous comment about Jim that I would hear from anyone.

"I started first grade with your brother," she said, "and he was an ornery little sh*t!" I broke out laughing. "I don't mean that he was mean or anything, just ornery," she continued. "I remember in the first grade

(75 years ago) there was a cute little girl with long blond braids and your brother and Tommy Anderson used to dip her braids in their ink wells."

"I remember your mother too," Mrs. Welker went on. "She was so nice. She loved those little kids." She was talking about the kids in our mom's day care group. "She used to bring them over to our garage (her parents owned Murphy's Bonded Service Station) for a soda pop. They were always so well behaved. I knew your dad too. He was smart. I went gambling with him once in Springfield."

Mrs. Welker is eighty-three now. She dropped out of high school in 1941 at age fourteen to go to work in her parents' garage at the corner of N. Main and Court Street, just a block and a half from the Reeds home (after 1950) on North West Street. In addition to their garage, the Murphys had a small lunchroom called Mary's, in their home, right next door to the garage. Lavonne said her mother's BBQ sandwiches were famous. Her folks started what eventually became Kersh's Restaurant, one of the few remaining businesses from that time. The building that housed Murphy's Service Station is still standing but it's vacant, run down and an eyesore. Any old building like that only serves as a sad reminder to locals of what Farmington was like decades ago. (That's why, when I left Mrs. Welker's today and drove by our old Reed family home at 154 North West Street, I was happy to see that it's been kept in good repair.)

Mrs. Welker said her home is 105 years old and "my grandparents, Clark and Hattie Murphy, raised ten kids in this little place." She herself was one of four children of Arnold and Mary Baxter Murphy. Tragically, her three brothers all died in infancy. She recounted that Jim cared for both her grandparents and her parents.

Mrs. Welker and her husband, Harold "Pud" Welker, had four sons—Bill, Tom, Mike and Evan—and one girl, Brenda. Pud passed away in 1976. She said he'd survived six heart attacks, then the seventh one finally killed him. She added that Jim had once offered Pud a job at his horse farm but Pud had felt he wasn't physically up to it. She said he did sometimes do odd jobs on farms, was on the police force for a time and was a cemetery sexton. Until she became too disabled to hold a job, Lavonne Murphy Welker had worked all her life, as a bartender and waitress at the Moose Club, at the American Legion and at Sonny's Place, owned by our brother. "Sonny was a great guy, but he was watching over me too closely, making me nervous. So I talked to his wife Donna about it and she made him stop it."

Lavonne was the third generation in the Murphy family to be cared for by Jim. Her son Mike became the fourth generation. He and his wife, Maxine, had a daughter, Ramona, who became the fifth generation. When

Ramona married, she had a son, James McFarland, who was the sixth generation. It's very unlikely that any doctor in American history has ever cared for seven generations of one family; when I jokingly asked Jim if there wasn't something he could do to encourage the young James McFarland, now 17, to marry and become a father, he had a good laugh.

In her straightforward manner, Lavonne began to talk about her medical problems. For many years, she's been plagued by the three most serious problems facing all Americans: diabetes, heart disease and cancer. She's had two heart attacks, the last in 2006. Her heart condition has necessitated the insertion of seven stents, three in her heart and two in each leg. She suffered from cancer of the bladder which was successfully operated on by Dr. Frinice in Canton. "I didn't sleep last night at all," she said. "I watched TV most of the night. I have trouble moving around. It's hell to get old but it's something we all gotta do." In spite of daily struggles with serious health conditions, Mrs. Welker has managed to surpass by several years the average life expectancy of her peers.

"I wouldn't be here at all if Jim hadn't taken care of me," Mrs. Welker continued. "He's one in a million." I knew she must have seen a lot of specialists over the years, so I asked her what the difference was between them and Jim. She reacted quickly, and loudly. "Oh hell, all they care about is making money! They don't care about you. When I go to see your brother he gets up out of his chair, greets me and shakes my hand and asks about me." "When he sees you does he have to look at your record?" "Oh No," she shouted back, "he knows it all without looking at it." Later, when I related this to Jim, he smiled and said he might have to look at a record to check on a patient's medications.

"I saw your brother on the first day he opened his office in 1956," Mrs. Welker told me. "His office was where Dr. Dimmitt used to be." I tried to correct her, telling her Jim's office was above the post office, (Dr. Dimmitt's office was one block east, above Jackson's Drug Store) but she wouldn't have any of that. "I was his second patient. When his receptionist took his first patient back, she (the receptionist) tripped over the phone chord and fell down." When I asked Jim about this, he laughed and said he wouldn't know because "I never go into the reception area. I don't think I've been in the waiting room more than a couple of times in the past thirty years."

Lavonne noticed my attention was drawn to the shoebox of pharmaceuticals, on her kitchen table, right in front of me. So she kindly offered a tour. At 83, Lavonne Welker is a poster child (poster elder?) for the miracles of modern medications. Here in front of me was a shoebox full of medicines, none of which were available to Jim Reed when he first set up shop here in 1956. While the drug companies have rightly come under a barrage of criticism during the past few years for such practices as blocking generic medications and hiding negative research results, there can be no question that the development of disease-specific medications over the past 50 years has been one of the greatest advances in the field of medicine. (And the most profitable, of course.) Those meds doubtless played a major role in Mrs. Welker's living two decades longer than the average woman born in 1927.

Glancing across Mrs. Welker's kitchen, I noticed three small loaves of homemade bread. "I make pies too," she said. "Your brother's favorite is chocolate. Sometimes he cuts into it as soon as I get it to the office. His wife's favorite is pecan. She's so sweet. She always calls and thanks me." Then Lavonne added the kicker. "I've kept all the newspaper clippings about your brother," she said, "but I don't know where they are."

Leaving Mrs. Welker's tiny home and her simple existence, it was impossible not to admire her upbeat attitude in the face of her serious medical condition. She's led a tough life. And she's a fighter. Maybe she learned it from her father. (She said her second grade teacher, Miss Palin, used to smack her left hand hard with a ruler to stop her from printing with her left hand. Her father saw her bruised hand, went to school and told Miss Palin that if she ever touched his daughter again, he'd throw her out the window!)

Lavonne has determination and hope. There is no one still alive in Farmington who has known Jim longer than Mrs. Welker: 75 years. He's doctored her for 53 of them. It's a rare thing, almost impossible to fathom. One has to wonder how many other Mrs. Welkers have been cared for by Jim for the past fifty years.

No one can ever know the exact depth and strength of the bonds between people like Mrs. Welker and Jim Reed. But do not think they are less than deeply personal. To several thousand folks in this Spoon River country, Jim Reed has been a "foul-weather friend," always showing up when times are bad. Jim's dedication, his know-how, his humility, his selflessness and his hometown roots are the reasons why he is beloved by people like Lavonne Welker.

Chapter 30: Ryer

There are two medical experiences you never forget. One is a serious illness of your child, and the other is the death of your beloved. You might forget some of the specific dates and details, but you don't forget the emotional impact. Kathy Garlish Donath, 47, has lived through both types of medical crises, and Jim Reed was there to help her, just as he has been there for her throughout her life, as well as five other generations of her family.

From 1956 to 1980, patients didn't schedule appointments to see Jim. It was first come, first served—which generally meant it was SRO. "When I was just a kid," said Kathy, "my brother and I learned patience and respect at Dr. Reed's office. Our parents told us to give up our seats every time someone older came in. The other thing I remember," she went on, "was having butterflies in my stomach while waiting to hear if doctor said I needed a shot. Years later I saw the same look of apprehension on my daughter's faces whenever doctor saw them for a sore throat or the like."

In 1979, when Kathy was 18, she married Bob Moke. Unbeknownst to anyone, Bob had been carrying around a deadly brain tumor since childhood. In his early twenties, he began having bouts of dizziness, accompanied by pain in his left ear. After awhile he sought help from an area doctor, who unfortunately failed to diagnose his problem. Seeking an answer, he arrived at Jim's office. Jim immediately suspected something serious and put Bob in the hospital for testing, where the tumor was confirmed.

Kathy was only 23 when she got the call from Jim asking her and Bob to come to his office. Jim also asked Kathy to bring her parents with her. "I've committed to memory the discussion with Dr. Reed," Kathy said. "He was kind and candid about what we were facing." The neurosurgery, performed by Dr. Patrick Elwood, was successful. But five years later, Bob began experiencing the same symptoms again. Tragically, the cancer had spread widely. There was nothing that could be done. Bob succumbed in 1992, when he was only 31. Kathy was also 31 and their two girls, Karrissa and Stefanie were eleven and eight.

L to R, Kathy Donath, her daughter, Stefanie Moke, and Eric Donath

Stefanie and her maternal grand-parents, Jan and Hank Garlish, in Stefanie's hospital room, Oct., 1999

The family eventually recovered from their horrible loss; Kathy got lucky and met another great guy named Eric Donath. They married and life was good—until a horrible day in 1999 when Stefanie, then 15, was involved in a life-threatening car accident leaving her in a coma. Kathy said the night it happened, the neurosurgeon told her that only 25 out of 100 patients survived an accident like Stefanie's, and of those 25, only four would make a complete recovery. She added that four days later, "Dr. Reed told me he couldn't predict the outcome." Stefanie remained totally unresponsive for nine anguish-filled days. Then, on the tenth night, she raised one finger at the request of a nurse. The family was thrilled. Four days later she opened her eyes for the first time. During the next few days, she slowly regained all her senses. Then she began two weeks of intensive physical, occupational, speech and cognitive therapy. "The neurosurgeon marveled at her recovery," Kathy said, "calling it divine intervention. I could see the relief in Dr. Reed's face when I broke the wonderful news to him." After a month, Stefanie returned home.

Divine intervention or not, once home, Stefanie's recovery was long and very tough. As a result of her trauma, she was as an infant in most ways, learning to walk, talk and feed herself all over again. Her therapies continued on an outpatient basis for six months and she also had a home tutor for five months. Stefanie's determination, family support and long rehab paid off. She eventually experienced a full recovery and her mother doesn't miss a day without giving thanks.

Kathy wanted to end her recounting Stefanie's hellish year of life on a humorous note, so she talked about one of her daughter's fondest wishes to return to socializing with her friends. When she turned eighteen, Stephanie pressured her mother to ask Dr. Reed if she could have a beer once in awhile with her friends. Her mother refused to mediate, but told her if she wanted to talk to Doctor about it, she could. So together, they went to see Jim and "Stefanie spoke right up," said Kathy. "I could see it was all Doctor could do to keep from laughing, and Stefanie was so thrilled when doctor told her he guessed it would be okay for her to have a beer once in awhile." Stefanie, now a strikingly pretty young lady, is due to graduate from Bradley University and become a teacher.

Kathy Donath's paternal great grandparents, Rosella Ingold Ryer and Walter Ryer, were the first of six generations to be cared for by Jim. Rosella was born in 1898 in Deer Creek, a small town just east of Peoria, while Walter (1896) was born in Farmington in a home on South Main, near the old C, B and Q railroad tracks. Like nearly all of Jim's long-term families, the Ingold, Ryer, Garlish clan had many connections to the Reeds.

Rosella's father, Theodore Ingold, owned a gas station across from Chapman School. Our brother Cotton Reed worked at the gas station for several years before entering WWII. Rosella's brother, also named Theodore but always called "Thede," was a successful farmer and a huge Cardinal baseball fan. I knew him when I was a kid and was in awe of him because he was the only person I knew who'd visited a big league spring training camp. The aforementioned family historian (and Kathy's mother) Janice Manual Garlish, is the younger sister of Marilyn Manual, a high school classmate of mine. Janice's aunt is Virginia Manual Thomas, who actually worked for Jim Reed, and whose husband Bill was one of Jim's closest childhood friends. Finally, Kathy's grandson, 8-year-old Owen Fresia, had a paternal great, great uncle, Jim Fresia, who was a former Mayor of Farmington and a sort of second father figure for my brother Harp and me. (Harp and I spent many hours in a clubhouse at the back of Fresia's Clothing Store.) To top off all the Reed connections, Kathy Donath lives in a home she and her husband bought from Donna Reed, the widow of our brother Sonny. (No, not that Donna Reed.)

Walter and Rosella Ryer were cared for by Jim until their deaths in 1975 and 1988, respectively. The Ryers had three daughters, one of whom, Mildred, married Elman Garlish, a local farmer. Mildred and Elman had three sons: Garry, Hank and Steve.

"I'll never forget when I was a young guy," said Steve, who's now 65 and living in Arizona, "going into Dr. Reed's on a regular basis for allergy shots. His nurse, Barbara Hedden, always saw to it that I didn't have to wait. That was very important because there were more social gatherings in there than at the Moose Club. This one muggy day," Steve went on, "Barbara stepped out from the back and motioned for me to come on back.

As she was walking in front of me, she blandly asked how I was. I replied that I would be better if it weren't for the damp weather. She reacted like she'd been shot! She turned around and looked at me with astonishment, thinking that I had said 'damn' weather. Nice young men didn't say those things at that time."

"On a more serious note," Steve continued, "when I was in my early twenties, my right eye starting bulging and I was having serious headaches. I allowed this to go on for about a year, for I was afraid it was cancer and didn't want to know. At one point, I had a cold or the flu and went to see Dr. Reed. He took one look at me and asked me who I was seeing about my eye. When I told him no one, he kind of 'let me have it.' He put me in the hospital that day for tests, and in short order I was moved to Peoria for neurosurgery from Dr. Elwood. He found a mucous sac that had broken through the sinus and was growing down the base of my brain. Had Dr. Reed not taken quick action, the sac might have burst and death would have been imminent. How do you properly thank someone for saving your life?"

"When I was young," Steve added, "I had asthma so bad that Dr. Reed recommended I move to Arizona. I did that in 1969 and I was greatly helped. But that meant my sons could never go to Dr. Reed. I wish he had been around to treat their bumps, bruises and broken bones. Farmington is very lucky to have had hometown doctors like Dr. Dimmitt, Dr. Jacobs and Dr. Reed. The day that Dr. Jacobs died in a car accident is one that will never be forgotten by those of us who knew him." Steve's mother, Mildred Garlish, now 89, recalled taking Steve to see Dr. Reed in 1956 when they were the only ones in his office. In retrospect, that may have been the one time in 54 years when Jim's office was that empty! [ed.note: it saddens me to report that Steve Garlish passed away in September, 2009.]

Hank Garlish and Janice Manuel were both born in the area, married in 1960, and lived here all their lives. Janice is 65 now, Hank's 68, and Jim Reed has been their doctor more than 50 years. They recall fondly his willingness to come out to their home to care for their two infants. They recall, too, Jim's liberal use of the gas pedal (Hank remembers "doctor driving REAL fast in reverse out of our driveway"). Janice remembers Jim opening his Trivoli in-home office after hours to see them, and "doctor's youngest boy coming into the office in his pajamas to check things out."

They especially remember the care Jim provided to their aging parents. Janice Manuel's mother suffered from arthritis-related ailments and osteoporosis. Janice remembers the time her mother was too ill to drive somewhere and Jim drove her himself. They haven't forgotten how helpful Jim was when the difficult time came to make nursing home plans for their parents. Janice and Hank have so many warm memories, as does their daughter Kathy, and Kathy's own daughter, Stefanie. With a little luck, Walt and Rosella Ryer's great, great, great grandson, Owen Fresia, will also have memories of Jim Reed. Maybe he'll even echo the wonderful words of his great grandmother, Janice Garlish: "Dr. Reed has taken care of each one of us as if we were his only patient." There aren't any higher compliments a family doctor can earn than that one.

Chapter 31: Riccioni

Bob Riccioni

Some of the younger folks around Farmington probably don't know who Bob Riccioni is. But if they're older, they know. Because Bob is one of the two most talented musicians ever to grow up in Farmington. (You've already met the other, trumpeter Jim Perelli.)

"I started playing the accordion when I was about six," Bob said. "I never took lessons. My dad taught me, just like his dad had taught him. It was almost like it was the national instrument of Italy." If you believe that some people are just born 'naturals,' then Bob was one of those. "I could read music, but I didn't really need to since I could play a song if I heard it once or twice," he said matter-of-factly.

Bob advanced so quickly with his squeezebox skill that when he was only 14, he won the Chicago Musicland Contest before a Soldier's Field crowd of 50,000. He entered the Korean War shortly after graduating from high school in 1952, and during Army boot camp training at Ft. Leonard Wood in Missouri, he was chosen to represent the base on the nationally televised Arlene Francis show, "Talent Patrol." After his discharge from the service, in addition to working for the Matthew's Music Co. in Peoria, Bob had three regular gigs on local radio and TV. (That's when I saw him in an unbelievable solo performance of " The Flight of the Bumble Bee.") While working in Peoria, Bob got a lucrative job offer from the Lowery Organ Co. in Chicago. "But I turned it down," he said, "because my wife and I had spent all our life in Farmington and we decided we didn't want to leave." (Without prompting, he added he never regretted that decision.)

Bob's grandparents, Joe and Elvira Riccioni, were born in the town of Gaggio Montano, Italy in the early 1880's. They became the first of six Riccioni generations cared for by Jim Reed. They were under Jim's ministrations for twenty years before they both passed away in the 1970's. Joe had been a coal miner, and like many others, he and Elvira came to the Farmington area from the mines of Pennsylvania. Joe and Elvira had a son, Hugo, born in 1913 in Farmington. He grew up, became a coal miner as well, and married Jessie Benns from nearby St. David. They were doctored by Jim for 45 years before they passed away in the 1990's. Hugo was eighty and Jessie lived to be eighty-four.

Hugo and Jessie had one child, Bob, born in 1933. He was a classmate of our brother Sonny for his first eight grades, but when Bob was 14, he had an emergency appendectomy and was forced to miss an entire year of school—making him a classmate of our brother Harp. Bob began dating a local girl, Jean Balagna and they were eventually married in 1954. Their only child, Karen, was born in 1956, the same year Jim Reed came to town. The entire Riccioni clan was cared for by Dr. Victor Williams before he died in a 1954 car accident. So, when Jim Reed came to town, he effectively inherited four generations of Riccionis.

One thing parents never forget is the first time their infant is really sick. When Karen was only two, her parents learned about Jim Reed's dedication. Little Karen awoke one day with early symptoms of a cold. Jean and Bob watched her closely that day, hoping to see improvement, but it didn't happen. Throughout the second day, her symptoms began to worsen, with congestion and coughing. Now her parents were quite concerned; but by that time it was too late in the day to take her into Jim's office. As the night progressed, Karen began having trouble breathing. In a panic, her parents called Jim at home. He came immediately.

Shortly after his arrival and a brief exam of Karen, Jim knew the villain was an upper respiratory illness. Karen was a perfect example of Jim's aggressive approach to the treatment of URIs discussed in the chapter, "The Clinician." He quickly started Karen on a course of antibiotics. After that he 'treated' the anxious parents by assuring them Karen would be fine in short order, and would be under his close supervision. More calming to the parents than anything else may have been the quick response from Jim. "He came right out to our home," Bob said, "in the middle of the night. How many doctors do you know who would do that? And he did it several times. He did it for me when I was real sick," he added.

Karen was fortunate to get through childhood without enduring any other significant health problems. But like most kids, she hated going for checkups. "I used to hide under Dr. Reed's examining table and they would have to drag me out." Who'd have guessed she'd grow up to work for Jim for over 30 years—and counting. After graduating from high school in 1974, Karen worked for a few months in the office of the strip mines. "But I didn't like anything about the place," she said, "so I quit and went to nursing school. I started with Dr. Reed in 1976 and been there ever since." One visit with Karen showed her to be friendly, straightforward, humorous and happy in her work.

"I wouldn't work in a hospital," she said. "I don't care for that kind of an environment. Dr. Reed and the other doctors here show us a lot of respect. Everything here is more personal," she added. "Doctor used to take us all out for a long lunch whenever one of us had a birthday. 'Uncle Phil' [Jim's brother] always joined us. But we had to stop the birthday parties when Doctor sold his practice to Methodist Hospital [1980]. "It helps a lot," Karen went on, "that we know all our patients so well. And while we take our work very seriously, we also know it's important to keep the atmosphere a little loose too. We've always dressed up at Halloween." Then I asked her about a roller skating story her parents had obliquely mentioned, and she started laughing.

"Hon"—she's the type who calls you Hon ten minutes after she meets you—"Doctor used to open an examining room door and holler 'GIRLS!,' which meant he wanted us fast, often to give a shot. So one day I called my mom and asked her if she still had my old roller skates. She did so I asked her to bring them down to me at the office. I also had one of those giant water guns that was sort of shaped like a syringe. Well, the next time Doctor hollered out, I came skating down the hallway carrying that huge gun that looked like a syringe. Everyone had a good laugh!"

"When you're working under very stressful conditions," Karen continued, "it helps a lot to lighten the mood a little. I remember the time a patient brought in a batch of peanuts he said were special ones he had grown himself. We all tried them and they were terrible. But Dr. Reed, being diplomatic, told the guy they were very good. So after the patient left, for the rest of the day I taped one of the peanuts to every chart Doctor saw."

When the talk turned to family matters, Karen's tone became more serious. She spoke of her two children: Greg, born in 1978, and Eric, born in 1981. (They became the 5th generation of Riccionis to be cared for by Jim.) When Greg was just three, he had such a bad case of the croup that Jim wanted to hospitalize him. To Jim and Karen's dismay, the hospital had no beds available. But Jim had an idea. "He showed me how to build a croup tent at home," she said, "and he came back to check on Greg several times." The child made a full recovery. Greg and Eric now have four children between them: Adriene, four; Logan, three; Brayden, two; and Owen, one. They are, of course, the sixth generation of Riccionis cared for by Jim Reed.

Bob Riccioni was in his forties before he needed help from Jim Reed for what became an ongoing malady: back pain. Most of us find it easy to empathize with patients suffering back pain. It's estimated that anywhere from 50%-80% of Americans have suffered from back pain at some point during their life, and that in any given year, 10% have back trouble. As you might suspect, since Jim has helped people with their bad backs probably as much as any doctor in history, he's become quite adept at diagnosing numerous types of back-related ailments. In recent years, specialized pain clinics have surfaced in our larger cities; Jim probably feels like he's been specializing in it for years, without any fancy title.

While one can rarely pinpoint with certainty the specific back pain triggers, Bob Riccioni feels his was caused by "the repeated lifting and moving of pianos and organs on the job at a Peoria music store. Toting around a heavy accordion may have also contributed to my problem." At the onset of back problems, the typical medical advice is to give the body a chance to heal itself. Bob tried that but it didn't help. The next step was a course of physical therapy. He pursued that diligently, but unfortunately without significant improvement. At that point, Jim felt some sophisticated diagnostic testing was called for, so Bob underwent an MRI which indicated that he had three herniated discs. Most physicians recommend back surgery only as a last resort. They feel, rightly so, that surgery is a judgment call which only the patient can make.

Like most patients, Bob didn't like the idea of surgery. So Jim recommended some lifestyle changes to help his back and instituted a regimen of pain medications. Knowing that the accordion was a major part of Bob's life, Jim didn't suggest he give up playing, and Bob didn't. Unfortunately, the discomfort level for Bob continued mounting, and he finally gave in to the pleadings of his wife and daughter. In 2001, at age 68, Bob's back was operated on by a Peoria neurosurgeon, Dr. Facet, who implanted three artificial discs. Bob was hospitalized for four days during which he experienced a lot of discomfort, though the surgery was pronounced successful. Bob's own evaluation was that the surgery "helped with the pain in the middle of my back but not very much with my lower back." So Bob returned once more to 'tough it out' mode, with the help of some strong pain medicines. He told me what he regrets most is no longer being able to indulge in long walks, his favorite form of exercise.

Bob's scariest medical problem happened ten years ago when he underwent a cardio stress test. For testing, Jim had referred him to Peoria cardiologist Dr. Thanad Shay, for whom Jim has the utmost respect. "The test results," said Bob, "showed I had one main artery that was 50% closed, but that the other arteries were in good shape. Dr. Shay wanted to operate on the one problem artery. So I did what I always did. I came back to get Dr. Reed's opinion. And boy, was I glad I did," Bob continued, "because Dr. Reed said he didn't think I needed the surgery. That was ten years ago and I haven't had a heart problem since. I went with Dr. Reed's recommendation as I always did and always will." Later, Jim told me that when two doctors have had a close relationship for years—as is the case with he and Dr. Shay—it's no big deal for them to disagree once in awhile. He added that he would never hesitate to disagree with anyone as long as he felt it was in the best interests of his patient.

"It's a little hard for me to believe," Bob continued, "but I've never been to another doctor for over 50 years, except for the specialists Dr. Reed sent me to." That sounded quite odd. "Haven't you ever been to the other young doctors working in the same offices with Jim for the past few years?" I asked him. "Oh," he responded, "I've met them and know who they are but as long as Dr. Reed is in practice, we'll continue with him."

In yet another example of lives interlacing in Farmington, Bob's wife (Jean Balagna Riccioni) mentioned that there were three or four other Balagnas living right on their same street, on route 116, just west of Kersh's Café. Jean's older sister Bea lived two doors west and was married to Chick Jacobus (Jim's oldest living childhood friend). Bea passed away a couple of years ago after a long bout with Parkinson's and osteoporosis. Jean expressed thanks for all the time Jim dedicated to her sister, a lot of it right in Bea's own home.

As I was preparing to leave the Riccioni home, Bob surprised me by asking if I'd like to hear him play a number. I felt pleased and even honored to receive a private performance. He settled in and hooked his accordion up with a fancy music computer board. (He didn't do that in the fifties.) I couldn't identify the tune, but unsurprisingly it had an Italian flavor to it. Later, when told about my private show, Jim said I may have been the last person to ever hear Bob play, because of the progressive back pain. For once, I hoped Jim was wrong with his diagnosis. So does he.

Chapter 32: Gilstrap-Kimbrell

Mason Patrick Griffith was born on April 21, 2006. Like every baby born into a loving family, he was the center of attention, at least for a little while. Mason's proud parents were Patrick and Mallory Gilstrap Griffith. His very proud maternal grandparents were Michael and Kimberly Gilstrap. And his very, very proud maternal great grandparents were Bob and Dixie Kimbrell Gilstrap. All were living in the Farmington area at the time of Mason's birth.

When Mason was two months old, in June, 2006, he became a patient of Dr. Jim Reed. At the time, no one knew the significance of that day: of the roughly 20,000 different patients Jim had seen during 55 years of practice, Mason was the only one to have two branches of his family tree—Gilstrap and Kimbrell—cared for by Jim for six generations.

Pearlie Vawter Gray and her husband, Matt Gray, celebrate their 50th wedding anniversary, June 12, 1970. Pearlie is the great, great, great, great grandmother of the boy whose photo graces the cover of this book.

The Gilstrap clan came from a rural area in northeast Missouri near Macon. Also living in that area was a family named Vawter. As time passed, a Gilstrap brother and sister married a Vawter sister and brother. Ralph Gilstrap was the first of his family to move to Farmington, drawn like so many by work in the coal mines. In 1938, he moved his family into a home on Cone Street, just a few houses from the Reeds. In 1943, the Harry Vawter family moved into town. Then in 1947 the Ray and Berniece Vawter Gilstrap family followed suit. Finally, the migration was completed in 1959 when Pearlie Vawter Gray followed the other family members. Pearlie, born in 1894, was the first of the six generations of Gilstraps cared for by Jim Reed.

Bob Gilstrap was nine years old in 1947 when his father Ray moved the family from Missouri to Farmington—not surprisingly for work in the mines. "Did you start dating Dixie Kimbrell as soon as you moved here," I jokingly asked Bob. "No," he laughed, "but I sure thought she was cute!"Since Dixie is a Farmington native and her husband has only lived in Farmington for 61 of his 70 years, we'll begin our Gilstrap-Kimbrell saga with Dixie.

Like so many patients interviewed, Dixie knew other Reeds before she knew Jim. "When I was young," she said, "and we were living on North West Street, your brother Sonny used to sort of supervise us kids when we'd play out in the street." (The streets were a common playground in small towns. Cars were slower and far between.) "And your sister Greta used to babysit me," Dixie added.Later, Dixie's family moved from North West Street one block east, on North Main, directly across from the Princess Theater and next door to Dr. Dimmitt.

Delbert "Deb" Kimbrell and his wife, Lillian, in 1955

My brother Harp and I worked at the Princess with Dixie's paternal grandfather, "Deb" Kimbrell. Yes, Deb. (It stood for Delbert.) I always idolized Deb because I aspired to his job: running a roaring, powerful vacuum blower after Harp and I had all the popcorn boxes out of the way. And then at night, Deb was the almost mystical projectionist, hidden away up a dark, narrow set of old wooden stairs. When Dixie was a teen, she had one of the theater glamour jobs, working the concession stand.

High school sweethearts, Dixie and Bob graduated from F.C.H.S. in 1956, just two months before Jim Reed opened his practice. Three years after marrying Bob in the fall of 1956, Dixie became pregnant. It was at that point that the Gilstraps really got to know Jim Reed. By then, Jim's reputation for never leaving his mothers-to-be in the lurch was well known, which helped put Dixie's mind at ease. Dixie's pregnancy and the birth of their son, Robert B. Gilstrap, in 1960, came off without a hitch. Dixie's confidence in Jim was cemented. That's why Dixie wasn't overly concerned when, as her second delivery date approached in August, 1963, Jim broke some slightly complicating news to her. One of the biggest races of his fledgling harness horse business loomed at the Illinois State Fair, and he had a top horse with a championship chance. He wasn't going to miss it. He gave Dixie an emergency phone number where he could be reached at the horse barn, and, if need be he would leave the fair and be by her side in a matter of minutes, since Springfield was a brief drive (at Jimspeed) from the hospital. But Dixie never had to use the number; very early on the race day, she went into labor and called Jim at home. They both rushed to the hospital. Michael Gilstrap was born without a hitch by 9 A.M....and Jim arrived at the Fair just in time watch his pacer, Gaytime's Best win a state title.

But let's return to 1959 and one of Dixie's early experiences with motherhood and Jim Reed. Like all young, first-time mothers, Dixie fretted about every little imperfection with her infant. She recalled taking baby Robert to Jim for a simple case of cradle cap, common for infants. "Dr. Reed assured me that Robert would be okay. He prescribed a special soap to use on his head." But when she returned home, in her state of worry she did what many young parents did. She went to the bible of baby care advice, Dr. Spock's Baby and Child Care.It said to put oil on the baby's head, and so she did. The cradle cap worsened. Back to Jim she went, terribly embarrassed. When Jim asked her what she'd done she confessed the whole story. "I wish," Jim joked, "instead of listening to Dr. Spock, you'd have listened to Dr. Reed!" For the next 45 years, both she and Bob would do just that.

Four generations of Kimbrells: From L to R, Maynard, his daughter, Dixie, her son, Michael Gilstrap and his daughter, Mindy

Deb Kimbrell died in 1955 at age 62. His widow, Lillian, was treated by Jim Reed until she passed away in 1966 at 72. She was the first of the six generations of Kimbrells cared for by Jim. (She suffered a broken arm in 1960.) Deb and Lillian had four sons: Maynard, Glen, Lawrence (Ozzie) and Richard (Mick). Strangely, three of the brothers developed aortic aneurysms.

"I think Dr. Reed saved my Uncle Ozzie's life," Dixie said, "because he diagnosed his problem so quickly and got him right to the hospital." Dixie's father, Maynard, a coal miner, "had never been sick and so he never went to Dr. Reed," she said. But, in 1993, at age 78, he died suddenly from an aortic aneurysm. Jim could do nothing to save him. Not long after that, Dixie's Uncle Glen also died suddenly from the same problem. Dixie's mother, Hazel Dikeman Kimbrell, died in 1964 at the young age of 49. Jim also treated Hazel's own mother, Nellie Dikeman, who outlived her daughter.

In 1956, Jim began doctoring the Ray Gilstrap family, including six of the seven children. From oldest to youngest, the seven kids were Bill, Bonnie, Bob, Betty, Barry, Ben and Byron.

"I remember my first visit to Doc," Bob Gilstrap said. "I'd had a minor accident while working one summer shortly after high school. I lost the skin off the tip of my right four-finger and he took care of me. He had just started his practice above the post office. A few years after that, early in my mining career, I dropped the upper half of a D-8 Cat radiator grill on my left toe. I wasn't wearing my safety shoes. It mashed my toe and it's a wonder it didn't do more. They took me to the closest doctor, which was in Williamsfield. He cleaned the toe up, bandaged it the best he could and sent me home. About seven that evening, the toe was still bleeding and needed some attention. Dix called the office and luckily Doc Reed was still in. She drove me to town and Doc had me sit on a table with my foot extended. He asked me how it happened and he wondered about my not being smart enough to wear steel-toed shoes. Then he got ready to put in some sutures. He got a syringe of Novocain and told me he would have to stick it in the very end of my toe, so I should 'hang on.' When he stuck the needle in and started to plunge in the drug it squirted out the hole in the top of my toe. He sorted of grunted and tried again. Same thing, eruption out of the toe. I'm thinking 'what the hell's going on' and he calls out, 'Barb, come look at this.' Barb Hedden, his nurse, came in and he gave the syringe another try and out squirted the drug. He did this a few times, and then they started chuckling. I finally kind of laughed and he grinned and said something like,'maybe we better fix this hole, eh?' Bottom line, he sewed me up and sent me on my way. What a guy! He was so comfortable with his patients, he was like a member of the family."

Ray and Berniece Gilstrap in 1939 with three of their seven children children. The infant is Bob Gilstrap, now 73.

Apparently the family head, Ray Gilstrap, was a piece of work. Bob was blunt in his assessment: "Our old man was outspoken, brash, independent and very demanding. He was seriously overweight and had emphysema and other medical problems. What with caring for Dad, all us kids and running the house, poor Mom would work herself into the ground. It would get so bad that sometimes Doc Reed would admit her to the hospital for a few days just as a vacation for her. He'd tell Dad she wasn't feeling well and needed to go in for close observation. The family always admired Doc for doing that. Nowadays, of course, he couldn't get away with that."

Then Bob described how his dad became completely devoted to Jim. Like other area miners and farmers, some of that devotion stemmed from Ray's admiration for the heroic way Jim reacted to various mine and farm disasters. Bob was laughing as he told me what would happen at family gatherings when the talk turned to health issues. "The old man," he said, "would get excited and say he wasn't going to listen to what anyone had to say unless he knew they had gotten their information from Doc. My Dad's strong feelings about Doc," Bob went on, "was the damndest thing you ever saw."

What made it remarkable was the fact that Ray didn't actually follow Jim's orders very well; warnings about obesity, for instance, went in one ear and out the other. Bob started laughing again when he said he'd "never forget the day I was driving around on the job and got a call from my office saying Doc needed to talk with me as soon as possible. So I pulled up to a pay phone and called him. Doc was excited. 'Dammit Bob,' he said, 'you've got to do something about your Dad, doesn't he do anything but eat!' "Look," I told Doc, "the old man's mother died when he was nine and ever since then he's done whatever he felt like doing. If I told him he needed to lose a lot of weight he'd just tell me to mind my own damn business."

Bob said that what the family always remembered was that "Doc cared so much about our Dad that he would go out of his way to talk to us about him." Bob's wife added a story along those same lines. "One day," Dixie said, "my younger sister, Cindy, was quite ill and made an appointment to see Dr. Reed. But then she got to feeling worse and couldn't make it in to his office. So, the next day, without being asked by anyone to do it, he just stopped by her home unannounced to check on her."

"I mean it," Bob interjected. "The old man would have fought for Doc." Bob's younger brother, Ben, echoed Bob's opinion. "Dad thought Doc was the greatest doctor in the United States," said Ben, "and I quite frankly agree with that statement. Doc is a man whose judgment our family trusted without reservation. I've driven back to Farmington from my home in Joplin, Mo.—a 250 mile trip—just to see him for help with my serious back trouble. Over the years, I've been to other doctors and none of them were able to help me. Doc has forgotten more than most of the others ever knew."

The Gilstraps, like all of Jim's patients I talked to, have been convinced of his diagnostic skills for many years. And with good reason: They've seen him at work. Bob and Dixie saw it when their granddaughter, Mallory, was a teenager. She suffered for weeks with a mystery virus. Jim referred her to a pulmonary specialist. After his exam, the specialist diagnosed her asthmatic. He prescribed some meds, but after a couple of doses she actually felt worse. So Mallory and her mother, Kim, returned to see Jim. When Kim told Jim what'd happened, he became very upset, telling her, "That girl doesn't have asthma and you should take those damn medications and flush 'em down the toilet." Jim has always been known for maintaining a cool, calm demeanor. But he also didn't hesitate to show his displeasure with what he considered inferior medical service rendered to any of his patients. Jim's original suspicion of bronchitis proved correct, and Mallory recuperated nicely following a course of antibiotics.

Bob enjoyed relating a story from several years ago about his adult son, Michael, who'd suffered for a decade with back problems. He'd gone to Jim off and on for help, but (stubborn like his grandfather) had declined to follow through with recommended testing. (Jim suspected a hip problem might be causing the back pain.) After trying to grit it out for a long time, Michael's condition worsened to the point where he could no longer work, in fact could barely walk. He finally agreed to see a Peoria specialist, but even after extensive testing, the specialist couldn't find the problem. And so Jim then referred Michael to the renowned Barnes Hospital in St. Louis. After an exhaustive and exhausting workup there, they told Michael the problem was… his hip! Recounting the medical misadventure, Bob broke out laughing. "After all that time and expense and testing, Michael ended right back at Doc's with the report from Barnes saying the same thing Doc had said at the start. So later I asked Doc how he had known it was the hip. He said people with that hip problem often start walking a little differently and he had seen that in Michael."

Bob Gilstrap spent his work career in the mining business, like his father before him. Starting as a union miner, he worked his way up through the ranks. He became a supervisor and in 1977 general manager of five area strip mines. In 1989, the last mine was due to close and Bob was offered a position in Arizona. With all his loved ones living locally, he refused to move. Instead, he formed a partnership with three other managers and bought the mine. They operated it until 1998 when he retired. "Doc had a lot of interest in the mines," Bob said. "One time I was in his office and we spent 55 minutes just shooting the breeze about the mines."

As manager of five strip mines, Bob's relationship with Jim and other doctors took on a new perspective. Bob sometimes had to determine if miners were legitimately off work because of an illness. Bob said he had to keep an eye on Jim because "Doc was a little loose on letting guys stay off the job. The reason I knew that was because I had seen him do it with my own Dad. I'll never forget the time I complained to Doc about one guy I thought should be back at work. A few days later I got a call from Doc saying that one of my other men would legitimately be missing work— because he was having heart surgery. I got a real bang out of that."

It's 2009 and although the high school sweethearts from the FCHS class of 1956 are getting older, Bob feels he and Dixie are in good shape except for some minor problems associated with aging. (Jim agrees with that assessment.) It is a good sign when Jim Reed doesn't recommend a yearly annual physical—and he doesn't with Dixie and Bob. They've learned when they need to see Jim and they've always had full confidence in any specialist Jim refers them to.

Bob and Dixie Gilstrap pose for their 50th wedding anniversary in 2006.

Bob Gilstrap and his wife, Dixie Kimbrell Gilstrap, are fortunate people; life could not have been much better for them during the past half century. They've been very successful in what's always been their first priority: family life—enjoying fifty years with their sons, their daughters-in-law, their grandchildren and their first great grandchild. Like most of us, they've endured many peaks and valleys over the past half-century. But unlike most of us, during those decades they've had one family doctor who's been there for them whenever they needed help. They remember every incident and they will remain forever grateful. "Like so many others," Bob lamented, "we dread what we're going to do when we no longer have this kind and gentle healer to care for us."

Epilogue

During the entire time I was writing this book, the most contentious national health care debate in our country's history took place; at times it was hard not to let this book material be colored by that debate. But my goals had always been more personal. My primary purpose was to tell the simple story of a country family doctor in the last half of the 20th century. I quickly learned, however, that there'd be nothing simple about it, because there's nothing more complex than human lives. It was still a pure labor of love, though, because I'd looked up to my older brother Jim for my whole life and this was a way to pay tribute to him. Furthermore, what heightened my love for this project was the intense, even intimate feelings Jim's patients so freely expressed. Above all else, I hope this book has sufficiently captured the real meaning and importance of the doctor-patient relationship.

Jim's primary interest in seeing this book come to fruition derived from his long-held belief that the general public (excepting people in the Farmington area) and even the medical profession didn't understand what a modern country doctor's life was really like. He wanted to set the record straight, so it pleased me to no end when Jim said this book had accomplished that—hopefully dispelling forever the stereotype of the country family doctor as little more than a kindly old gentleman leisurely stitching cuts on rambunctious five-year-olds, soothing unhappy babies, and commiserating with seniors about their various aches and pains.

I understand why, for his patients, Jim's persona ascended to the status of near sainthood. He's saved many, many lives, and those lives in turn have deeply touched many others. Jim Reed's dedication to his patients has been total; any time, night or day, any place, under any conditions. They know he's sacrificed much of his own personal and family life for them. When his guard is down Jim has admitted his awareness that his career has been unusual. But, he also knows full well that it has not been unique, because he appreciates medical history.

In the first half of the 20th century, dedicated hometown doctors were plentiful. Farmington had two before Jim: Drs. Jacobs and Dimmitt.

They may not have had Jim's modern medical know-how, but they gave everything they had to their patients. Wherever there was suffering, they were there. Whenever help was needed, they went. They were dedicated to their patients, and as a result, their patients were devoted to them. Jim enjoyed listening to old doctors talk about their experiences, and he never forgot their stories. When ice and snow made driving treacherous for him, he thought about the old doctors spending hours in their horse-drawn buggies. When he had miracle drugs at his disposal, he thought about the old"ice house" treatments for asthmatics. He never divorced himself from the past. He took the best human qualities of the old doctors and made them his own. I had no intention of addressing—at least in any detail—the numerous problems plaguing our national system of health care. This is not to say, however, that there aren't lessons to be learned by the profession of medicine from the life of Jim Reed.

Occasionally, some matters become so clear as to be self-evident. I believe I happened upon two of those while working on this book. One is that the profession of medicine and most importantly, patients, need more Jim Reeds—or more precisely, doctors with the characteristics of Jim Reed, especially of course in rural America. The other truism is that nothing should ever come between the doctor and his or her patient—not governmental bodies, not churches, not insurance companies, not family members, not medical corporations, and not money. The degree to which any of those factors is allowed to infiltrate the doctor-patient relationship is the degree to which quality health care for all patients will be diminished.

One large question lingers—especially in the hearts of Jim Reed's patients. Will we ever again see the likes of a hometown, country doctor like Jim Reed? Jim's patients answer with an unequivocal "No," and I fear they are right. Our society has changed a great deal since Jim Reed became a doctor in 1954.

The great chasm between the personalized medicine of 1950 and corporate medicine of 2010 is epitomized in the words of Peter Neupert. A Microsoft executive in charge of creating software for health care providers, Neupert served on President George W. Bush's Information and Technology Committee. "At its core," said Neupert, in the July 19, 2010 edition of Newsweek, "health care is an information-management business." No disrespect to Mr. Neupert, but to put it bluntly (as small town senior Midwesterners are apt to do) he doesn't seem to have a clue. An information-management business? There are a few ideas I'd like to drum into Mr. Neupert's head:

- The focus of health care has moved away from primary care to megacorporations dominated by specialized medicine. The foundation of any health care system must instead be a highly skilled, massive program of primary care physicians, adequately funded and staffed.

- Doctors cannot function as they should while under constant threat of being sued. Litigation reform is a must.

- The cost of medical education for students must be subsidized to a great extent, so that career choices are not influenced by financial concerns.

- Medical schools need to divest themselves of all activities not directly related to the only mission for which they were established; namely, the education of students.

In the 1950s, America's perfect family doctor worked his way into the hearts of TV viewers in the mythical personage of Marcus Welby. But life is not television and life's never perfect. Jim Reed, who has likely come as close as anyone to being the ideal family doctor in real life, did not appear spontaneously out of anyone's imagination, and all the computer technology in the world will never produce his kind. We won't see his likes again without individual sacrifice, desire, and determination. But moreover, those virtues must be cultivated within revamped educational systems, and supported through wise policy planning. Maybe then, there's a chance.

Seventy-five years ago, in the midst of the Great Depression, Jim Reed was a scrawny young boy in Farmington, Illinois. Jim, his parents, and his ten brothers and sisters depended on welfare to eat, to live. Everyone in the family (except of course the toddlers) pitched in to help. Twice a month, Jim set off to the nearby city park. He made that walk alone and carried a large, empty bucket. Once at the park, he stood in a long line—people of all ages waiting to receive their government soup allotment. His bucket filled, Jim made the solitary walk home.

Since the Depression, few American children have had to do what Jim did. Most adults today would be too embarrassed to tote a soup bucket... and who would think of asking a child to do it? Jim still remembers those walks to the park. "I didn't feel embarrassed," he said. "Everyone was in the same boat and I was just doing what had to be done." He was eight years old. Can there be any question that growing up during those tough times played a key role in Jim's character development?

Fifty-five years later, on September 1, 1990, Jim took another walk to the same park. But this time he didn't walk alone. On this occasion, he led a large, proud army of family members to a park overflowing with people gathered to honor him. Two hours later when the crowd had scattered, there was no longer a Farmington City Park. There was Dr. James M. Reed City Park.

One by one on that memorable evening, grateful speakers stepped up to the microphone and paid respects to the family doctor they knew so well, and loved so much. Jim sat there quietly, but a little uncomfortable with the attention. Finally, it was his turn to speak. He hadn't prepared any remarks and didn't use any note cards. No teleprompter, no TV camera. Just Jim, his family and his patients. As the sun began to set, he rose and looked out over the crowd, most of whom he'd known for decades. Then he spoke from the heart. "It has been my honor to serve you all these years. I've never thought I was anything special. I always thought I was just doing what a doctor was supposed to do." And that was it.

The folks gathered that night weren't surprised by what Jim said. To them, he was just being the same person they'd always known. But they didn't agree with him. They all knew the person standing at the podium was something special, and they knew why. This book has been about those "whys." Why he came home to practice. Why he remained humble. Why he was an outstanding diagnostician and clinician. Why he made house calls. Why he was totally dedicated to their care. And, most importantly, why he was deeply admired and respected by his thousands of patients. By October, 2010 (coincidentally, the same time Jim ended his practice in Farmington), I felt I had pretty much answered all the "whys." And happily, Jim agreed with my assessment. That was it then: the book was done. Yet, in spite of all the good feelings, I was nevertheless left with one nagging regret. I'd never had the opportunity to experience a face-to-face emotional exchange between Jim and one of his patients. Then fate stepped in.

On a crisp October Saturday in 2010, Jim, myself, and four other family members decided to grab a late lunch at one of his favorite dining spots: Pico's, a quaint, family owned Italian restaurant in Norris, a hamlet just five miles south of Farmington. We entered a small, unoccupied room off the main dining area. Along the south wall was a group of five or six booths. The only other seating was one of those long, narrow tables used for banquets—since there were six of us, that's where we landed, with

Jim, my daughter Elise and I on the north side, and Jim's daughter Cindy, my wife Mary and my sister Greta Gay, across from us, close to the row of booths.

It was a nice setting. We had privacy and there was none of the noise that passes as music in most places. After we'd been there about twenty minutes, a middle-aged couple with an elderly lady entered the room. The younger gal recognized Cindy and stopped to chat for a moment before sitting at the last booth. Then, almost as soon as they were seated, the older woman screamed out loud enough for everyone in the place to hear: "Dr. Reed is here! Where is he?" Rising slowly from her booth, she again shouted, "Where's Dr. Reed, I've got to give Dr. Reed a hug!" Leaning over to Cindy, I asked who those folks were. Cindy whispered that the elderly lady was Mary Alice Page, who was almost totally blind. The couple was her son, Gary, and his wife, Valerie. Meanwhile, Mrs. Page had begun, chair by chair, to slowly feel her way around the south side of our table to the north side, where Jim was seated, all the while proclaiming that she had to "give Dr. Reed a hug!" Eventually she reached Jim, who hadn't said a word and seemed a little ill at ease with the public fuss. After receiving her hug and chatting for a minute, she calmly returned to her booth. Later, I learned Mrs. Page was the former Mary Alice Wake and that she had known Jim most of her life, having been one year behind him in school.

During the car ride back home to Decatur that day, it occurred to me that what I'd witnessed resembled one of those news clips of a visiting potentate in a parade with roadside well-wishers pressing against barriers to get close enough for a touch. But, in my mind, what made the "Pico's moment" an even more moving experience was that it was an unplanned, spontaneous outpouring of pure, honest emotion. I felt like I couldn't have scripted a more appropriate ending for the book.

As Jim Reed nears the end of a long and glorious career, his legacy, in the minds of many, will be the superior level of family medical care he provided to thousands of folks in and around his rural hometown. If nothing else, that alone is deserving of a place in a classic textbook of "how-to-do-it medicine." But his legacy should not—and does not—stop there. His true legacy is his humanity, and it will go on living inside people he touched, in the form of heartfelt, deep emotions of gratitude, respect, admiration and devotion. It is what he gave to them and what, in turn, they gave back to him.

In 2009, Jim stands in front of the city park named in his honor.

Funeral Blues

by

Rudy Reed

Climb down from combines and tractors. Walk awhile in acres of silence. Remember his soothing touch when you notice fading scars. Stop assembly lines. Close bars. Draw drapes. Turn daylight to dark. Walk slowly once around Dr. James M. Reed Park. Uncage his pigeons. Watch them soar into an overcast sky. Wonder if his soul is there. And why he had to die. Free his racehorses. Watch them run wild. Let teachers talk of his greatness with every child. For an hour or a day, let your heart weep. And bleed. For my brother, Jim Reed. Without him, go inside yourself when you ail. And feel low. Search your soul. In there you can find part of my brother Jim. For half a century a part of you was inside him. Never forget suffering of loved ones. Recall how he cared for them. And watched over them. On weekends, on holidays, in the middle of the night. Never forget dreadful feelings of doom. Until the moment he came. None of that will ever be the same.

Acknowledgments

While there were many, many people who played important parts in the making of this book, my deepest appreciation goes to my brother's patients. They were more than gracious and willing to share their stories and deep feelings about Jim. Simply put, without them, this book would not have been possible.

The book would also look much different than it does were it not for the months of painstaking editorial work of Robert Reed, whom I'm also proud to say moonlights as my son. And my daughter, Elise, spent many hours on the cropping and placement of photos, as well as trying to educate me about computers.

On a personal note, I'm delighted to be able to thank two old, dear hometown friends. Bob Gilstrap, a FCHS classmate, took the time to educate me about the history of coal mining in the Farmington area. Jim Perelli, my first male teacher as well as my first coach, was pleased to share with me his knowledge of the history and important contributions of Italians in the life of Farmington.

For their reviews of various book sections, I'd like to thank my family physician, Dr. Gregory Totel, my brother and sister-in-law, Jim and Phyllis Barr, good friends Susan and Fred Mosedale, Heidi Majors, Marian Wrinkle, Marti Kunski, John Schleper, Don Carmichael, George Batson and Mary and Clark Waldmeir. I also benefited from the helpful comments of retired University of Kentucky professor Carolyn Thompson, a high school classmate of Janet Reed. I'm grateful to Linda Picone, a Minneapolis writer-editor—and my daughter's close friend—for her kind and wise advice to this first-time author.

A very special thanks goes out to Cynthia Reed, the daughter of Jim Reed, for all of her help with the nuts and bolts of scheduling, tracking down details, etc. And for their encouragement throughout this project, heartfelt thanks to my brother, Warner, and my sisters, Barbara Jeanne Osborn, Marcia Lou Little, Greta Gay Kumlander and Alicia Rose Aden. For his assistance in taking old family photographs and making them presentable for publication, I'm grateful to professional photographer Bryan Reed, Jim's son.

I'm convinced librarians are an underutilized community resource, and those in Farmington, Peoria, Decatur, Galesburg, the University of Illinois and the Farmington Museum provided much help to me.

For their continuous support and encouragement throughout this project, my deep thanks to my immediate family: my daughter Elise and her devoted husband Norman Wondero and my son Bob and his lovely partner Tracey Burton. Finally, without a very special lady named Mary by my side for fifty years, none of this would've been possible.

CPSIA information can be obtained at www.ICGtesting.com
Printed in the USA
LVOW081550090213

319418LV00005B/9/P